Afghanistan

A Memoir from Brooklyn to Kabul
Book I 1968-1980

Cat Parenti

To Cie,

Enjoy!

Love,

Cat

2/10/20

Afghanistan

A Memoir from Brooklyn to Kabul
Book I 1968-1980

Cat Parenti

Forchianna Publishing
Radford, Virginia

Forchianna Publishing
Radford, Virginia

Forchianna Publishing
P.O. Box 1363
Radford, VA 24143
www.MagnificentU.com/forchianna-publishing/

Ordering Information: Quantity sales. Special discounts are available on quantity purchases by corporations, associations, and others. For details, contact the publisher at the address above.

ISBN 978-0-9964310-8-8

Cover Design: Christy Collins
All Interior Photographs: Copyright © Cat Parenti

Printed in the United States of America

10 9 8 7 6 5 4 3 2 1

This book was typeset in Gentium Book Basic

All of the events in this book are true. The characters are composites. Names, places, and dates have been changed to protect the innocent, and the guilty, for they too deserve mercy.

According to the Sufis, Islamic mystics, the word "afghan"
refers to the spiritual station of the soul characterized
by one who has achieved true purity.

Table of Contents

Acknowledgments

All of my thanks go to my daughter, Chandra, for her love and support, Jamal, the late love of my life, the late Nick Pappas, my first mentor and editor, my friends and family who encouraged me, especially Terri Gibbons, my editors Brandi Stewart and Judy Silvaggio, the team at the Quantum Leap Program, and my publisher and author success consultant, D. Takara Shelor, without whose help this book would not have been published. A special acknowledgement goes to HRH, the late Prince Ali Seraj of Afghanistan, a friend whose life, unknowingly, was parallel to mine.

Introduction

Due to stultifying Catholic schooling, I lived an internal childhood life through dreams, visions, and imagination. Teachers accused me of daydreaming and I was. Because my grades were all A+, they never could say nor do anything else. I viewed the world from inside of myself as if I were seeing a movie, not a part of the movie merely an observer. Afghanistan awakened me.

All of my childhood visions were like an energetic skein inexorably pulling the warp and weft of my life forward, where I didn't know. But some part deep inside of me, knew I was on my path.

Afghanistan, the very scent, sight, and sound of those days, forever lost but now drowning me in wave upon wave of memories. A hushed reverence hung over the entire city of Kabul. Sounds were absorbed by the purplish brown hulks of the mountains. They ringed the city like the edges of a crater, broken on occasion by the solitary piercing wail of the call to prayer.

"Afghanistan: A Memoir from Brooklyn to Kabul" is a greatly expanded two-volume version of my previously published autobiography, "Afghanistan: Blood and Honor." They recount my intermittent twenty-four-year odyssey between New York and Afghanistan.

This first volume covers the years from 1968-1980. Politically, this timeline goes through the rule of the kingdom of Afghanistan by King Zahir Shah and President Sardar Daoud Khan's Republic of Afghanistan.

I wrote "Afghanistan: A Memoir from Brooklyn to Kabul" in order to portray the love and beauty of the Afghan people and their country shown through my experiences in this now much-maligned land. The shocking stark, wild beauty of the deserts, lakes, and mountains with their villages huddled at their feet. The beauty of the sometimes reddish brown earth or the sand color adobe homes whose monotony was broken by intense splashes of color in the clothing of the men and women plus the magnificent multi-color carpets and hand embroideries in their homes filled me with fascination.

Love and beauty existed in the traditional greeting to each other, in the eyes of lovers, husbands and wives, those of parents towards children, in the religious mysticism of the Sufis, the Afghan laws of asylum, their hospitality towards foreigners as guests in their country and countless daily life activities that imbued these qualities.

In addition to love and beauty, two other recurring themes in both of these books are "blood" and "honor." In this first volume, there is the purity of the bloodlines kept by the preferred marriage to first paternal cousins, the blood of male circumcision and the virgin bride on her wedding night.

"Honor" is a pervasive theme throughout Afghan culture. The king honored God/Allah. Ministers and the nobility honored the king. Guests were honored by the host through the hospitality of food, shelter, and protection, if necessary. In return, guests honored the host by devoting all of their time and talents to him and his family. The guest/host relationship was inviolate even if the host lost his life in the process.

Children honored parents, and men and women honored each other. When a woman discovered that she was pregnant, she went to her husband and said, *"I hath the honor to tell thee that I bear thy child."* The husband responded, *"This is the greatest honor that thou canst bestow upon me."* Servants honored their masters and in return were honored by their own children.

Their love, beauty, honor, respect, intensity, and kindness flowed from their spoken words. There is no way to transport the reader back in time to the Afghanistan of the past, without a transliteration of their spoken words in italicized text.

The women I lived and, interacted with were not abused. They were treated with honor and respect within the confines of their culture that was very ancient, largely agricultural, having a love of nature, a strong belief system religiously and culturally. Afghanistan was barely touched by outsiders. This is the culture that I have portrayed in this book.

Having said this, abuse of women physically, sexually, mentally, emotionally and intellectually has existed since the beginning of time worldwide and has always been abhorrent to me. It is only now that violence and abuse of woman and children are being recognized and dealt with in many countries of the world.

I have used the name of God and Allah interchangeably for I believe that there is only one Creator no matter the name. The word Koran, I have rendered Quran.

Several words need clarifying. The singular noun "Afghan" and the plural version "Afghans", refer to people, not to objects. The adjective "Afghan" must be followed by a noun such as an Afghan carpet. The currency of Afghanistan is called "*afghanis.*"

Having lived in many countries around the world, I have used British spelling in the book, eg. *theatre* instead of *theater*.

I was raised in Brooklyn, NY by Polish Italian parents who came through Ellis Island. I was the translator between my grandparents who spoke no English. Both my parents spoke English without accents, well my father had somewhat of a Brooklyn accent. So Catholic school = Latin, the base of most western romance languages. Catholic high school = French. Fordham University Catholic College = Russian taught by native Russian speakers. I am not a religious person but very spiritual. At that time, Catholic schools were the best and my parents could afford them. I love languages and they have always come easily to me. Every time I came to a border of a foreign country, I would sit with the local customs officials who spoke English and learn 30 phrases of the local tongue.

During my life, I have made a study of Christianity, Judaism, Islam, Hinduism, Sikhism, Jainism and some Native American beliefs. All of these religions acknowledge a Supreme Being. None of these religions commands us to kill people or commit suicide to attain heaven. All say love God and your neighbor, not the perverted slaughter of Muslims, Christians and anyone else who does not subscribe to the narrow, feudal, radical, insane interpretations of the Quran by Al Qaeda, ISIS or any of these other groups currently running rampant..

I had the privilege and honor to be married to two Muslims. I am a New Age Christian. Both of these men told me that conversion on my part wasn't necessary. According to the Quran, they were allowed to marry believers such as Christians and Jews. Infidels were people who were atheists.

This book series is a tribute to the Afghan people for their courage, their faith, their love, and the beauty of their souls.

CHAPTER ONE

Thė First Timė

"The voyage of life is the story of separation,
Loneliness is a soundless wave,
Don't take the trip alone, my love
And don't leave me alone."
Jalaluddin Rumi, Afghan Sufi Poet

I had been in Kabul for several months in 1968 until the night that marked the beginning of a series of events that completely changed my life. On that day, I was in the bazaar, as usual, buying jewelry and embroideries while checking on the progress of my tailors who worked in a tiny wooden cubicle perched on a mud embankment. I had my own export business creating western clothes incorporating Afghan embroideries that I sold to Henry Bendel's and Bloomingdale's in New York.

When I got back to my rented house, Mowlowdowt, rushed to my bedroom, lit the stove and brought tea. He sat and talked with me about the progress of my work, and any household business I needed to know. These daily discussions ended when my guests arrived for the evening, or I went to my Afghan friends' homes to enjoy good food, music, and company.

It was eleven o'clock, on that fateful Thursday night. I did not intend to leave my home on such a cold November evening. No one had come to visit me and I had no invitations. I was bored and wide awake with an indefinable anticipation. I decided to go to my friend Exalted's club. The full moon was resplendent in silver finery as I walked the deserted streets. The night air was clear and crisp and the road before me was a gaudy, silver ribbon. In contrast, the mountains and the two-storey houses, together with their shadows, resembled sharp, chiseled, black stone giants.

I entered the small, dimly-lit, crowded club that always smelled of stale wine, cigarettes, and hashish. In the hazy darkness, I found a group of other exporters whom I knew from Europe and America who called out to me. Hans from Holland was animatedly describing his day at the carpet bazaar to Christine and Tom, Peace Corps volunteers. Morrie, my previous roommate in a local hotel, nursed his Czech beer and smiled. Tom asked what I wanted to drink, and I joined them, talking, joking, laughing and drinking.

Morrie teased me because I always got great prices for Afghan goods. I told Morrie that it was because I spoke some Dari and knew how to bargain with the shopkeepers. I offered to teach him some rudimentary Dari and invited him to come to my house the next morning. All shops were closed on *Juma* Friday, the Muslim Sabbath, and we could spend the day together.

The club was one of a small handful in the "modern" section of Kabul. Clubs were looked upon as unlawful and a stain upon respectable society. For the few "Westernized" Afghans (less than two percent of the population), the Club provided a place to see, be seen and have access to foreigners. On Thursday nights it was jammed, and this Thursday was no exception. The club was always dark with only a little red exit bulb over the bar. The glass dance floor, illuminated from beneath, occupied the middle of the club. On the right side, there was a space for the band, and an area with small wooden tables and chairs, each with a tiny candle in the center of the white tablecloth.

This was the last night in Kabul for the owner Exalted's Peace Corps friends. He was busy dedicating Neil Young songs to them. This put us all in a festive but poignant mood. I glanced towards the bar with its dim red aura and saw several men seated there in a smoke-filled haze. My blind gaze was riveted to one of them as I felt a powerful force emanate from him. While chatting and drinking, I tried to understand what drew me to that one indistinguishable figure and what excuse would bring me to the bar without being obvious. As I wrestled with these thoughts, a tall stocky, platinum-haired German, whom I knew as one of the few foreigners in Kabul, approached me. Heinz asked me to dance and I gladly accepted. I noted the surprised look that flitted across his pale features. Our conversations were limited to a few comments about the weather, or my export business and then a polite goodbye. I could tell from the way he looked at me with his flat, blue eyes that he wished for more but I was not interested. I rose from the table, and Heinz led me onto the dance floor. The music was a fast American disco beat and Heinz grabbed me around my waist and began to whirl me around.

When the music stopped, he guided me to the bar and said, "Cathy, I have a friend who wants to meet you."

My head was whirling from excitement and the next thing I heard was Heinz saying, "Ms. Cathy Parenti, I would like to present His Highness Jamal Mahmood Yusuf Khan.

The man I'd felt drawn to rose and turned towards me. I found myself looking into the face of the most handsome man I had ever seen. His name meant "Beloved Lord Joseph of Divine Beauty," and in truth, never was another so aptly named! Just then the band began to perform the song "The First Time I Saw Your Face" by Roberta Flack and Donnie Hathaway, and I thought how appropriate this was.

Jamal was very tall, broad-shouldered with a slim waist and narrow hips. His hair was a mass of thick, dark black curls flecked with gray that fell to his collar. He had a dark-gold complexion, with regal features. His dark-brown eyes ended in points; a Roman nose with slightly flaring nostrils and a pair of perfectly formed full lips in the exact shape of most Buddha images completed this picture. A huge, thick black mustache that curled upwards towards his sideburns, commanded his face. His pale-blue silk shirt, navy-blue, cashmere jacket and charcoal-gray pants, as well as his buttery black leather shoes, were of the finest French materials and style. He had a fierceness to his features that recalled the wild and unchecked beauty of a black panther about to spring. This fierceness was thinly disguised by an outward veneer of civilization. His bearing spoke of great pride and dignity with an inner core of strength ... that of people born to rule and used to having their commands obeyed.

In the brief instant that I took all of this in, a star burst in the center of my forehead and planets collided. Suns and moons died and were reborn. I felt the pages of my mind rifled backward at incredible speed. This was the man I had dreamed of since I was thirteen years old! In my dreams, I was married to this same tall man with a dark-gold complexion, and his country was at war.

CHAPTER TWO

The Cement Flowerpot

*"Afghanistan was a violet color on the world map and
my soul was drawn to that little-known country over
and over again."*
The Author

The visions and dreams began in Brooklyn, New York where I was born. A large red brick Brooklyn apartment building that housed forty-eight families was my first home. When I was three years old, my mother allowed me to go down the four flights of stairs alone to play with the other children, under the watchful eye of some neighbor.

The front door of the apartment building was flanked by two long rectangular gardens full of young trees and hydrangea bushes. An old, imposing, cracked cement flowerpot guarded each garden. One day, tired of playing tag, I put grass and leaves into one of the empty flowerpots, stirred it with a stick while I pretended to cook. A curtain descended before my eyes that revealed an ocher color plain, with purplish brown mountains in the distance. I felt as if I were looking at a movie of myself. I was a twelve-year-old girl in a black dress. It had dark red embroidery with small coins, silver beads, and silver buttons. My hair was a mass of tiny braids. My feet were bare, and I stood by a pot hanging over an open fire enveloped in its smoke and stirred its contents with a large geometrically carved wooden spoon.

I was interrupted by my mother calling me from what seemed like a very far distance. I wanted to turn towards her voice, but I was riveted to this beautiful place. The calling became insistent. Minutes and then centuries passed. The scene before me began to fade. And to my surprise, I found myself again in front of the flowerpot. I never mentioned this to anyone, but continued to play the flowerpot game until age five, when I lost interest.

In grade school, when the teacher asked us to name three countries in Asia, everyone said, "China, Japan, and the Philippines."

I always responded with, "Afghanistan, Pakistan, and India."

Afghanistan was a violet color on the world map, and my heart was drawn to that little-known country over and over again, although I had no explanation for it. An inner voice incessantly repeated, "I am going to Afghanistan."

Always fascinated with gypsies, when I was twelve, I wrote a paper on their origin and received an award for it. Every Halloween, I joyfully dressed as a gypsy. I wore a flowing multi-colored skirt, a peasant blouse and my hair was in a ponytail on the right side of my head with Cleopatra eye makeup and a deep red lipstick.

At age thirteen, I had my first dream of my beloved. I beheld in awe a very tall man with dark-gold skin. I felt that he was my husband and we were very much in love. His country was at war, and I was helping him defend it. This same dream that put me in a state of longing and wonder continued until I went to Afghanistan.

Nomadic Pashtun Woman and Baby

At eighteen, a girlfriend and I went shopping in Manhattan. We passed a storefront advertising palm reading. My friend was very excited and persuaded me to go with her to get our palms read. But the minute we entered the store, I knew in a flash that the gypsies were not the people I had been seeking all these years.

10

I subconsciously sought the Pashtun nomads who trekked with their flocks of sheep, goats, and camels from the searing plains of southeastern Afghanistan in the summer to the cool mountains of northwestern Pakistan, and then back again in autumn.

After graduating from Fordham University, I had a job as an administrative assistant to a vice president at Panasonic. One late September afternoon, as I sat in the shade of a tree on the stoop of the brownstone that I rented, I watched a man several doors down hauling drywall and other materials to the front yard. He smiled and waved. I waved back, and he asked if I would like to tour the brownstone that he just bought.

The windows and chandeliers were original Tiffany glass. The three-storey building had carved mahogany balustrades. When we reached the top floor, Bob Miller asked if I wanted to look at some of the artifacts that he brought back from various countries around the world. There were Tibetan thangkas, Hindu saris, and mirrored embroidery from Pakistan. There were also piles of Chinese silks, Turkistan brocades, and Kashmiri shawls. Then Bob pulled out a long dazzling white cotton tunic with tiny, hand embroidered, geometric designs in white silk. Bob said that this was called *peeran*. It was the white on white wedding shirt of the Pashtun grooms (the indigenous Afghans) of Kandahar in southern Afghanistan. Suddenly, the room disappeared, Bob disappeared and I was riveted to this tunic that was surrounded by a white light expanding and contracting. Stunned by my reaction, I felt again that I was looking at myself in another life.

I came back to the present when I heard Bob ask, "Didn't you ever want to travel?"

"Of course," I replied as excitement coursed through me.

"I know of a group going overland from England to India. It takes six months. Are you interested?"

"Absolutely," I replied without hesitation and my inner voice started singing, "I am going to Afghanistan!"

I got all of my visas and vaccinations, took a leave of absence from my job, paid for my place on the Land Rover, packed my bags, sublet my brownstone apartment and threw a big farewell party. My friends were convinced that I had lost my mind.

"You are going to travel around the world with complete strangers? Are you insane? What will happen if you get sick? The people in some of those countries are savages! You may be cut up and put in a stew pot!" These were some of the comments at the party. But I was inwardly driven to take this journey and countered all of their fears with, "I am going to Afghanistan."

I was fortunate that no one asked why, for I had no answer. Little did I know that this was the beginning of a journey that would irrevocably change my life.

And that journey had brought me here, to the man I had dreamed of. I was drowned in sense of timelessness. I knew with certainty that we had known each other before, in centuries long ago, in civilizations more ancient than this one. A feeling of awestruck wonder possessed me as I began to greet him in Dari.

But I was interrupted by his deep resonant voice with an Oxford English accent overlaying the Urdu tongue, saying with acute distaste, "Madam, I am not a Kabuli!"

This meant that he was not from Kabul. Taken by surprise at his rudeness, my temper flared and I retorted, "I greet everyone I meet in Kabul that way!"

He sniffed and said "Huh!"

After that inauspicious beginning, we both climbed onto our barstools facing the bartender. I toyed with my half-empty wine glass provided by Heinz who then beat a hasty retreat. Jamal savored his Johnny Walker Red scotch.

After a short interval, without looking at me, he said, "Madam, would you care for a Dunhill?"

Not sure if he was referring to a drink, I asked, "And what is that?"

He produced a maroon and gold box of cigarettes, opened it, and offered it to me. He looked down the end of his nose, and said, "Obviously not properly educated!"

I accepted the cigarette and allowed him to light it. No one had ever offered me a cigarette without putting the pack in front of me. Besides, I was only an occasional smoker, and unfamiliar with this English brand. I remained quiet waiting my chance. There was palpable electricity growing between us. He bought me another glass of red wine.

I thanked him and said, "Would you like a Djarum?"

"And what is that?" he asked testily.

I pulled out my pack of clove filled cigarettes from Indonesia, offered him one and replied, "Evidently not brought up in the correct manner!"

He snorted, and I could hear him suppress a chuckle. Then I turned toward him and said in Pakhto, his own language, *"Well, Sahibzada* (Noble Lord), *and how art thou this evening?"* Since his name told me he was an Afghan, I knew he would have spoken either Dari or Pashto. Hearing the British accent, I guessed correctly that it was Pakhto, the language of the Afghans in Pakistan and India. They were colonized by the British. Afghans in Afghanistan speak Dari, the language of Kabul which he rejected and Pashto.

Amazed he burst out, *"Thou speak my tongue?"*

I just smiled and said nothing.

"By God, Madam, you are unusual for an American!" He hurled the last word from his mouth as if it were an epithet. Easterners usually follow a vehement statement like this by forcefully spitting. However, Jamal was much too cultured for that.

Then in a gentle tone, he asked, "Would you care to dance?"

We rose and I allowed him to escort me to the dance floor. They were playing a popular Pakistani tune that had a cha-cha beat. Jamal's movements were like a rippling stream that sensuously caressed the shoreline. He never missed a step. I knew then that I must be with this man no matter what, and began to wonder what his mustache would feel like when I kissed him. I felt a compelling force binding us together for eternity.

The following thought crossed my mind. *If he is not married, I will marry him. And if he is married, I will have a child by him.*

We spent the remainder of the evening drinking, dancing, and exchanging many, insolent remarks, all of course prefaced by *"Khan Sahib"* ("Lord Gentleman") on my part and "My Lady" on his. I called him primitive. He said I was uncivilized. I said he was ignorant, and he retorted that my upbringing was sorely lacking. I called him "crossbred," a grave insult to those who pride themselves on keeping their bloodlines pure for generations. He "cast doubts on my father's identity." On and on and on we fenced as he interspersed this game with his history.

He was a Pakhtun (the Pakistani cousins of the Afghan Pashtuns) of the Yusufziais, the largest tribe in Pakistan. He began in Pakhto, *"The great state of India hath witnessed my birth, Oh My Lady."*

"In which place hath that occurred, Oh My Lord?"

"The ancient kingdom of Oudh, that they now call Uttar Pradesh."

"So what occurred that My Lord who is a Muslim was born into a Hindu kingdom?"

"Oh My Lady, know thou not the history of India and Pakistan?"

"Somewhat, My Lord, my knowledge is such that Pakistan was a created state by the British for Muslims that lived in India, is this not the truth?"

"Yay, My Lady. But there was much more. We art originally from Afghanistan. My family fought against the Delhi dynasty for Babur Shah the ruler of Afghanistan in the 15th Century. When my ancestor declared victory, Babur Shah told to him, 'Take thy horse and ride from sunrise to sunset in one direction. Then make a circle, and this land wilt be thine to rule.'

Switching to English he continued, "Thus, was the reward for my ancestor. Generations to follow lived in and ruled the kingdom of Oudh. When the British came, my grandfather founded a university there."

"Oh My Lord, were thou educated in Oudh?"

"Yay, My Lady, all of my male ancestors as well as my brothers were, and then we finished our education in England at the University of Oxford."

"Do you still call Oudh home?" I asked in English.

"No, My Lady. It was the work of the British that destroyed the unspoken pact of peace between Muslim and Hindu. They fomented much trouble until these brothers fought each and another. Then the great Muslim state of Pakistan was born from their blood. The home of my family is now that of Hyderabad in Pakistan."

"Is that where you came from at this time?"

"Nay, we were in Europe buying Mercedes Benzes and Rolls Royces for our family."

Despite our mutual insults, I was transfixed by him. The more time we spent together, the more time I wanted to spend; I sensed that he felt the same. All this time, the sexual tension between us was mounting as electric fire jetted from our eyes.

Around four o'clock in the morning, I stood up, offered him my hand, and announced, *"Khan Sahib,* thank you for a most interesting evening. I am going home."

Jamal jumped off the bar stool and replied in Dari, *"Madam, 'twould whiten my face to escort thee."* He paid the bill, and we walked outside into the cold, clear, indigo night. As we were leaving, one man emerged from a group of tourists and said, "Sir, you are a beautiful dancer and so is your partner."

Without hesitation, Jamal replied, "No sir. My partner is a beautiful dancer only when she dances with me, and together <u>we</u> dance beautifully."

Jamal was insulted that a stranger in a public street no less, would presume to mention me to him. In his mind, I already belonged to him, and it was his right only, to talk about me. Speaking of a wife, sister or lover in a public place was something he and other Afghans never did, even with their own families, let alone with a stranger.

Jamal woke his servant Sattar who was asleep in Jamal's black Mercedes. Sattar, a tall, ropy Pakhtun with short, black hair and a Charlie Chaplin mustache, leaped out of the car to hold the door for us and then got behind the wheel. We tooled through the moonstruck streets; the Mercedes engine a mere purr as I gave directions to my home. Jamal instructed his servant to stay in the car, and he got out and came around to open the door for me himself.

I unlocked the gate and we went into the winter garden deprived of all its leafy finery. We walked under the bare boughs of the trees as the tension between us reached an unbearable pitch. Coming into the light of the full moon, we slowly circled each other. We were two wary panthers inhaling each other's magnetic perfume. I drank in every feature of that magnificent face. With a barely perceptible motion, we advanced towards each other until I felt his breath upon my face. His eyes burned into mine as our lips touched. In a flash, I was drowning in his arms our lips and tongues inextricably meshed. I felt as if I were melting, and leaned into him for support. His legs were vibrating. We continued, in awe of our passion, without speaking, for what seemed like an eternity.

I broke the spell when I pulled back, smiled, stood on tiptoes and love bit his ear. He sprang back as if electrified, gripped my shoulders in a vise, furrowed his brow and shouted, *"Don't <u>do</u> that woman! Dost thou wish to be raped?"*

I smiled again and replied, *"By thee, Khan Sahib, yay!"*

15

He was dumbstruck by my openness but recovered himself and whispered, "Come with me now then, for tomorrow I leave for Pakistan."

The urgency of his utterance charged through me. Even though I wanted him more than anyone I had ever met, I balked at having a one-night stand with a nobleman who was used to having his every wish granted, and had all womanhood at his command. I invited him to stay with me for several days. He declined since he was with his family. For him to take a lover in the open was considered a blemish on family honor, since love affairs were conducted with the utmost discretion.

When I remained silent to his proposal, he became very formal, kissed my hand and said, "Very well, My Lady, it was my pleasure to meet you."

He turned on his heel, went out of the gate into the car and waved goodbye as Sattar drove off. The setting moon with its harlequin face, mocked me from the now violet sky, glinting star patterns on the moving Mercedes. I stood there in shock, watching him go, every cell of my body still pulsating. I was surprised ... and intrigued beyond belief. I couldn't understand how could just walked away. Like that!

I was shaken to my core, never having expected to be knocked so off-balance by anyone. However, the constant thrill of discovery, deep curiosity and craving to learn more had been my constant companions, welling up and overflowing in me from the very first moment I left New York.

Three Cups of Tea

"Oh Kabul, my Kabul!
Awake from your violet slumber to a pink-orange dawn,
Ringed by your moonscape mountains,
You await the call to prayer to cast off the dust of dreams and begin your day."
The Author

Every color in this mountainous land was clear and bright due to the altitude and lack of modern pollution. The clouds were a smeared silver frosting on the azure cake of the sky on the day I met Dustin and his girlfriend, Susan, in 1969. Everyone called her Sunshine due to her personality. We decided to travel together.

They were going to India to "get enlightenment" like many other Americans who were influenced by the Beatles and Maharishi Mahesh Yogi. They were nice people. We traveled, ate, cooked, laughed, joked, smoked hashish and generally reveled in life. They asked me to come to India with them but I knew my path was in Afghanistan.

Dustin was a psychologist and Sunshine a nurse. They had taken a year off to travel. He was medium height with waist-length, straight brown hair that he wore in a braid. Sunshine had curly, blonde, short hair. She was five feet tall and petite. They were from San Francisco and flew to Spain where they bought a Volkswagen minibus and were traveling overland to India for the winter. We met in Turkey.

The minibus was outfitted with a bed, a wood-burning stove and a tiny sink. The area under the bed in the back of the van was used for storage where my backpack filled with clothes and toiletries, audio cassette tapes, and a mini tape recorder was stashed with theirs.

The first thing that we noticed about Turkey was the children. The little boys, ages seven and eight, already had western suit jackets that were exact replicas of their fathers. Each one hawked their wares up and down the streets and in the bazaars. Their expressions were those of wizened adults; tiny lines had already formed around their eyes and mouths. I had never seen such sobriety in children and hoped that these children were an exception. However, I soon learned that child labor existed in many third-world countries where mortality rates were high. The idea was to have as many children as possible to support the family. Schooling, outside of Quran reading and basic mathematics, was a privilege to be paid for by those who could afford it. At age seven, almost all children took on the responsibilities of adults.

The Turkish men were avid bottom pinchers and laughed at Sunshine's and my protests. I was glad to leave Istanbul.

The breath of yesterday welled up in me when I saw the harbor of Ephesus. It transported me back in time. I could see Turks, Jews, Arabs, and Romans milling around the streets. Because of time shifting the earth, the natural harbor was now about three miles inland.

I was searching for something, perhaps the well center of the human race or the cry from the first breath of humanity. I wouldn't find it here. The feeling of being in another era tried to creep in and take over, but it wasn't far back enough for me. I knew that the sum of humanity was found in a further past. When I met myself in history, I'd know.

Walking among these ruins, breaking the gauzy, hovering mists, I smelled the ancients and their ways pressing upon my body drawing me deeper into past civilizations. The "grandeur that was Rome" left its massive imprint upon the earth in heavy columned remains. I came to a shelf-like ridge where the remnants of a stone hut stood. Then I climbed an extremely narrow, stony path, winding upwards and covered by pine trees to such an extent that I had to creep on all fours. The path, however, only led to a higher ridge. It was typical of the sly Turkish mountains; always leading me to believe I'd reached the top when one more ridge peeked out from the next bend.

Outside of Izmir, in the south of Turkey, Dustin stopped the bus and we camped for the night. We were on the edge of a tobacco field where three women stood a little ways off and smiled at us. I approached them and greeted them with the traditional greeting of *Selam Aleikum* (May peace be upon thee). Everyone bowed and smiled. In the next instant, I realized that was the only phrase we had in common. These simple agriculturists spoke a Turkish dialect unknown in Istanbul. The Turkish spoken in Istanbul was as foreign to them as English. Undaunted, we communicated with our hands and facial expressions. I asked them how old they were and each one told me with their fingers that they were twenty-six, seventeen, and sixteen. They were fascinated that I, too, was twenty-six and proceeded to touch my face, my hair, arms, and clothes, laughing all the while. I did the same to them, feeling their hands calloused from picking tobacco and their faces leathered from always being exposed to the sun. The sixteen-year-old disappeared into a large garage-like structure and returned with a shot-size glass of hot, black, sweetened tea for me. All of the women insisted that I drink three glasses.

The women were dressed in incredibly colorful blouses and skirts of a floral print over loose pantaloons. Tied on their heads, each one had kerchiefs resembling nuns' veils. The sixteen-year-old was sandy-haired and freckled. She reminded me of a chunky Midwest farm girl. The two older women were married. They told me this by pointing to their wedding bands and drawing mustaches with their fingers on their upper lips. I wore several rings so they asked if I was married. I shook my head no. Their faces registered surprise that I was still unmarried at my age. It was dusk by the time I finally returned to the van after many goodbyes. I felt satisfied that I was able to communicate with them but sorrowful that it was so limited.

In eastern Turkey, we camped in the courtyard of a crumbling ruin of a castle, a leftover from the Crusades. Early in the morning, I decided to explore what was left of a turret. I climbed the fragments of a staircase and walked into a narrow passage that was perched over the sea. I came out at the other end and felt as if I were standing at the end of the world thrust out over the turquoise waters.

I heard the crunch of pebbles. As I turned, I was faced with an incredibly fierce, furious-looking Turk. He had dark-brown skin, cruel, black eyes, and a thick, black mustache that ended in points. He wore a white shirt with an open neck and balloon sleeves, as those worn by pirates in the seventeen hundreds. Over this was a red, white and black checked wool pullover vest. His black balloon pants were shoved into black, calf-length boots. On his head was a large, white turban wrapped around a multi-colored pointed skull cap.

I held my breath as he strode passed me and stood on the end of the promontory, resting one leg on the mushrooming rocks. He turned to look at me. My skin crawled and my stomach twisted at the hideous look in his eyes. I fled down the passageway, leaped from the crumbled stairs and ran to the bus. Dustin and Sunshine were just having their morning tea as I burst upon them, spilling out my fear. Dustin dashed out of the bus and up the passageway, but no one was there. I had no clue what Dustin thought he'd have done if he had met the Turk.

Later that day, we were having tiny cups of the thick bitter coffee claimed by all countries in the Middle East, when an elderly Turk approached us and asked in excellent English if he may join us. Dustin pulled up a chair and we answered the usual questions about where we came from, where we were going, and how we liked Turkey. We all said that we liked Turkey very much ... especially the kindness of the villagers.

He gave us a broad smile and said, "It is our pleasure to serve you."

I told him about my escapade with the man in the ruined castle.

"Other people have reported a similar man in that same place. No one wears that type of clothing today. It is very old fashioned. The local people believe that it is the ghost of someone who committed murder there more than one hundred years ago."

Hearing his words made the hair on the back of my neck and on my arms stand up and chills run through my body.

* * *

Next, we ventured into Iran. Our trip there was uneventful. The people in Teheran were extremely rude in their simple dealings with us. They verbally pushed us around in order to serve us and get rid of us as fast as possible. We were shocked and angry at their behavior, but since we didn't speak Farsi, we couldn't discover the source of their displeasure. It was only after we got to Afghanistan that we learned from some tourists that the Iranians had been badly dealt with by the flood of tourists going through Iran to India. The tourists thought nothing of stealing from the Irani merchants. I guess since we were Western tourists, the Iranians lumped us together with the others.

The women here wore the *chador*, a huge, sheet-like garment, unlike the simple headscarves of the Turkish women. The *chador* was worn over their clothes, and they held it over their noses and mouths with their teeth. I was very curious to see what the women wore underneath the *Chador*, but they just moved along the streets hardly looking at me.

By contrast, the Irani villagers were wonderful. The men stood in small groups smiling in welcome as young boys shyly *Selam*ed us and offered us *chai* (black tea) to "quench the travelers' thirst." Women were nowhere to be seen. The further east we traveled, the fewer women we saw. It seemed as if entire countries were populated by men.

At the border, we gave our passports and visas to the sour Irani Customs officials who stamped them and threw them back at us. Puzzled by their hostility, we hoped the Afghans had better manners.

We crossed the border into Afghanistan. An old man showed us some of the oldest windmills in the world. They looked different from any windmills I had ever seen. An extended adobe wall was broken by vertical wooden poles with horizontal slats. The speed of the turning slats was controlled by several bunches of tall reeds that leaned vertically against the slats. Underground rooms were used to winnow grain churned by the windmills. This was explained to us later by the customs officials after they made sure we were seated with very sweet *chai*.

Before we entered the customs office, we saw a sign outside that read, 'Five dollars per vehicle entrance fee and currency exchange seventy *afghanis* to one U.S. dollar.' We had already been told by some tourists that the currency rate in Kabul was one hundred *afghanis* to the dollar. Consequently, we weren't eager to do a large transaction here.

The customs official, who was tall with black, longish hair, dark copper-colored skin, and black eyes, smiled and greeted us in broken English. He asked where we were from and we smiled back and said, "America," and handed him our passports and visas. All went well until he insisted that it was five dollars per person to enter Afghanistan. We shook our heads in refusal and he dug in his heels. I could understand his point. He tried to get as much money as possible out of tourists since God alone knew how long he'd be in this barren place with just two other customs officials for company. The average salary in Afghanistan was fifty dollars per year.

Unwilling to pay a total of fifteen dollars for three people, we coaxed him outside of his own office and pointed to the sign. When he saw that he was beaten, he shrugged his shoulders and said: *"Parwa nist"* (It doesn't matter, or forget about it). Later we learned that this was the most common saying throughout Afghanistan.

We went back indoors and the customs official offered us more tea and brought out a chunk of hashish. He broke it in two. It was black with a golden-colored center and the aroma filled the office. Then he handed us silver dollar-size pieces. Smiling and chatting, Dustin and he ate theirs while Sunshine and I saved ours to smoke later.

This was the opportunity to learn thirty useful phrases in the local language. Dari is an ancient form of Farsi, the official language of Iran. The customs officials were thrilled that we wanted to learn their language and helped us to write down and repeat the phrases during the time that they stamped our passports. They couldn't do enough to assist us with our questions about Afghanistan. After changing ten dollars into *afghanis,* the officials didn't even check our van.

We noticed a European man in a suit and tie who they put through all sorts of difficulties: checking his papers, his vehicle and his driver. By the time we cleared customs it was dark, and he was still being searched.

We drove several kilometers past the border towards Herat, the western capital of Afghanistan. The black, moonless night and the non-existent road made it impossible to travel further. We came upon a lonely *caravanserai* buffeted by high winds and decided to spend the night. These were inns of a sort that were used by men driving caravans. It was a single-storey adobe edifice with approximately ten rooms. The largest room served as the *saloon* (the living room) and had to be entered first. Red carpets in black geometric designs covered the floor. The whitewashed walls had small chinks of mirrors glued to them.

Six Afghan men were squatting in a circle, some smoking *chillums* (cylindrical, four-inch, vertically-held pipes) made of clay; others fingered *tassbee* (prayer beads) over egg-sized tea bowls. A small candle in the center of the carpet stood in a cracked dish. Because of the many pieces of mirrors on the walls, the room was well-lit by the candle's reflection.

After leaving our boots at the door in line with the others, we entered the room and greeted—everyone with *Selam Aleikum*. The reciprocal greeting, *Wa' Aleikum as Selam*, was returned with smiles, and everyone made room for us to join the circle. A ten-year-old boy, who looked like he was from Mongolia, appeared with tiny cups and a minuscule teapot of *qawa*, a traditional green tea served with crushed cardamom seeds. The men were exceptionally polite and friendly. The local toll collector, Abdul Selam, spoke English.

Afghan names, no surprise are different from ours. Afghans do not have last names. When they arrived in Western countries and were asked their last names, they merely took the name of the town, city or village they were from. For example, instead of Cat Parenti, they would use Cat Brooklyn. The word "Abdul" is a short version of "Abdullah" meaning "Servant of Allah." Instead of using Allah/God after every "Servant of," Afghans use the attributes of Allah such as Servant of the Creator, the Peaceful, the Clement, the Mighty etc. These names are used by men. Abdul Selam means "Servant of the Peaceful." These two names are not used separately.

Women have the same names without "Abdul" and usually with an "a" at the end in addition to names of flowers, the moon and the stars. Some examples are Halima (meaning the Clement), Shirin Gul (Sweet Rose), and Sitara (Star).

Abdul Selam had a dictionary of Dari, Pashto, and English. The former two were the national languages of Afghanistan. We started to have what became a very familiar conversation throughout the East. "Where are you from? Where are you going? What is your name? Where is your family? Are you married?"

After we got through this bit of conversation, I asked this man, "Tell me, sir, about the custom of leaving footwear outside."

The toll collector replied, "This is to show respect for the home by not bringing in the dirt of the streets." He then laughed and said that an Afghan curse was to call someone *Khak-ay-sarak* (Filth of the streets).

I asked, "What is the meaning of this custom of pressing three cups of tea upon us? We've seen this from Turkey to here."

He replied, "This is the courtesy of Islam; that of honor to the guest. The first cup is to quench the thirst, the second is to show friendship, and the third reveals the host's generosity to his honored guest."

When I remarked that the tea boy had Mongol features, Abdul Selam began to explain to us about the Afghans. The Pashtuns, the indigenous Afghans, are the largest group and speak Pashto. This is a language unto itself probably from the Scythian and Parthian languages of this region. Then there are the Tajiks, who speak Dari, an ancient form of Farsi who came from Iran originally. Finally, there are the Hazaras, so named for the *hazar* (one thousand) troops quartered in Afghanistan by Ghenghiz Khan. They speak Hazaragee, a combination of Dari and Turkic. These Mongols intermarried with the locals. In a war with the Pashtuns, the Hazaras lost and were pushed into the central part of Afghanistan that is very mountainous with caves and is called the Hazarajat. The Hazaras, who are Shiite Muslims like the Iranians, have all the menial jobs in this mainly Sunni Islamic country.

After myriad tiny cups of green tea, drunk while holding sugar coated almonds in my mouth, I needed to find a toilet. I spoke a few words of Dari to our new friend Abdul Selam. His reply was to call the tea boy. The boy brought a lantern and led me outside around the back of the building to an adobe hut attached to the *caravanserai*. He pulled aside a sackcloth curtain that covered a doorway and flashed a lantern into a bare adobe room with a one-foot-square hole near the far corner. This was the toilet. Near it was a pile of fine sand and what looked like a teapot, minus the lid and handle, filled with water. These were to be used instead of toilet paper. The tea boy started to leave and I stopped him, smiled and signed for him to set down the lantern. For some reason, he interpreted this to mean that I wanted to kiss him. This boy who barely came up to my chest put the lantern down, grabbed me around the waist and pulled me up against him.

He said in English, "Come on, I Afghan!"

I laughed at the ridiculousness of the situation and said, "*Nay nay!*"

He released me and I took the lantern.

The following day we drove into Herat, the western capital of Afghanistan. It was gorgeous. Walled adobe houses, along grassy, tree-lined banks over small streams, stood on the outskirts of the city. The main street was graveled and had paved sidewalks. Shops without fronts sold everything from food and clothing to auto parts, all displayed in geometric procession. The three of us were grateful that the Afghans were amazingly friendly, without the bottom pinching of the Turks or the pushiness of the Iranians. Everyone smiled and said, "*Selam Aleikum.*"

It was a cloudy, cold winter day. We passed the big fort that dominated the town. Everything was a blue-gray color except the offerings of the fruit sellers, whose electric-orange tangerines were stacked in huge pyramids on the ground.

Herat belonged to the Persians until the sixteen hundreds when, through the efforts of a Kandahari, called Mir Wais Hotecki, it became part of Afghanistan. Here, the people spoke Dari. At the bank, they gave us eighty-three *afghanis* to the dollar.

The few cars we saw belonged to tourists. The Afghans walked, rode bicycles, or used striking horse-drawn carts painted in a multitude of colors.

The horses were decorated with beautiful red-knitted little balls, tassels, and sleigh bells. The men's headgear was either the turban or a *karakul* (lambskin) cap. They wore long, flowing pastel-colored tunics that hung to their calves. These garments had round necks, straight sleeves to the wrist and side slits from the hips down. The voluminous pantaloons fell into graceful folds and tapered at the ankle.

This traditional outfit was called *peeran/tambon* (tunic and pantaloons). The *peeran* is the long tunic worn by both men and women. The *tambon* are drawstring pants that fall to the ankle and are worn under the *peeran*. In the center of Kabul, women wear white elephant pants cuffed in white lace. Women wear vibrant colors and are compared to the setting sun and the men wear pastels and are compared to the moon. Over these clothes, the men threw European overcoats, leftovers from World War I or II. Some just hung carpets over their shoulders to keep warm and to advertise their merchandise.

The women wore the *chadoree,* a complete veil that dropped over the top of the head resembling a tent. A small embroidered cap fit the head. The veil had minute vertical pleats that cascaded down the back and sides to the feet. At the front, a small mesh grill covered their eyes. The rest of the front piece was not pleated but embroidered and hung down mid-thigh. Underneath the *chadoree* were calf-length flower print dresses and the same style solid colored pastel pantaloons as the men's. The colors of the veils were brilliant red, blue, green, rust, and gold.

Women in Chadorees

We went on foot to examine the shops. We marveled at the fruit shops where the merchants sat among their geometrically stacked pyramids of ripe pomegranates, quinces, apples, persimmons, and bananas. Green grapes were hung from the ceiling resembling incense braziers adding to the perfume of the shops. We loaded up on their bountiful wares.

Then we stopped at a pharmacy to stock up on penicillin and Entro-Viaform against dysentery, a prevalent scourge of tourists and Afghans alike. The cost was a penny a pill with no prescription needed. Because I spoke a few words in Dari, the druggist was impressed and gave me a chewable vitamin C tablet as a gift. I did not know it was pure ascorbic acid and when the bitterness hit my tongue, I did a little dance. Everyone laughed at my reaction.

We decided to explore the jewelry shops. In one of them, the owner invited us to sit down and he played his *dutar* (a two-string, lute-like instrument), while Dustin accompanied him on sleigh bells. I loved his jewelry and picked out an old, silver bracelet with carnelian and moss-green agate stones with five rings attached to it by silver chains. Unfortunately, the rings didn't fit me. The owner of the shop replaced the rings with some from another set he had. In the transfer, one of the rings cracked and he had to send it out to be soldered. His first price was four hundred *afghanis*. I held out and he said three hundred and fifty. I started walking out of the shop and he exclaimed, "For you My Lady, best price two hundred!" I grinned and retrieved my prize.

Fruit Seller

Although we had sweaters and light jackets, we were unprepared for Afghanistan's twenty to thirty degree Fahrenheit winter weather. In Europe, Greece, Turkey, and Iran winter was just beginning. Tourists on their way to tropical India didn't want to be encumbered with heavy clothing.

The sheepskin coat bazaar had a few shops chock full of coats with sheep's wool on the inside. The outside skins were heavily embroidered. They were fabulous to look at and just what we needed. There were also embroidered sheepskin boots. However, nothing fit us. We agreed to wait until we got to Kabul where there would be a bigger selection.

A baker smiled, gave us the *Selam* and invited us to examine his oven, a large hole in the center of an adobe platform. He squatted on the platform over the oven and pointed to a roaring fire below. After a few minutes, he used a peeled stick to pull a loaf of flatbread off the wall of the oven. Out came this brown oblong-shaped bread that was about one-quarter of an inch thick in the center and one inch thick around the edges. The center was scored similarly to a pie. He smiled and handed it to us saying, "*Naan.*" We each bought a loaf from him for a penny apiece and he gave us a piece of hashish as a gift.

The Afghans are exceptionally patient and kind. Hashish is legal there and it is offered to you wherever you go. The baker fell in love with me and of course assumed that Dustin had two wives since no unrelated men and women are seen together in public. In broken English, he asked Dustin how much money he should give him for me. I told him in Dari that I wasn't for sale. He was amazed! He laughed, shook my hand and wished me luck on my journey to Hindustan. With a grin and a snap of his fingers, Dustin said, "Just when I was about to make some money."

Thē Bi·Lēvēl Tōilēt

*"The baking of bread is considered a very holy work.
Bread comes to mankind from the heart of God/Allah
to bring Light to the soul."*
Afghan saying

The next day we had our first Afghan meal in our first Afghan restaurant outside of Herat. This place was a huge two-storey adobe structure with a balcony that swerved around the upper floor.

The middle-aged proprietor came forward with a smile and we all gave the *Selam*. He directed us to the upstairs part of the restaurant where there were rough, raw wooden tables and chairs. Nobody else was on this level. It was reserved for families, so the women could lift their veils and eat without being stared at by 'strange men.' He asked us in Dari what we wanted.

I gave the traditional response in Dari, indicating that we were hungry.

With a smile that split his face, he commented on my ability to speak his language and disappeared downstairs. We sat talking, enjoying the scenery and the activity below.

An extraordinarily handsome man came upstairs and passed by the table. He greeted us with a smile. As he walked by, an incredible aura of roses wafted over us. Several minutes later he reappeared and stood by our table. He was six-foot-two, muscular with dark, copper-colored skin, black hair, huge black eyes, a Roman nose and full lips that were almost hidden by a big black mustache. His dazzling teeth matched the color of his traditional long, white cotton tunic and brilliant white cotton pantaloons. The shirt had an embroidered silk geometric design down the front resembling the shirt Bob first showed me in Brooklyn. A tan leather belt with two curved daggers protruding from it and two bandoliers of bullets across his chest completed this outfit. His head was topped with eight feet of white cotton turban and a pink rose was tucked behind his right ear. He wore a gold watch and had a gold ring with a turquoise stone on his right hand. He made a very impressive presentation.

With a smile on my face, I put my fingers near my nose and inhaled. He began talking rapidly in a language that I later learned was Pashto, the second language of Afghanistan. I didn't understand him but he pulled out a tiny glass bottle with a cork stopper and handed it to me. I removed the stopper and the aroma of roses encircled us as we passed the bottle around. We were all smiling and nodding. I tried to return the bottle to him but he refused with many protests insisting that we keep it. We did so with more smiles and nods and repetitions of *tashakor* (thank you).

Later we learned that, in Muslim countries, if you admire something, you must be given it no matter the cost.

Lunch arrived as several large oblong *naans*. They placed one in front of each of us. On this was served a portion of rice and lamb with carrots and raisins. There were also tiny dishes of lamb stew with potatoes, an extremely spicy stewed spinach dish, and of course *chai*.

This time it was plain black tea, served in short, thick, clear glasses from France. Each glass contained sugar that resembled shards of rock candy. This was beet sugar that melted very slowly. Your last cup of tea was as sweet as your first. Hungry, we fell to the food using pieces of our bread as utensils, in the same way we had observed the men downstairs doing. It was plain but tasty. The entire meal cost fourteen cents.

After all the tea, I needed the restroom. When a waiter came around with more tea, I asked him in Dari where the bathroom was. He pointed to the wall. All I saw was a quilt hanging there. I asked him again and his answer was the same. I went over to the wall and picked up a corner of the quilt to discover a door. I opened the door onto a bare room with a rectangular hole in the adobe floor. As before, I noticed the pile of fine sand and the water pot. When I went to relieve myself, I looked down and saw the identical "toilet" on the first floor! Thank God, no one was using it! If they looked up, they would've seen my naked bottom and simultaneously gotten a "bath" from me!

Laughing hysterically about the toilets, we paid the bill, climbed aboard a horse-drawn cart and rode back to the van.

To show respect for the meal and the cooks, food is eaten with the right hand and without the use of utensils. The first utensil is the spoon. Forks and knives came later in this culture. The left hand that is used to clean your body in the toilet always remains in your lap.

We decided to treat ourselves to a hotel before going on the road to Kandahar the next day. The Super Hotel had a room with three single beds. We threw our sleeping bags on top of their blankets not trusting to lice and other odious crawlers. Exhausted and full, we fell into bed and slept cozy and warm for a change as it was quite cold making sleep in the van uncomfortable.

The next morning was another crystal-clear, sunny day with a brilliant periwinkle sky. We sauntered across the courtyard into the Super Hotel's restaurant, and super it was! The dining room was a large whitewashed clean room with unvarnished wooden tables and chairs. Breakfast consisted of fried eggs, Afghan bread with unsalted butter and orange marmalade plus *chai*. It was a feast for our western palates.

The owner, a graduate of Kabul University, brought out our order. He was only too happy to practice his English on us, asking how we liked his food and if we thought other tourists might be pleased. We assured him that the brilliance of serving something akin to western food would endear him to the tourists expected to inundate Kabul in the spring.

After our meal, we drove along the road to Kandahar, the southern capital of Afghanistan. I observed the barrenness of the plains and the vastness of the mountains with small dun-colored villages huddled at their feet. Seized with poignant awe at the might and majesty of the earth, I asked Dustin to stop. Climbing over a small hill about fifty paces away, I dropped to my knees with my arms outstretched and acknowledged the work of the Supreme Creator in all His Majesty and Glory. The words "How beautiful Thou hath made the earth, Oh Lord," coursed through my mind. I prayed fervently, praising God for about five minutes; something I had not done, except by rote, since childhood. A feeling of great peace descended upon me: a peace of the soul that comes when we feel we are in paradise.

We stopped for lunch in the tiny town of Girishk and walked up five crumbling stone steps into an adobe restaurant. Everything was adobe including the seats that were embankments jutting out from the walls. On the walls were hand-painted, colorful floral designs. We chose one of the rooms, removed our shoes and sat cross-legged on the embankments covered with carpets. A small boy brought a huge platter of saffron rice with small dishes of stewed lamb and potatoes and the now familiar, delicious Afghan spicy spinach.

Some Afghans came up to us and smiled, showing us cards of Paul Bunyan and the astronauts Neil Armstrong and Buzz Aldridge. They resembled the baseball cards that we collected when we were kids. Two of the men were dressed as women and it was obvious they served as women for the men. One, who was in his teens, had large black eyes rimmed with kohl and long lashes. He held a part of his shawl over his face, similar to the Irani women holding the *chador*. He was especially delicate looking, tall and slim. The other was obviously a young man with a mustache who had a very soft voice, a pearl earring and a heavily embroidered *peeran*. We had a smiling session and the Afghans left.

After the meal, we drove into Kandahar, parked and walked around the town. We came upon a shop selling *peeran*. The owner, Assad, spoke some English. He invited us in for *chai*. Assad brought out what resembled the black sole of a man's shoe. It was a piece of hashish. He said that this quality was five dollars per kilogram and machine pressed. Then he brought out a hard, black patty that he said was hand pressed and cost ten dollars per kilo. He inquired if we wanted to buy some to sell in Europe on the way back. We laughed and said we were on our way to India right now. We finished the *chai* and left. Dustin remarked on the flourishing hashish business that must be going on among locals and tourists. Since hashish was legal in Afghanistan, many European tourists had a thriving hashish business that stretched from Afghanistan to Europe. Amsterdam is an open city where any and all drugs may be purchased, used legally and are taxed. Some Americans also tried to buy and export hashish, on a minute scale since it was and still is illegal to export drugs to the United States. They were usually caught at the border leaving Afghanistan.

Kandahar was a twelfth-century walled city breathlessly standing on the ochre colored plains. Women were nowhere to be seen. Boys and men from age six to sixty were hustling to make money. All of them tried to take us to a hotel, sell us hashish, or change money. Merchants came out into the streets cajoling us to enter their shops and peruse their wares, promising the best prices. We disliked the pressure here, so opposite to Herat. The Kandaharis were not unfriendly, but their smiles faded with a handshake. After escaping the melee of merchants, we loaded up on fruits, vegetables, cookies, pasta, and beans and started driving towards Kabul. On the way out of the city, we saw pastel-colored adobe buildings lining the road. Some were green with turquoise geometric designs and others, pink with yellow designs. A dry river bed was our campsite for the night.

In the morning, I took a walk up the clay riverbed and came upon a herd of camels. There were many babies. A nearby stream ran into a large algae-covered pond where many tiny fish darted in and out of the spinach-colored water. I stayed for a while thinking that I had finally made it to Afghanistan. But why? Why was my coming here so important? With these thoughts turning over and over in my mind, I meandered back to the van.

King Prŏtěcting Frïěnd

"Anyone can knock at any door and
Must be cared for by the owner of the house
For three days."
First Law of *Pashtunwali* (the law of the indigenous Pashtun Afghans)
is *melmastia* (hospitality to the guest)

After settling into the Sinha Hotel in Shar-ee-Now (New City) in Kabul, I wandered around the neighboring shops. I found a beautiful brown sheepskin coat with rust-colored silk embroidery outside and brown lamb's wool on the inside. This would definitely keep out the Kabul cold. It would also double as a mattress and pillow at night. Schooled in the Afghan method of bargaining, I knew not to show any interest in a particular item or the price would be astronomical.

Starting my conversation in Dari, I said, *"Selam Aleikum."*

"Wa' Aleikum as Selam, Khanum (My Lady)."

"Art thou well?"

"I thank thee, Khanum. Art thou also well?"

I nodded. *"Tell me Oh Master Shopkeeper, how much wilt thou take to part with this coat,"* I asked as I pointed to one I had no interest in.

"Oh Khanum, for thee, the best price is thirteen hundred afghanis."

"Nay, this is very expensive."

"But here, Khanum, is a coat just for thee for only twelve hundred afghanis."

"Oh Master Shopkeeper, the quality is very poor."

"Nay nay, it is good. What price wilt suit thy desire?"

I pretended to mull this over and turned and pointed to the coat I wanted. *"My desire is to procure this coat for six hundred afghanis."*

"Nay Khanum, the cost of this coat just for thee is eleven hundred."

"Nay Oh Master Shopkeeper, seven hundred is the price I desire to part with."

"One thousand, because thou speak so artfully."

I smiled and thanked him as I walked out of the door and attempted to cross the street.

Laughing, he came out of the shop and said in English, "Yes, Khanum, special price, seven hundred and fifty!"

I pretended to consider this as I returned to the shop and pointed to the vest that I had seen before.

"'Tis five hundred. But for thee Khanum, 'tis a gift if thou wilt give me eight hundred afghanis for both," he said with a satisfied air in Dari.

I started laughing at how he came down, in a second, from five hundred *afghanis* to fifty. He was making money on the deal for no shopkeeper anywhere will give merchandise away. I paid him and put on my warm coat and carried the rolled up vest. We smiled and *Selamed* each other and I am sure both of us felt that we'd made a wily bargain.

Outside, the orange setting sun gazed at the now chocolate mountains, tingeing their folds with cinnamon. I reconnected with Dustin and Sunshine and they congratulated me on my purchases. We went for a meal in the Khyber Restaurant, a favorite of tourists. Here, in a room as big as a football field, we found imitations of western food. There were thin steaks, roasted potatoes, a cauliflower stew and even rhubarb pie in "steam table" like pans. This was such a feast after so much Afghan food! We ignored the fact that it was lukewarm. Eventually we were to discover that the Afghans wanted to imitate Western habits but they never could get it quite right. There were no candles under neath the chafing dishes! After the meal, Dustin and Sunshine returned to their van and I went to the pension I secured for the night. We planned to meet in the morning.

My roommates, Morrie and Bill, were in Kabul from Australia to export *jezails* (antique guns) and carpets. The 3 of us had the "dormitory", a very large room with 3 single beds loosely grouped around the *bokharee* (wood burning stove). November in Kabul was between 45 and 55 degrees F in the day and 25 to 30 at night. With no central heating, we all slept in our clothes and sleeping bags with our sheepskin coats for covers. As the night wore on, the fire in the *bokharee* dwindled and the cold seeped into the room, complete with frost on the inside of the windows. Like hibernating animals, we burrowed even farther into our sheepskin coats and dreaded getting up in the morning.

The following morning, Dustin, Sunshine and I went to a shop that sold antique jewelry that some tourists in Europe had recommended.

The shop was owned by King Protecting Friend. In the large, rectangular front room, all kinds of silver, antique jewelry hung on the walls and rested in the glass cases strewn about the shop. As we entered, a young servant, Mohammed, who was tall and well-built, with a shaved head and face, approached us. We gave each other the *Selam* as King Protecting Friend called, from his office in the back, "Come, come."

King was a bear of a man at six-foot-five with a huge head of pitch-black hair, large mustache and the creamy, rosy skin color of the Neapolitan Italians. King had very large brown eyes, a Roman nose, and full lips. He wore a milk-chocolate brown suit with white pinstripes, a dark-brown tie and dark brown leather shoes that offset his white shirt. He was smiling and the kindness of his soul flowed from his eyes. I smiled back and immediately felt an affinity for him.

He introduced us to a friend of his, the Seer, who was five-feet-ten, with olive skin, a pencil- thin mustache, and short black hair. He had on a dark-blue suit with a light-blue shirt and red tie. King spoke little English but the Seer had studied in the United States and his English was equal to ours. My gut, which is never wrong, said *"no"* to the Seer's friendliness.

Dustin explained that an Englishman, Malcolm Hardcastle, who he had met in Holland, recommended King. Malcolm was one of King's customers. The Seer translated everything we said. King lit up when he heard the Englishman's name and poured out a river of Dari. The Seer said King would be happy to help us with any jewelry business. We answered King and the Seer's questions about who we were, where we came from, where we were going, and how we liked Afghanistan immediately followed.

After much *chai* drinking too close to noon and Kabul's thirteen-hundred-foot altitude, we were famished and went to lunch.

Afterward, we walked back to King's shop and he asked if he may drive us anywhere. We told him we wanted to go grocery shopping. He drove us in his dark-blue Mercedes and surprised us by insisting on paying for our purchases because we were guests in his country.

We asked King about this custom and he said in Dari, "*First law of Pashtunwali* (the laws of the indigenous Pashtun Afghans) *is melmastia* (honor to the guest)." Both King and the Seer were Pashtuns.

The Seer took over and said in English, "King is your host. He is bound by *melmastia* to shelter and feed you. Anyone can knock on any door and must be taken in and fed for three days. At the end of this time, the person thanks their host and leaves, or states any business that needs to be done."

Astonished, I burst out, "But why would you do this? Don't you fear for your lives and property?"

The Seer translated for King and both laughed. "You see Catee-*jon*, we have no fear. As we do for others, so Allah will do for us in paradise. The second law is *nanawatai* (protection). This means that anyone can ask anyone for protection and it must be granted."

"What does '*jon*' mean?" I asked.

The Seer said, "It is a term of endearment. It means, 'dear' or 'life' or 'body'. You can say this to family members or friends or lovers."

"Okay, King-*jon*," I said, feeling even more endeared to King.

"I like this word 'okay', Catee-*jon*. Okay, okay," King repeated and we both laughed.

"But suppose that an enemy asks for protection," Dustin asked.

"The law of asylum must be granted even if the person who grants asylum loses their life in doing so. In Afghanistan, our word is our bond."

"What happens if someone refuses?" Dustin continued.

"Then he is no Afghan and we will cast him out from among us. The third great law we have is *badal* (revenge). Revenge is taken against those who have stolen land, money or the honor of a woman." ˋ

"Do you kill people for these transgressions," I asked, thinking about my New York friends who called these people savages.

"No, first we make them pay fines. If they refuse, then it is up to the person who is wronged to decide what to do. Everything is decided on a case by case basis.

"So there is no central law," Sunshine asked.

"Yes, the three great laws of hospitality, asylum, and revenge are our central law. But they are applied on a case-by-case basis with the people involved before we seek to involve a *kazi*, a judge as you have in America," the Seer replied.

After we made our purchases, we returned to the van with many thanks to King.

He replied in Dari with a smile, "*Thou art my honored guests.*"

We were filled to the brim with love for the Afghan people as we drove to the Ansary Hotel where Dustin and Sunshine decided to stay for their two remaining nights. The Ansarys were a family close to the Prophet Mohammad and their lineage is revered. We were met in the lobby by three brothers as well as their two male cousins. Everyone was completely drunk. They began spouting to us in English on how very close their family is to the Prophet Mohammad since their ancestors assisted him when he fled from Mecca to Medina. I wondered at this "closeness" since alcohol was forbidden by Mohammed. They wanted us to join them but since Afghans are not used to consuming liquor, we took one look at their bloodshot eyes and red noses and were convinced to forego this little gathering.

Dustin and Sunshine said goodnight and headed to their room which was about the same size as mine, complete with a wood burning stove. I walked back to the Sinha Hotel.

The next day, Dustin, Sunshine and I met at King's shop. I purchased some antique, silver jewelry from him. King produced a bottle of acid to test the quality of the silver. He put one drop of the acid on the underside of a bracelet and it turned gray-black. The Seer explained that this meant the silver was "sterling." Then King proceeded to show me the different colors associated with fine and mixed silver. The Seer said that a blue or green color indicated that the piece was brass, copper, or iron, and only coated with silver. King suggested that we set up a business together. He agreed to collect and ship jewelry that I would sell in America. We would be partners. I thought that was a great idea. The Seer left and King gave me a sterling silver necklace as a gift for my purchases. It was a huge, heart-shaped locket with peacocks and flowers carved on the lid.

"'*Tis for thee, Catee-jon. Thou art my sister,*" he said in Dari, his eyes overflowing with love.

I was overcome with emotion receiving such a beautiful gift and thanked him profusely.

Then he said that he wanted to show us Kabul before Dustin and Sunshine left. King took us to lunch at what once was the summer palace of the king called Bagh-ee-Bala (High Garden). It was on a hill overlooking the city. The interior was whitewashed with vaulted ceilings and hand-painted floral designs on the walls. Beautiful, old carpets covered the polished stone floor. The chairs were wood with mother of pearl inlay and had brown leather seats and backs. Platters of roast chicken with carrots, potatoes, and peas were carried out to us, accompanied by Italian white wine, and orange sherbet for dessert. With much laughter and enjoyment, we devoured our meal.

Afterward, King drove us past a Russian-built mosque. He said that nobody goes to that mosque since they do not want to be too friendly with the Russians. We also passed Qargah Dam that had villas alongside for rent plus another western restaurant. King asked what we were doing for dinner and we explained that we were going to cook for ourselves since this was Thanksgiving in America and we usually spent it with our families.

He said, *"Thou must think of me as family."*

Then he promised to rent a villa and *"give much foods. You bring all Americans you like. Then everyone family."*

He laughed at our surprised faces. We couldn't believe such generosity towards complete strangers. Then we all shook hands. "Aha," I thought, "the law of hospitality is at work."

King held onto my hands and examined them. The water in Iran and Afghanistan was extraordinarily hard and my hands began to look and feel like old, cracked, dried leather. King produced a small tin of hand cream. He said, *"You take, gift for you."* It was wonderful, very thick and oily. Soon my hands were smooth and soft again.

That evening, Morrie, Bill, Dustin, Sunshine, and I went with King in his dark blue Mercedes to Qargah. The villa was a series of ground floor rooms similar to our nicer motels. The electric heaters in each room dispelled some of the winter's frosty night. I preferred the *bokharees* (wood-burning stoves). King provided two-hundred-proof brandy. Feeling warm and cozy, we began chatting, laughing and joking. Then the food arrived from the Qargah Restaurant. It was roast chicken and French fries with green beans and carrots in a spicy tomato sauce.

When we were gorged to the maximum, King lit up a *chillum*, a handheld vertical pipe with some premium hashish. The effect was incredible. I left my body and visited other planets and star systems. King began playing his harmonium, an accordion-like instrument in the minor scale. The harmonium sits on the floor when played. King's right hand worked the keyboard as his left controlled the accordion-like pleats. The droning of the classical songs and his deep basso profundo voice carried me away to another century when I lived as an Afghan.

We all were in a dream state for what seemed like an eternity as King went on playing and singing. Although I couldn't understand the words, there was no mistaking the emotions of love found and lost. I was mesmerized; it all seemed so familiar even though it was totally foreign to anything I had ever heard. I understood it on a soul level. I had met myself in history at last! I was so comfortable among the Afghans. I had no fears and looked forward to each day as a new adventure. I decided that there was no need to go to India after all.

My friends had long since passed into other realms on clouds of brandy and hashish but King and I were wide awake and felt as if we were alone in the world. I searched his face for some sign that maybe he was the man that I had dreamed about for so long. But outside of sisterly love, admiration for his talents and appreciation, I felt nothing. It was well after midnight when he drove us back to our hotels.

The next day, I went to King's shop and, holding my hands, he gave me the Afghan kiss among equals or relatives (kisses on the right, left and right cheeks), and said in Dari:

"*Catee-jon, how art thou?*"

"*I am well, Oh King Protecting Friend, and how art thou?*"

"*By the grace of Allah, very well. What desire may I grant thee today?*"

I grinned at him and said in English, "My desire is to have some boots made."

He replied in Dari, "*It wilt be my honor to negotiate a good price.*"

We smiled into each other's eyes and I felt my heart go out to him and the word, 'Brother' touched my mind.

He said in English, "I must do. You my sister" and his eyes began to fill.

Shocked I asked, "Why, oh King-*jon*?"

"Oh Catee-*jon*, my sister is with Allah."

"What happened?"

"She took the smallpox when she was fifteen. She do everything for me. She make my food, my tea, prepare my clothes, everything."

The Seer entered the shop and we all greeted one another. I told him what King had just said. The Seer bowed his head and said, "Karima was King's favorite sister. She was put in charge of him and they loved each other very much. The closest relationship between family members is brother and sister topped only by relationships with God and the beloved."

I bowed to King and said in Dari, *"I am honored by thy trust in me to tell me thy heart, oh King-jon."*

"Tis my honor, Catee-jon."

The Seer made a phone call and excused himself. King and I went by car to a main crossing where a huge, dilapidated adobe and wood building leaned to one side as if in a drunken stupor. The roof over the veranda sat at a rakish angle to the building. This was the boot-maker Sayeed's shop.

His eyes were red, his speech slurred and his brain seemed clouded with hashish. Sayeed was thirty years old, five-feet-eleven-inches tall, and of medium build. He had short, black hair, and resembled most Afghans but his eyes were bloodshot. He joyfully welcomed us and insisted we have tea before business could be transacted, obeying the first great Afghan law of honor to the guest. Sayeed looked and acted like a man under the influence of some intoxicant. Perhaps he was forced to marry someone against his will or his wife had a miscarriage; a common reason. I felt sorry for Sayeed, that a man so young would be a *charsee* (a hashish addict).

King had Sayeed measure my feet and I picked out some black suede pieces with tiny pink and red embroidered rosebuds scattered over them. Sayeed said the boots would be ready in three days.

King and I went to the Marco Polo Restaurant that was named after the Italian explorer who traveled to China bringing noodles to the west. It reminded me of a Brooklyn pizza parlor! I mentioned this to King and he told me that the Seer had been to New York and was enamored of pizza parlors and came back with the design. There were Formica and stainless steel tables and booths with red and black décor. While we were eating, King asked me to teach him English. I agreed. In return, he would help me improve my Dari. At that moment, Morrie walked into the restaurant and sat down with us. We all talked and joked and then he said he was having trouble with Customs and his visa. King called for a telephone and after a few sentences in Dari told Morrie that he had an appointment with the President of the Customs House. He called his nephew who arrived in a white Mercedes to drive Morrie to Customs. With another five-second phone call, he got Morrie's visa extended for fifteen days in order to get his shipment out to Australia. I felt that King was justly named; he could do anything.

Back at the shop, Sunshine and Dustin arrived and we told King that we wanted to make Italian food for him to repay him for his kindness. He insisted on paying for the groceries. We walked the bazaar, and Dustin asked King if he knew a good mechanic because he was having problems with the van's transmission. To his amazement and pleasure, King offered to take him to his personal mechanic in the morning. We completed our purchases and agreed to meet King later that evening.

CHAPTER FIVE

Thė Tûrtlénėck Şwëâtėr

"On a gray leafless bough,
A black crow is perched
In the autumn dawn."
The Author

Sunshine wanted to go shopping for a turtleneck sweater. We entered one shop and the merchant showed us a black polyester one. She tried it on but it was too big for her. The merchant told us to come back in an hour and he would have the correct size sweater. Thinking he was clever, he cut out the tag of the size five sweater and put it into a plastic bag that had a size four sticker on it. Sunshine tried it on and of course, it was still too big. The merchant, not about to give up a sale, said, that for twenty *afghanis,* he would take it to a tailor to alter it. We started laughing at his insistence and refused. He cajoled us with sweet words and sweet tea until we gave him the money and off he went. Half an hour later, he returned with the "altered sweater." "Altered" was the correct word! The entire sweater was puckered because it takes a special machine to sew polyester. When Sunshine tried it on, it was so tight that the merchant ripped it all out trying to make it fit her. We couldn't help ourselves and collapsed, laughing at the ridiculous situation. Knowing he was beaten, the merchant asked for fifty *afghanis* more and said he would bring a size four. We watched him go into another shop, purchase the correct size sweater and return with it for Sunshine. Of course, it fit perfectly. The merchant was happy that he made a sale and a small profit. Sunshine was pleased with her new sweater. We all smiled and *Selam*ed each other.

Sunshine and I walked to King's shop and shook our heads while we talked about Afghan merchants' tenacity but willingness to please when bargaining with customers. We met Dustin at the shop and while we waited for King, told him the whole story. Dustin burst out laughing and told us he experienced the same thing when purchasing a wool vest that morning! We agreed that bargaining was deeply embedded in the Afghan character and everyone is expected to play the game. I must admit it is much more entertaining than entering an American store, picking out an item, and bringing it to the counter to pay; all this with a minimum of conversation.

King agitatedly burst into the shop and rapidly made for his office. Startled, I burst out in Dari *"What ails thee, Oh King Protecting Friend?"*

"My jewelry hath been taken without payment."

"Who hath done this terrible wrong to thee, my brother?"

"My servant says some people from Teheran. The cost to me was six thousand dollars for very old pieces of silver jewelry in my possession."

"Wilt thou call the police?"

"Nay, my sister. These ones called by the name of police art not effective."

"What plan hath thou to take possession of thy goods?"

"First 'tis my duty to seek out the bread maker. From him I shalt procure much naan. I shalt go on foot to see to its distribution to those in the city who art in need. Then inshallah (God willing), I shalt receive guidance to my next action."

"Why wilt thou distribute naan?"

"The giving of alms to the poor renders us pleasing in the sight of Allah." (This meant that Allah would be more inclined to help him recover his stolen property).

We consoled him as best we could and told him that the Italian food would cheer him up. He smiled at us. Sunshine and I returned to the van to prepare the meal on the propane stove. The tomato paste was from China and very bitter. I used some sugar to sweeten it. Ever the cook, I had carried some dried Italian herbs in my backpack all the way from New York. I didn't want to miss my favorite foods while traveling. Afghan meat was freshly killed each day before dawn and consumed the same day owing to a lack of refrigeration. Afghan meat is not aged like ours. The ground beef was very mushy and the meatballs wouldn't hold. The parsley looked different from ours but I thought it was just a local product. I chopped it up and put it into the meatballs along with the raisins, bread crumbs, beaten egg and minced garlic as I always did. Because of the high altitude and low amount of propane in the tank, the food took three hours to cook versus the usual half hour. We brought the pasta and the meatballs into the shop and Dustin, Sunshine, King and I sat down to eat. I took a mouthful of meatball and spit it out into my hand. It tasted like soap! What I thought was parsley was actually cilantro, something I never had before. Cilantro was in almost every Afghan dish either as a fresh herb or the dried seeds known as coriander. Everyone laughed at my first taste of cilantro.

I looked at them and said, "*Parwa nist* (Never mind)!" which caused more laughter.

A group of European tourists entered the shop, followed by the Seer. King brought out a bottle of cognac and we all started drinking. Tongue loosened by alcohol, the Seer told us that he had a Master's Degree from Berkeley and spent three years in the States studying police work. He also traveled quite a bit in Europe and spoke several languages. He said he had an important government job here.

His inexhaustible repertoire of riddles and jokes kept us all laughing. When he offered us some hashish, we demurred because he was a government official. But he lit up a *chillum* (a vertical clay pipe) and passed it around. We told him that we felt uncomfortable smoking hashish with a government official.

He replied, "What does my job matter when you are all my friends?"

One of the tourists said he had bought some beautiful antique silver jewelry from some Iranians near Kandahar. When they arrived in Kabul, they showed the jewelry to the local merchants in their attempt to purchase more and were directed to King's shop. King and the Seer had a quick conversation and made several phone calls. Then King offered to drive me back to my hotel so he could pursue his jewelry that was stolen from him by the Iranians.

When we got there, the gate was locked. It was near midnight. Unfazed, King slammed the thick chain around a few times to attract the attention of the servant inside. When that didn't work he simply snapped the chain in two with his bare hands. We approached the main door made of wood with glass panes in the upper part. I was sure that it was locked.

King said, "*Parwa nist.* I break glass."

Horrified at the thought of his being hurt, I exclaimed, "Oh no!"

But the door was open.

He embraced me and kissed my hand in gallant old-world fashion and said, "Good night, Catee-*jon*, my sister, see you tomorrow."

I had the same dream again. I saw a very tall man. He was my husband. His country was at war and I was helping him. I was taken from this dream before dawn by the call to prayer.

The *Muezzin* (the man who calls the faithful to prayer five times per day) uses a loudspeaker on top of the mosque's minaret to make the announcement. I put on my sheepskin coat and went out onto the balcony of my hotel room. There in the crisp, cold, clear November air I looked to the mountains in the distance and pondered my dream.

The main street in Shar-ee-Now was called 'Chicken Street' because, in the past, a huddle of adobe shops sold live chickens. Now, it was the main thoroughfare for tourists to purchase handicrafts. Towards the end of the street was a *naanwai* (a baker).

On the left side of Chicken Street were two large shops that belonged to a couple of Pashtun brothers from Pakhtiya, an area in southeastern Afghanistan. Both of them were well over six feet tall and handsome. Their thin black mustaches curled upwards towards their chiseled cheekbones, over which sat piercing black eyes. Each one wore velvet and gold thread embroidered vests over their traditional clothing and the customary eight yards of black silk wound around their skullcaps. They opened up the first shop that sold handicrafts from Nuristan, a remote area in northeastern Afghanistan. Outside of the shop, many heavy, squat hand-carved wooden chairs with animal gut seats were lined up on either side of the doors. Inside the shop, were piles of red silk wedding shawls, hand embroidered on thick, undyed cotton backing; heavy, black ten-meter dresses with fuchsia embroidery; and carved silvery-metal glasses and water ewers. I chose several of each for export with the shopkeeper's assurance that more was to come.

After the crossing, stood the fruit stalls. For me, the bazaar was a living theatre where I went to feast my eyes, ears, and nose. On the right side of the street, just past the street crossing called Chera-ee-Treboz Khan, was the mouth of the small vegetable and fruit bazaar. In the front on either side, two stalls carried all the varieties of fruit in the country. It was stacked in careful pyramids on a wooden platform. Unlike the fruit stalls in Herat that were level, these platforms stood two feet high in the front and rose on an incline to five feet in the back. There the merchant sat cross-legged amid clusters of squat glass jars filled with homemade cookies the consistency of hardtack that had no taste. The idea was to dunk them in sweetened tea. There were also hard candies, imported Pakistani toffees (one of the legacies of the British), and boxes of wooden matches from Russia that blew up in your face when you struck them, as well as bottles of sweet cloying hair oil from India.

Suddenly, the perfume of persimmons, oranges, and peaches enticed my senses. The fruit merchant and I exchanged the traditional greeting and the radiance of his soul was reflected in his eyes. I pointed to the persimmons and he insisted that I take one as a gift. I tried to pay him but he refused with laughter. Thanking him for this sweet treat, I stepped off the pavement into the dirt lane of the bazaar.

The next two stalls were the Afghan equivalent of the "general store" and carried fresh eggs, sold individually for a penny a piece. Imported, but by now rusted, Pakistani and Indian, canned goods of fruits and vegetables and dusty packets of dehydrated Knorr soups from Switzerland were available. The stalls also carried American tin foil, and jars of *turshee* (fiery pickled vegetables), eaten with rich stews and rice dishes.

Further along, two stalls on the right acted as butcher shops. Various cuts of lamb hung in the open suspended from meat hooks with their customary quota of flies. Since refrigeration is a rarity in almost all of the country, the Afghans remedied this by building an underground store room with cupboards and counter space to keep meat cool. The animals were brought to the market at dawn every day. They were killed in the Islamic manner by first praying and then slitting the throat, allowing some blood to fall onto the ground before the throat was completely cut. The Afghans call this meat *halal* (legal for consumption). After death, the animals are skinned, cleaned, carved up and brought to the various butcher shops around town on *karachees* (huge, wooden plank open carts with tractor-size tires). The men pulling the *karachee* were Hazaras, Shiites from the Hazarajat in Northern Afghanistan who were second class citizens and relegated to menial work. Their once powerful khans or lords were pushed into the barren areas of central Afghanistan by the indigenous Pashtuns (Afghans), never to regain their positions.

Bread Seller

The morning was still cold as it threw off the chill of a desert-like night. The pullers wore their wrinkled, raggedy-layered and repatched *peeran tambon,* (traditional outfits) all soft and gray from constant washings. Strips of rags were wrapped around their hands for warmth against the sharp winter air. Their static faces and black, almond eyes sunk in epicanthic folds were identical to the round, flat, buttery bread they made with tiny, black nigella seeds in the center. The hushed dawn of time on the barren Mongolian steppes from where these people came, has left an indelible print of timelessness and antiquity rooted in solemnity, upon their features. Their faces, ageless yet aged before their time from the harshness of the weather on the open plains and the mineral hard water, were crossed and scored. These lines were accentuated by clouds of powder-fine dust raised by the *karachee* in its constant meanderings. The breath from their noses formed small temporary icicles on their sparse mustaches as they pulled the steaming chunks of freshly killed lamb through the bazaar. I watched the Hazaras advance and noticed their headgear. Their stubble-ridden heads as if in a nest were surrounded by several yards of soft handwoven gray color cotton, twisted lengthwise and wrapped around their skulls. The *karachee* lumbered towards me and stopped. Repulsed, I hugged the adobe wall to avoid being smeared with the dripping mass that exuded the sickening sweet smell of fresh blood and seeped into the greasy mud in front of the butchers' stalls. The porters unloaded their cargo. Mesmerized, I held my breath to keep from gagging as they trundled by on their journey. Hooves, tails, and innards were carted away to be prepared as stews in huge pots and sold to porters, *karachee* pullers and other vendors at lunch for two *afghanis* a plate. By nine o'clock in the morning, no meat left in the market is worth buying because the quality cuts are already in the stewing pots of Kabul's households.

Hazara pickle sellers

I trudged along the muddy hilly lane where the vegetable merchants squatted amidst large piles of geometrically stacked vegetables in brilliant colors. Electric-orange carrots, glaring red radishes, snow-white cauliflowers, royal-purple baby eggplants, bright-green peppers, yellow potatoes and onions, spring-green peas, white and mauve turnips, and scarlet plum tomatoes flaunted their brightness in front of my eyes. Ropes of garlic hung like mobiles from the ceiling.

A boy of twelve years of age had the responsibility of carrying an empty, square metal gallon can to the lone water spigot that stood four feet off the ground on the street outside the bazaar. This spigot was connected to Kabul's drinking water system. The boy filled the can and returned to throw water on the vegetables to refresh them and used the rest of the water to keep down the dust of the lane. He did this every hour or two depending on the weather that day.

My merchant, Nafass Siddiq, had the last stall on the left side of the lane. He knew from the subtle change in the hubbub of the bazaar that I was near. He immediately leaned out over his vegetables and began his call to me in Dari with a big smile.

"Oh Khanum! Bya Khanum, bya!" (*Oh My Lady! Come, My Lady, come!*)

All the while he flapped his hand as we do to shoo birds away ... the Afghan gesture for come closer. He was a Tajik: the second largest group of Afghans. He was five-feet-six, medium build with a pale-yellowish cast to his skin. He had traditional European features and black eyes that ended in an Asiatic slant showing a Mongol strain in his Caucasoid lineage. He was wiry with brown hair and a Fu Manchu style mustache that ran parallel to his dimples when he smiled. He wore charcoal-gray traditional clothes, a black western suit jacket, and a pale-gray turban of soft hand-loomed cotton.

The minute I smiled and greeted him in Dari, he started piling kilograms of his best vegetables in front of him. He glanced at the other merchants with slight disdain and no small amount of pride because his was the stall I chose to frequent. That I was a foreign lady who spoke Dari, was an accomplishment in his eyes.

Nafass Siddiq was lord and master of his little world. He sat there daily, like a king dispensing largesse and held samples of his choicest vegetables as if they were rare fragments of ancient statues, for my inspection and approval. The entire time, he kept up a gay chatter on their firmness and freshness.

There was a small brass scale that held up to fifty kilos, with individual weights for measuring. He first placed the vegetables in question on one side of the scale and with an expert eye, placed the one, two, or five-kilogram weight on the other side. He hoisted the scale high in the air and then proceeded to throw on or remove tiny gram weights as necessary. This process was accomplished in a matter of seconds and he rarely had to add or subtract a weight more than once to get the scale to balance. Most Afghans are not able to read and write but they positively can count and measure.

In front of the merchant, a pile of coins served to make change after a purchase. A wad of bills was kept in a tight roll in an inside pocket of his suit jacket. At the end of my daily purchase, I insisted that he keep the change but he always returned it to me with many thanks and a smile, with the addition of a handful of some vegetables as a gift for having "brightened his eyes with my presence."

After my purchases, I clambered back up this narrow, rocky, muddy lane to a chorus of "*Selam Aleikums*" from the other merchants.

I strolled along the streets and passed a teahouse. Everyone smiled and greeted me and I returned their "*Selams*."

On occasion, I came across my own people. These were Americans who joined the Peace Corps. They taught the Afghans helpful agriculture methods, dam and road construction as well as English. These people were my age, with good and open natures. Yet I was never interested in them. Their fascination was with technology and the rapid progress civilization brought. My interest was in being with the Afghans and I was comfortable adjusting the cloak of their ancient ways around my shoulders.

CHAPTER SIX

Thirty Birds

"Prayer puts the believers on the path to Allah,
Fasting takes us to Allah's door
But only the giving of zakat (alms) to the poor
Allows the believer to enter Paradise."
Muslin belief

I passed another *chaikhana* (tea house) with its raised platforms that served as both a table and a seat. The teahouses reserved for men are called "newspapers of brick" since all news/gossip is exchanged within. Women get "the news" from merchants they frequent in the bazaar, their relatives, and friends.

A local merchant sat cross-legged on the platform with an old man sitting in front of him. The merchant gestured for me to come over, and made a place for me facing the old man. He introduced him to me and we gave each other the greeting. A tiny teapot appeared along with a heavy, squat glass almost half-full with crystal, clear pieces of beet sugar to drink my tea through. The merchant, while chatting with me, filled the glass with tea and told me that this old man, Baba Ali, was a famous storyteller. I asked Baba Ali to tell me a story while the merchant translated.

"The mythical bird of paradise is called the '*Simurgh*.' The word means 'thirty birds.' A flock of thirty birds decided to search for the *Simurgh*. When they reached paradise after many trials, they were ushered into the presence of the *Simurgh*. The birds experienced a revelation. They saw each other as the *Simurgh*, they saw the *Simurgh* as one and they saw themselves individually comprising the *Simurgh*. They had discovered the meaning of Allah as the One and the Many simultaneously."

I thanked them both and we all smiled at each other. I felt as if I had received a precious jewel to be treasured and scrutinized whenever I wanted.

There was very little to do in a 12th-century culture. Walking to the bazaars for food or merchandise and to the post office provided entertainment as well as exercise and a chance to further explore the culture. I preferred to walk the bazaars alone or with tourist friends or roommates. Sometimes when I walked to the old section of the city to pick up mail at the Poste Restante, I stopped to eat lamb kebabs from the stands along the Kabul River. On the way, as I passed the tomb of Abdur Rachman, one of the kings of Afghanistan, I saw an old man coming towards me.

I addressed him in Dari, *"Oh father dear, from whence hath thou come?"*

"Oh my daughter, I come from prayer near the place of this great king."

"But my father, why dost thou pray here?

"Because of the emanations of the soul of Abdur Rachman, many people seek Allah's help here."

"Oh my father, I am an Issawee (believer in Jesus). *I desire to know what the Muslims believe about prayer."*

"This is the easiest of answers daughter mine. Prayer puts the believers on the path to Allah, fasting takes us to Allah's door but only the giving of zakat (alms) *to the poor allows the believer to enter Paradise."*

"I thank thee for thy wise words, my father, may thou walk in the peace of Allah."

"There is no thing to say me thanks, my daughter, the thanks belongs to God alone. May Allah protect thee."

In the old area of Kabul, called Jad-ee-Maiwand, the ancient bazaar sat baking in the sun. The big wide thoroughfare running through its center accommodated four lanes of traffic - two lanes in each direction. Ancient Russian buses and taxis, a sprinkling of VW Beetles, Mercedes, and one or two Land Rovers, as well as bicycles, horses, donkeys, and people on foot, all swarmed together.

Each side of the street was studded with small shops huddled side-by-side. Behind the shops was a warren of twisted, dirt lanes with crumbling one-storey adobe buildings, divided into a room of ten by ten feet. It was to this place that the Hazaras flocked when they came to Kabul to look for work as day laborers, porters, sellers of pickled vegetables, and movers. The areas were divided by chalk marks and for two cents they had a straw pallet and a roof for the night. These "hotels" were run by brother Shiites. Here, the Hazaras felt safe from their Sunni enemies. To the Sunni Pashtuns, the rulers of Afghanistan, Hazaras would always be second class citizens. The Shias are a religious minority who believe that Ali, the son-in-law of the Prophet Mohammed, is his rightful successor. They accused the Sunnis (the Afghan religious majority) of torturing and killing him and his family. The Sunnis believe that Abu Bakr, a close friend of Mohammed, is the rightful successor. The centuries' old hatred runs deep between these two groups.

To show their contempt for Sunnis, whom they regarded as the murderers of Ali, the Hazaras wrote the names of Mohammad's Sunni successors on the soles of their shoes grinding them into the filth of the bazaar as they walked.

Sheep's wool was one of the mainstays of the Afghan economy. It was used by the people as rugs, tents, hats, vests, coats and boots as well as exported to Europe and the United States. Men sheared the sheep and the women spun and wove the wool. Small girls, under six years of age, carded the wool. Afghan rugs are, for the most part, red with black patterns in geometric designs, and are created by the nomadic Turkmen.

Dried Fruit Bazaar

I watched in fascination as Uzbek felt makers laid out wool fibers, dyed black or red. Then they saturated them with water and rolled them into flat sheets of material. Heavy rocks were placed on the felt and it was kept saturated until the fibers adhered to each other. The pieces were hand-stitched together with yarn and embroidered in abstract shapes.

Dried apricots, raisins, mulberries, pistachios, almonds, and walnuts were sold locally and for export.

Farmers, in their pastel-colored traditional clothing and colorful embroidered skullcaps, gawked at the dazzling bolts of material in the cloth shops. Unable to resist, I pawed through Russian flowered cottons, their huge pink roses blooming on vibrant green, red, and indigo backgrounds; hand-loomed, blinding-white Afghan cottons; brown Nouristani wools with maroon and indigo embroidery; Bokhara brocades in sea-green, gold, violet, peach and fuchsia; Chinese turquoise, royal blue, silver, and black silks; French velvets in purple, green, red and black; and American synthetics in every color of the rainbow. I was a pirate on Treasure Island who had just found the gold! These bolts of explosive colors all vied for the most prominent place in the shops. The bazaar also housed shops selling cooking utensils, leather goods, sandals, meat, bread, spices, and silver and gold jewelry.

Mustached city men in traditional *peeran tambon* wore Western suit jackets topped by rakishly-set *karakul* (lambskin) caps. Towering, bearded Pashtun tribesmen in voluminous shawls of eight-foot silk, black or white turbans, made a furrow through the crowd. Beardless Uzbeks strolled through the lanes in their vivid, multi-colored *ikat* silk coats. These coats held closed with fabulously carved silver belts were multi-colored tie-dyed and then hand-loomed on simple wooden looms. *Ikat* is the name given to the way these fabrics were created. Blue eyed, tall Nuristanis, remnants from Alexander the Great's Afghan visit, in their homespun woolen clothes with thick maroon and navy embroidery, walked straight ahead. Hazaras with huge trays bearing jars of pickled turnips, beets, and chickpeas carefully balanced on their heads, hawked their wares. Proud tribal women floated in and out of the crowd with their heavily embroidered and silver decorated dresses. There was a sprinkling of city and village women enveloped in their *chadorees* (veils) amid horses, camels, and donkeys on slippery-when-wet, twisting lanes, swirling with clouds of dust in the dry spots.

As I strolled around, the variety of colors and costumes overwhelmed me. I had never seen any clothing like this and I was determined to get some for myself! On the practical side, I also knew that no one in New York had ever seen anything like this either. My mind devised a plan to bring some of these fabulous costumes back to America to sell and of course, keep the best ones for myself.

Jad-ee-Maiwand the Old Bazaar

I perused the shops of Jad-ee-Maiwand until I came upon a jeweler's stall. Mohammed Aziz had a wooden cubicle painted robin's egg blue. The shop was just large enough for two to squat in comfort while he was perched on his adobe embankment, tending the fire in an old brazier. The ever-present-in-all-shops, clear forty-watt, naked light bulb, hung from the ceiling. There he sat, the master craftsman, with his thirteen-year-old son who was his apprentice. Aziz was in his mid-forties, blind in one eye, the other clouded by cataracts. He was medium height, thin with a scraggly, black mustache and beard. A racking cough completed the picture. This came from years of breathing charcoal and silver dust in the tiny, airless stall. The delicate silver jewelry he made looked ludicrous in his large calloused hands. Aziz worked with lapis lazuli, an indigo-colored, semi-precious stone (plentiful in Afghanistan) and light blue turquoise. I entered his shop and began the greeting in Dari that was always the same, no matter what your business or with whom:

"*May peace be upon thee. How art thou? How is thy life? May thou never be tired. May thy life be long. May only good news reach thee.*"

The greeting is done at the same time by both parties. Aziz sent his son, a younger clear-eyed version of himself, minus the cough, for tea. A rickety wooden chair appeared for me from the next adobe stall. Only after the obligatory three cups were consumed, was it considered polite to discuss business. I took a ring from my index finger for him to size and explained in Dari that I wanted a ring made for my father.

Oh Khanum, assuredly thy hand is much smaller than thy father's isn't it?"

"Yay, Oh Master Jeweler, the ring is for my father's little finger," I said laughing.

Aziz laughed too. *"And what jewel dost thou wish to procure for thy father's ring?"*

"Turquoise suits my father."

"Thou hath chosen well, turquoise protects the wearer from the evil eye. I shalt procure the best turquoise for thee."

I thanked Aziz and thought how I had heard the Italians in New York speak of *"malocchio"* or the "evil eye." I knew that my father did not believe in such things, but I was sure he would be amused when I told him this story.

"And when may I claim this ring?"

"In three days' time, inshallah (Allah willing), *wouldst thou bestow the honor upon me by staying in my poor house 'til thy father's ring is crafted?"*

"The honor wouldst be mine, Oh Master Jeweler," I said as I bowed and smiled.

Buyers are invited into the seller's home until the goods are ready partly due to *melmastia* (hospitality to the guest), and partly to ensure that the seller will be paid. As a foreigner, if I decided not to pay my debt, there is no family here for Aziz to approach. Of course, I loved the Afghans so much that such an idea never entered my head.

Suddenly, the *shamol* (the north wind) gusted around the corner. The insistent powder-fine dust permeated every crack and crevice of Kabul. Herders hastened to house their animals and people bolted doors and windows in vain. I quickly helped Aziz close up shop. We laughed and talked about the *shamol*. After all, Kabul was simply a cluster of small khaki colored adobe houses huddled together for safety on the barren plains, dwarfed by the purplish brown mountains standing thousands of feet high at their backs. When the *shamol* died down, I brushed the dust from my hair and clothes.

Dusk rested its rosy glow on the shoulders of people heading home. As the last rays of the sun passed over the hand-thrown bricks of the shops, a sudden coolness descended. I felt a stir as the vendors geared up for the final rush of the day. People bought last minute snacks of roasted corn, roasted chick peas, or sugar-coated almonds. Others purchased a few potatoes or carrots for supper. The bazaar was my favorite place to be at the end of the day. Merchants took in their wares, small boys fanned the biting smoke of the charcoal fires in front of the kebab shops, and lines formed at the bakers to buy freshly baked bread. Buses roared down the streets sending clouds of exhaust fumes into the clear air, forcibly disgorging their sardine packed passengers. The river flowed past the money market while men made the *wuzu* (the partial ablution before prayer). First, they washed their hands, then inside the mouth, inside the nose, over the head, wrists to elbows, ankles to toes on top and also the soles of their feet. Children played along the river's banks and women washed clothes. Within a half hour the sun had disappeared and, as if by magic, the streets were silent with only the haze of smoke emitted by the wood-burning stoves, disturbing the air. Packs of stray dogs foraged through the refuse heaps, arguing over bits of food. The black sky held many multi-colored, brilliant silver stars and colorful planets were visible to the naked eye.

CHAPTER SEVEN

Sister Wives

"Hand-in-hand we will stand,
Shoulder-to-shoulder we will go, my heart sang,
When I first saw you in a crowd,
Your glance set fire to my heart,
Your smile was like the leaves of a tree that blocked my path.
I thought you were only a temporary distraction,
But my heart sang on, hand in hand we will stand,
Shoulder to shoulder we will go,
When you threw your wild glances at me,
I didn't understand your meaning,
But my heart sang on, hand in hand we will stand,
Shoulder to shoulder we will go,
And now you are going my beloved,
With my rival to his home,
Just as Fate is giving in to my rival's desire,
So are you."
Afghan lover's lament

Mahmood, Aziz's son, led me to the back of the bazaar through a warren of rock-strewn, dusty sometimes muddy lanes lined by twenty-foot-high adobe walls with only an occasional wooden doorway. We sidestepped the piles of refuse left at various points along these walls and made our way to Aziz's house, a sprawling two-storey adobe structure. There I met Aziz's parents, his wives, Roya and Suroya who were sisters, his five brothers, and their wives and children.

Everyone stood up when I entered the *saloon*, and Roya, the chief wife, came to within a foot of me. She was in her early thirties, five-feet-six, with large black eyes and her hair in a long black braid. Roya was seven months pregnant with their seventh child. Suroya, her sister-wife, stood a little off to the side. She was a few years younger with the same build and looks.

Roya stared into my eyes for a full fifteen seconds. Then she cried, "*Amshir-jon!*" She flung her arms around me.

I turned to Mahmood who spoke some English and asked, "What is the meaning of this word?"

He smiled at me and said, "This means 'sister, the one who shares my mother's milk'."

Delighted to be so readily accepted as a sister. I went around the room and greeted everyone individually in Dari. Aziz entered the house and it was time for the meal. Roya sat at the head of the "table" that was a piece of tanned leather covered by a white hand-embroidered tablecloth. She insisted that I sit at her right, the place of honor for the guest. Everyone else took their places with Aziz on the left side towards the end. Roya, her sister wife Suroya, her mother-in-law, sisters-in-law and daughters kept up a lively chatter among themselves. The men spoke occasionally, but I noticed that Aziz did not speak unless directly addressed. When I asked Roya, "Why?" She replied that women are the rulers of the household and the men are like guests and should relax and enjoy the food without any worries of daily problems. We all sat cross-legged on the carpets as the food was brought in by the men. Aziz, his brothers, and sons did the serving, since the women and girls had prepared the food. We all ate together. There was a huge spinach *pullow* (rice with meat buried inside) with a leg of lamb in the center, a platter of green herbs of coriander, dill, chives, and mint as well as a tureen of yoghurt. Roya put food from her dish into my mouth with her right hand showing honor to the guest. When someone wanted more food, they first came and placed some on my dish before helping themselves as custom dictated. The guest must be satisfied before anyone else and is expected to eat three platefuls. I was groaning after the first! When I refused a second helping all of the women exclaimed in concern thinking that I must be ill, or I didn't like their "poor food" etc. I had to explain to all of them that I loved Afghan food but Americans just don't eat that much with the exception of holidays. They were appalled and thought that Americans were starving. Mahmood, ever my translator, explained, that not to eat until stuffed brings shame upon the host/hostess. "Oh well," I thought, "there goes my waistline," as I picked up a piece of bread.

The family rose before dawn and prayed. The women busied themselves with breakfast. Mahmood and his father ate a breakfast of *naan*, a fried egg and many small bowls of black tea half filled with sugar. One of Mahmood's four sisters, Dunya, who was one year younger than he, was assigned to his upkeep. Love shone in her eyes as she brought him his tea, served his food, washed and pressed all his clothes and was his confidant in all his problems. A very close bond existed between them as with all brothers and sisters in Afghanistan. I thought of dear King and the loss of his sister. Mahmood brought her gifts as well as anything she needed from the bazaar, took pride in her embroidery skills and was always praising her. Dunya was Mahmood's favorite sister. She patiently waited for him to return home, warmed up his food and didn't sleep until he was under their roof again. I pondered the very close relationship between brother and sister here in the East. American brothers usually teased and fought with each other. I saw no indication of this in Afghanistan. I believe this relationship prepared two people on how to act in marriage since there was no chance of dating beforehand. Marriages are arranged by the parents.

After Breakfast, father and son went to work. Even though he was thirteen years old, Mahmood was in complete command of the shop. He knew all of the prices by heart and haggled with customers as well as or better than Aziz.

During the two days I was there, I learned that Roya and Suroya contributed financially to the family. Both created fabulous embroidery that they sold to an upper-class Kabuli woman who designed clothing for the nobility and foreigners. This money was theirs to save for a daughter's trousseau, to buy a piece of land or to augment their jewelry collections that could be sold piecemeal when money was needed for themselves, the family or the children.

I was introduced to Habiba, who came to the house to collect her latest embroidery pieces. She was a tall, slim, exceedingly beautiful Pashtun woman with jet black hair to her waist. She spoke perfect English as did her husband, Suleiman who was a diplomat. They had been stationed in New York City for several years. We became friends and she invited me to her home for many delicious dinners.

It was Friday, the Muslim Sabbath, and the men were in the *masjid* (mosque). The bazaars were closed. Meanwhile, the women were busy in

65

the courtyard around the fountain. They were preparing the midday meal. While the lamb was pressure-cooked, the vegetables and grains were cleaned and prepared. Whole spices were ground in a wooden mortar and pestle. They drank many small bowls of sugared black *chai* flavored with crushed cardamom seeds. The women started this preparation early since without modern conveniences these complicated meat and rice dishes took hours. I loved to sit with them, smoke the *hookah* (water pipe) and listen to their gossip.

They were very curious about me and asked many questions in Dari.

"And what may I ask is thy age?" Roya asked me.

"My twenty-sixth year hath been reached."

"And how many children hath been given to thee?" she continued.

"My children art unborn as yet."

"How hath thou reached this age without children?" Suroya asked surprised.

"A husband hath not been given to me."

"And dost thy father still feed and clothe thee at this age? Why hath he not found a husband for thee?" she asked astounded.

"In Amrika, after women graduate from the middle school or the university, they canst live and work outside the home and gain money with no help from any other person."

"W'Allah (By God) this hath not reached my ears!" both Roya and Suroya exclaimed simultaneously and the others nodded in agreement.

Then it was my turn to question them in Dari. I teasingly asked them how they live with one husband between them. They laughingly respond that it works because they are sisters and close in age.

"'Tis well," I replied, *"But if a man takes a non-related wife who is much younger than the first wife, then what occurs?"*

Suroya said, *"The first wife becomes a shaitan (devil) and all of the family's lives art blackened."*

"Dost thou both sleep in the same bed at the same time as thy husband?"

They burst into raucous laughter at the thought of this. When they recovered, Suroya explained, *"Nay Oh Catee-jon. 'Tis the law that one night the husband sleeps with one wife and on the next night he sleeps with the other. Come and I shalt show thee our rooms."*

Both of them escorted me to the second floor and showed me individual bedrooms identically decorated except with different colored quilts. I thought the identical decorations were because they were sisters and asked them about this. They explained that, according to the law of Islam, both wives must be treated equally. What is given to one must also be given to the other so as not to show favoritism. They also said that it was common for a man to take his wife's sister as a second wife to help and be company for her. This reduces household chores and disagreements.

As promised, on the third day, Aziz told me that my father's ring was ready. I said goodbye to the family and the women clamored and cried at my leaving and begged me to stay. We had passed a very pleasant time together. I promised that I would visit again and followed Aziz out to his shop.

The ring was perfect. It was sterling silver with a beautiful turquoise stone. I thanked Aziz, paid him and returned to my hotel.

CHAPTER EIGHT

Uncleji Ji

"This day (Thursday) is before Friday,
a very sacred day to all Muslims.
On Thursday, we give alms to all who ask.
On Friday, we close our shops and businesses and sit amongst our families
and pray in the masjid (the mosque).
This alms giving is so that all may be in joy
with their relatives and have food to share."
Servant of the Creator

Before Dustin and Sunshine left for India, they wanted to go to the Intercontinental Hotel with some of our friends for an expensive bon voyage meal. The Intercon, as it was called, was the equivalent of our Hilton Hotels. We went to our English friends' Betty and Bobby's hotel to pick them up. Betty and Bobby were English tourists whom we met in the Khyber Restaurant when we first arrived in Kabul. They warned us that everyone who eats at the Intercon comes down with dysentery and they escaped this mishap by a hair's breadth themselves. My gut started grinding at just the thought of it! We decided on one of our favorite spots, a tiny adobe restaurant in the old section of the city. We gorged on *mantoo*, a Mongol specialty, steamed dumplings stuffed with ground lamb and spices. Scattered on top, were cooked carrots and lentils with *qrut* (a sour yoghurt sauce) blanketing the dish.

The owner of this cubbyhole restaurant giggled as he watched us enjoy his food. He was a burly Uzbek, clean shaven with small black eyes that ended in points. Beautiful-Names-of-God laughed with delight, called down blessings upon us and wished us well in our travels when we praised his food to high heaven. Dustin asked for the toilet and Beautiful-Names-of-God led us out the back of the restaurant and pointed to an outhouse across the yard. While we waited, two men brought out several huge cooking pots. A small boy of seven stood inside one of them on two filthy rags while throwing sand in the bottom of the pot. Then he "skated" on the bottom of this cauldron to "clean" it. At that sight, Betty lost her lunch. I looked at Sunshine and Bobby, shrugged my shoulders and said, "*Parwa nist* (Never mind)!"

I had grown tired of Afghan food, so one evening I went to a restaurant with Bill and Morrie. It was owned by a German woman and her Afghan husband. It looked like all the old movie sets of Germany in the nineteen thirties. The booths were upholstered in wine-color satin and accommodated eight people. The tables had snow white tablecloths on them and tiny candles nestled in small glass ashtrays were surrounded by fresh flowers. Little lamps hung overhead that gave off a dim glow. The restaurant was famous for its Vienna schnitzel, creamed cauliflower, and home fries. They also served apple juice from fresh pressed apples.

The Afghan waiter, whom I later learned was the owner's son, spoke, Dari, Pashto, and German but very little English. He was six-feet-one with a long narrow face, olive skin and a closely-cropped head of black hair. He was dressed just like any waiter in a fancy restaurant in Europe or the States. He had a snow-white shirt, thin black string tie, black trousers and highly polished black shoes. The only hint that he was the German woman's son was his perfect command of the German language.

After the Vienna schnitzel, we asked him what he had for dessert.

He replied, "Compote," that I knew as a combination of stewed fruits.

After a long wait, he came back with a plate of apple strudel.

Suspicions aroused, I pointed to the strudel and asked, "What is this?"

"Compote," he replied.

He thought that this was the English word for dessert. We gently corrected him and he smiled and laughed at his mistake as he thanked us in German. The strudel was delicious.

While King was out of town, I came down with the inevitable parasitic dysentery that plagued most foreigners. The terrible cramps, loose stools, fever and accompanying nausea made my body weak. The owner of the hotel suggested that I go to the Ministry of Public Health for a stool test.

At the Ministry, I was directed to a nearby hospital where an Afghan doctor motioned for me to lie down on the examining table so he could tap my stomach. He was five-feet-ten, medium built with large soulful brown eyes, and a shock of short thick black hair that fell onto his forehead. He tapped around on my stomach for a while. Ticklish, I started laughing. Then he asked if I could give him a stool sample. I pulled this clean quart glass jar from my knapsack and the doctor's eyes grew huge. He frantically motioned "no" to me while handing me a two inch by two-inch matchbox for my stool sample. I realized that the doctor thought I was going to fill the quart jar for him! We looked at each other and both burst out laughing. After I submitted my stool sample, he gave me a paper and told me to take the sample to a laboratory in Jad-ee-Maiwand.

I motioned to him that I had a sore throat. I sat down on the examining stool in the whitewashed examining room with its lone table and stuck out my tongue. The doctor came over and hugged me. I started laughing as I pushed him away wondering if sticking your tongue out was a prelude to Afghan lovemaking! He took my hand and led me into a larger examining room and stuck his tongue out for me and tapped his throat to indicate he understood my problem. He left the room, returned with a glass and gargled. He again showed me his tongue and handed me the same glass. I gargled and somehow survived the vile taste. I could not stop laughing. I never saw a doctor take the medicine with the patient!

I walked over to the old section of Kabul, and up a flight of stone steps to the laboratory. I was greeted by Light-of-Mohammed. He was five-feet-eight with a full head of straight thick black hair, swarthy skin, clean shaven, huge black eyes, a Roman nose and a full formed mouth and lips covering excellent white teeth. He had wonderfully shaped hands and his long fingers showed grace, culture, and attention to detail. We greeted each other and he smiled at my Dari. He said that my pronunciation was very good. I gave him the stool sample and he told me to come back in three days for the results. We said goodbye with many blessings and I walked back to my hotel.

It was December. The snowcapped mountains and the fresh cold air made me homesick for New York and Christmas. I decided it was time to go home. I planned to fly from Kabul to Tashkent in the Soviet Union, then take the Trans-Siberian Railroad to Moscow and work my way down to London where I had my return air ticket to New York. This would give me a chance to practice my Russian that I had studied at the university.

Before I went to the Russian Embassy to get a visa, I called upon Rao, a Hindu who owned a travel agency with his brother. They had been in Kabul for many years, were well-respected and known for arranging flights and hotels for Embassy personnel and businessmen traveling in and out of Afghanistan. I had gotten their name and address, plus an introductory letter, from a Pakistani family in New York. Both of these families were long-time close friends. In Eastern countries when introduced to someone through a friend, you automatically are accepted as a friend too.

Mr. Rao, the uncle, was a typical middle-class Hindu complete with western clothes, a bowler hat and a rolled umbrella. He wore rimless bifocals, was clean-shaven and short with a slight paunch. His head was bald and he had the dark skin of those of the subcontinent. The continuous smile on his face reminded me of a beneficent Buddha statue. We made quite a contrast, he in his English clothes and I in my embroidered *peeran* (tunic) over jeans and boots.

Daddyji (Respected Daddy), as he introduced himself to me, was six feet tall with a jovial manner. He shook my hand, read my letter and turned it over to Uncleji. He excused himself and said that he had a previous appointment.

Uncleji, as I affectionately called him, assured me that he knew the Russian consul and would be happy to escort me.

We got into his black Volkswagen Beetle and arrived at the Embassy a few minutes later. We were met by the Consul himself.

He was a big burly man who resembled the Russian priest who taught me Russian history in the university. However, the resemblance stopped there. This man had cold disdain oozing from every pore of his body. Mr. Rao explained what we wanted and he left us in the barren waiting room for twenty minutes while he locked himself in his office. I was sure that he was running my name through Interpol, the European equivalent of the FBI.

The Consul invited us into his very sparse office that contained a simple desk and two chairs with a shortwave radio blaring Communist propaganda. He started to write my name from my passport onto the visa.

He said in English with a heavy Russian accent, "'Cathy' that is like a Russian name, 'Katya'."

"*Yes, it is,*" I replied in Russian.

His head jerked up and he almost smiled before he became very serious again and continued writing up the visa.

He asked me, "In what hotel are you staying?"

I answered him in Russian, "*The Sinha Hotel.*"

This time he looked at me amazed and asked me in Russian, "*Do you speak Russian?*"

"*Of course,*" I responded in Russian.

"*Where did you learn my language?*"

"*I studied it for three years at Fordham University in New York City.*"

"*Why?*" he asked.

"*My mother is Polish and my father Italian. I spoke both languages growing up and I wanted to learn Russian.*"

"*Are you happy with your hotel?*"

"*Very.*" As I thought, "Oh-oh, here comes the inevitable invitation."

"*Would you accept my invitation to dinner?*"

"*No I have much to do before I leave for Tashkent,*" I replied forestalling any further "invitations."

"*Please call on me anytime you wish to practice your Russian.*"

The Consul rummaged around in his desk and thrust a bottle of Russian champagne at me as a present.

I laughed, picked up my passport and we said goodbye. Rao was ebullient. I could see that his estimation of me had risen considerably.

The next day I went to see Rao to give him my itinerary. His office was my mail drop for letters to and from the States. Uncleji invited me upstairs to his home above the travel agency for Indian-style tea. He told me that his wife was vacationing in India and their two children were studying in the university there. The tea was black and boiled up together with cardamom seeds and condensed milk. He explained that in India they get their milk from the black water buffaloes whose milk is rich and the closest to it that he could find in Afghanistan was American canned condensed milk. The tea was tasty but I didn't care for canned milk no matter how rich. Then Rao booked my flight from Kabul to Tashkent.

I decided to go to an Afghan movie. I always loved foreign films and spent one day a week in the Bleecker Street Cinema in Greenwich Village in New York City. I was excited to see what Afghan movies were like. The theatre was crammed with men only. They all turned to stare at me until the film began. I felt uncomfortable, but curiosity about the film won out.

The movie was Pakistani like the American films in the fifties. There was the muscle-bound innocent hero and the busty heroine temptress with Cleopatra make-up. I found out that these films were produced en masse in India and Pakistan and any attempt at anything remotely sexual even kissing was cut from the film even though the heroines poured on clothing exposed all her charms. The film was predictable, his parents refused to let them marry, she dies from a broken heart and he grieves her death. The sets were fantastic and very colorful with multiple waterfalls and rivers that appeared whenever the hero and heroine even approached each other. However, the attending music was raucous with women singing in traditional falsetto voices. Running water replaced any interaction even remotely sexual. That was my first and last visit to an Afghan movie theatre.

My roommate, Morrie, informed me that when he took his shipment of antique Afghan guns to Customs, he was told that he needed to first go to the Kabul Museum to get them tagged and approved for export. We grabbed a taxi to get more information, only to find the museum closed for lunch. Formerly a King's palace, it had six stories of fitted gray block stones. The surrounding gardens were beautifully terraced and had tiny connecting bridges and archways. Each garden had its own water fountain with stone benches and trees surrounding it. We sat down to wait, common with all Afghan negotiations.

When the museum reopened, we were ushered into the director's office that had a beautiful high, arched ceiling. He was very gracious and offered us *chai*. Morrie explained that he wanted to export and sell antique guns in New Zealand. The director, a kind distinguished looking man, explained that what Customs told Morrie was correct. In order to ship anything out of Kabul, it must be first brought to the museum to be tagged. We thanked him and caught a taxi back to Shar-ee-Now so

Morrie and his business partner, Bill, could arrange to have their shipment brought to the museum first.

The taxi driver was hilarious in a frightening sort of way. After I greeted him in Dari, his face lit up like a Christmas bulb and he began chattering away oblivious to the fact that I had exhausted my Dari repertoire. He insisted on driving while looking back at me and talking. This gave both Morrie and me nightmares. Other taxis, horse-drawn carts, bicycles, and pedestrians careened away from us at the last possible second. We tried to make him face the road but failed. I think that was when I got my first gray hair.

CHAPTER NINE

Meat and Fat

"Tell me, tell me, tell me, Oh Life of Mine!
Tonight, open your heart to me
Tell me what is in your heart.
Your lips are my sweet stories
And those lips of yours are my greatest desire,
Tell me, tell me, tell me, Oh Life of Mine!
How long should I wait for you?
Oh Life of Mine, why are you leaving me?
Tell me, do you love me or not?
Tell me, tell me, tell me, Oh Life of Mine!
Afghan lament
Radio Afghanistan, Kabul 1970

Sunshine and I went into a small grocery shop. The shopkeeper was five-feet-three with a burnished copper complexion, blue eyes, and a mustache. He wore a light blue *peeran tambon* (tunic and pantaloons) with a gray western suit jacket over his shoulders. On his head was a yellow-gray *karakul* (lambskin) cap. I greeted him in Dari and he smiled in delight while returning the greeting. The shop sold everything from Russian box matches to rope. There were the usual hard candies, canned fruits, and vegetables from Pakistan, plus the extra added attraction of American Coca-Cola bottled in Afghanistan. Sitting empty in their wooden cases along the back wall, we spied the familiar glass coke bottles, heavily scarred as if they had been used for bowling pins! Afghan coke tasted like tincture of benzoin. However, we were sick of *chai* and orange soda and asked for two bottles. The only safe water here was boiled and we had no means to do so.

The merchant disappeared into the back room. We turned back to the front of the store and he seemed to materialize in front of us. Both

Sunshine and I did a double take. Even though no words were exchanged, he could see by our expressions that we were surprised and confused. Then the first merchant came out of the back with our cokes and all four of us started laughing as we realized that they were identical twins who were even dressed alike! The warmth poured from their eyes as they handed us our cokes and with many *"Selams,"* bows and smiles we left the shop still laughing.

Sunshine and I headed to the Sinha Hotel to pack up my things and transfer them to the Mustafa Hotel around the corner. This was a newly built white stucco tourist hotel closer to Chicken Street with the shops that I frequented. I took a room on the second floor for twenty cents a night so I could have a balcony. There we sat and watched the street scene. We tourists called this "Afghan television."

The room had a polished crushed stone floor and two single beds, with homemade pallets for mattresses and hand-loomed coarse white cotton sheets. The pillow was hard as a rock and I put it under the bed preferring to use my sheepskin vest instead. The blanket was a coarse scratchy woolen affair that I thought appropriate for horses. I left it on the bed but covered it with my warm sleeping bag. There was a small wooden night table between the beds and two straight-backed chairs.

Cokes in hand, we pulled the chairs onto the balcony. It was sunset. Under violet clouds, a gossamer rosy pink haze swathed the horizon and melted into the azure sky. The pungent juniper and cedarwood smoke gave an acrid odor to the advancing night air. A phonograph scratched out Afghan popular songs raucously puncturing the usual quietly-humming streets. People strolled in and out of shops and restaurants at a relaxed pace. They were winding up the day's transactions to get home to their families before the night air began to bite.

It was after seven o'clock when Sunshine and I decided to go to King's shop only to find his friend the Seer. Somehow, Sunshine and Dustin were given one week transit visas instead of the tourist visas they needed to complete shipping their sheepskin coats to San Francisco. We explained all this to the Seer and he told us not to worry. He promptly wrote a letter to a friend who worked in the Tourist Visa Police office and told us to go there the next day. Sunshine and I thanked the Seer and went back to the van to join Dustin for our last night together.

The following day, when Sunshine and I went to the visa office, we found it closed for lunch. Down the block, to a tiny kebab house, we went and ate lamb kebabs with *naan* and a bowl of creamy yoghurt that was more like sour cream. Fifteen metal skewers with three tiny cubes of lamb and three cubes of lamb fat on each skewer equaled one portion. We skipped the fat.

After lunch, we returned to the visa office and located the Seer's friend. Yacub was tall and slender with black rim glasses and a brown *karakul* (lambskin) cap on his head. He immediately wrote up their visas after reading the Seer's letter. He told us to follow him to another office to have the visas stamped. There were about fifty people crowded into this small room around a desk where a man named Rasul sat. He was a middle-aged, portly, bald man with horn-rim glasses, reminiscent of the typically frustrated overworked bureaucrat.

When Yacub presented him with the passports, he responded with, "What is the matter with you? Didn't you tell them that they have to pay a fine?"

Yacub tensed in anger, but because Rasul was his superior, said nothing.

He turned to us, handed back the passports and said, "I am sorry. I can do nothing."

Angry, I snapped the passports out of Yacub's hand, and Sunshine and I returned to King's shop. The Seer was still there, and we told him what happened. He made a two-second telephone call. Giving us a scrawled letter, he told us to go back to Rasul. This time I turned on all of my charm as well as a few Pashto words. Rasul fell apart. He looked at us as if he had never seen us before as he processed the passports. Then he asked to see my passport and made a great show of studying it. He asked, reeking "charm," how long I would be in Kabul and what did I think of his country? I gave him a glowing description of Afghanistan, especially the kindness and hospitality of the people. He thanked me effusively while signing the visas and before he could get around to asking me to dinner, Sunshine and I backed out of the room with many thanks. We skipped back to the van where Dustin, Sunshine, and I said our goodbyes promising to write each other.

I climbed up the Mustafa Hotel's wide steps to the office. The manager, a Tajik with six fingers on each hand gave me the phone. It was

Mr. Rao telling me that all flights to Tashkent had been canceled until further notice because of a blizzard. *Oh well, I thought. I guess I am not supposed to go to Russia right now. I still had four weeks left on my ticket to New York and pondered what to do since I had to renew my Afghan visa to stay here any longer.*

That cold December night, a messenger came to my hotel room and relayed that King had invited me to a party. He arrived at eight o'clock and we drove for twenty minutes to a house on the outskirts of Kabul.

King hit the horn. A servant opened the brown wooden gates in the nine-foot-high adobe wall and we drove into a lovely, spacious garden. We walked under a grape arbor as the servant carried King's harmonium into a large house. We left our shoes just outside the door and entered the *saloon* where the floor was covered with very expensive silk Persian carpets. Hunting scenes, fruit trees, flowers, and sayings from the Quran were woven into them. An old European style couch stood against one wall. Eight young women were crammed on it with a horde of children all under the age of ten, climbing all over them. The women had waist length, straight black hair and large liquid "eyes like those of gazelles," as the favorite saying went. The remaining floor space around the walls, where the rest of the men and women sat cross-legged, was heaped with huge pillows, bolsters and cotton-stuffed pallets with bright floral cotton or velvet coverings. As King and I entered the room, all forty people rose in a circle. We stopped before each person giving them the traditional greeting. They smiled and laughed with delight at my limited Dari, pleased that I made an effort to communicate with them.

I squeezed myself onto a pallet while King took his place on the carpet in the center of the room. There were two other musicians playing *tabla*, or hand drums and *rebab,* an ancestor of our violin.

The Seer was there with his wife. He took me by my hand and introduced me to her. He said that I had to be careful because she was a Ghilzai. I looked blank. Everyone laughed at his teasing. Then the Seer explained that the Ghilzais are a mixture of Turks and Pashtuns, called Ghorids and are very fierce fighters. I looked at his wife and she indeed did have a Mongol slant to her eyes. I pretended to tremble and this made everyone roar.

The next hour was spent talking, laughing, and waiting for the remaining guests as we ate roasted chickpeas, raw almonds, and a soft white sweet cheese similar to Italian ricotta. It was garnished with yellow and pale green raisins. Eating was interspersed with smoking hashish and drinking brandy.

Johnny Walker Black and Red scotch was also available and the Afghans took full advantage encouraging me to do the same. I surprised them by refusing. They had seen American films where men and women drank in their homes and at restaurants. I explained that I only liked wine or beer. Shocked, they wouldn't believe me and pressed scotch on me at various intervals only to be met with the same refusal.

As the hubbub died, King and the other musicians began tuning their instruments. King hummed and then sang his own compositions. Although I did not understand most of the words, there was no mistaking the joyous emotions. As he sang, there were exclamations of praise and laughter at his double entendres, interspersed with applause. After each thirty minute piece, King told anecdotes and jokes amid more laughter.

I heard my name and turned to see Suleiman, Habiba's husband, a new arrival to the party. We greeted one another and he sat down next to me. Then he began to explain about Afghan classical music.

"You see, Catee-jon, music just like everything else in this world is divided into masculine and feminine. The major scale represents the masculine notes and the minor scale the feminine. Classical Afghan music consists of a beginning that is slow in tempo and masculine. The middle has many variations on the main theme and the tempo is very rapid; this is the feminine part. The end of the piece is again slow and masculine. Male and female are reflected as separate but interdependent entities. People say this music represents the relationship between lovers - happy, angry and then happy again."

"Thank you for this explanation, Suleiman-jon. All I know is that these sounds together with King's voice carry me away into another world and another life."

"Yes, perhaps you were one of us in another time, Catee-jon. I have never met a westerner as comfortable with our culture as you seem to be. Tell me Catee-jon, why did you come to Afghanistan?"

"Suleiman-jon, I am not sure. I always wanted to come here since I was a little girl. I don't know why. I am seeking something, what I don't know."

"May Allah, in His wisdom, guide you."

Then I said, "I do know that I want to buy jewelry from King and sell it in New York."

"What a splendid idea!" he cried.

King started singing and we both turned back to the music.

All the while, the children played games, munched on the snacks and fell asleep where they were. No one put them to bed. They remained with the guests and the family until the adults slept too.

Meanwhile, huge pieces of bread called lawasha were brought out draped over the servers' arms. At first, I thought they were long brown pieces of material. They were placed on a cloth on the carpet in front of us for several people to share. It was then I realized that this was bread, like a huge chapatti capable of covering a large dining room table. Then the kebabs arrived. Hundreds of thin metal skewers punctured tiny grilled cubes of lamb and fat.

I asked, "Why is fat served?"

Suleiman replied, "This shows honor to the guest. We have a saying, 'I will give you meat and fat.' This indicates the wealth of the host. His animals have plenty to eat and are well cared for."

At midnight, after more singing, the hostess announced, "The food is ready."

I could not believe that what we already ate were mere appetizers! We were led to a room off the saloon taken up with one huge table groaning with the choicest dishes. There were huge pullows of rice with whole chickens or legs of lamb buried inside with a myriad of spices. Some pullows were yellow from saffron, others green from spinach and cilantro, while others were caramelized with slivered carrots and raisins gracing their tops. King came to my side and pointed out that this last dish was their national dish called qabili pullow. It was known as "bejeweled rice" because of the carrots, raisins, whole cinnamon sticks, cloves and cardamom seeds that "bejeweled" it. There were many other succulent dishes including cooked vegetables and one with dumplings swimming in a yoghurt sauce perfumed with garlic and dried mint; and, of course, naan. Everything was seasoned to perfection!

After this meal, when we could hardly move, King again took up his harmonium in the center of the room and began to play and sing.

Hours later, the hostess brought out all kinds of desserts. There was a rose water and cardamom pudding; deep-fried pretzel-shaped dough swimming in more rose water; deep fried dough in the shape of elephant ears; a sweet egg omelet dusted with ground cardamom seeds; and baklava, a flaky pastry filled with ground walnuts soaked in honey with just a hint of amber essence.

Around four o'clock in the morning, King again took up his position and began to sing and play. Towards dawn, he began to weep. It was infectious. Many of the people became misty-eyed and some of the women cried openly. I realized that he was singing about the tragedy that befell his family. King's father was a court noble during the reign of King Nadir Shah. In a mini-revolt, Nadir Shah was replaced and King's father was made prime minister. King and his family moved into the palace. Several years later, the usurper was overthrown and all his associates were killed. King, his father, and brothers were tortured. All were killed except King who was a youth at the time. He, along with his mother and sisters, were spared and continued to live in their grief and shame in Kabul.

As the pink-orange haze of dawn crept over the horizon, we all fell asleep where we were. The last thing I remember was our hostess pulling quilts over us as I sank down onto a pallet, cushioned by huge pillows, and slid into a field of peaceful dreams.

The next day, I went downstairs to the restaurant and a young Portuguese man from a nearby table acknowledged me. I smiled and he asked in very broken English if he could join me. He was a medical student on sabbatical. His name was Ronaldinho. He was five-foot-nine, and powerfully built from playing soccer. He had jet-black wavy hair, porcelain-white skin, and pale, ice-blue eyes. Since English was torture for him, we discovered a common language, French. Ronaldinho said he was going to Pakistan and onward to India. I thought it would be a great idea to spend some time in Pakistan before my flight to New York. I chose Pakistan to get my exit visa because it was easier than facing the paranoid Iranians who were sure everyone was in the drug trade. They made entry and exit visas as difficult as possible.

Ronaldinho was happy to have a traveling companion who spoke his language. We skipped off to the bazaar to purchase some trunks for my shipments to New York.

The trunk bazaar sat in the middle of Jad-ee-Maiwand. The few paved streets in Kabul came to an abrupt halt here. They dissolved into small twisting dirt lanes among a warren of tiny shops selling tin, silver, and brass objects of every size and kind. The metal trunks ranged in size from two-by-three feet to eight-by-ten feet. I chose a medium size one for two hundred and fifty *afghanis* (two dollars and fifty cents). The man selling the trunks was hilarious. He jumped up and down on his products to prove their durability. We laughed at his antics.

The shop next door sold locks. They were one-inch square pastel colored locks for only twenty cents. Ronaldinho bet the locksmith that he could open any of these locks with the key from his hotel room that had a similar looking lock. The locksmith told Ronaldho that if he could do that, he would give him a lock free of charge. Ronaldinho proved his point and the surprised Afghan gave him a free lock.

Then it dawned on me. All of the locks on all of the hotel rooms had nothing to do with security; they were just pretty colored locks! Ronaldinho then took me to a Chinese locksmith. His locks cost fifty cents but were individually made. "Only the Afghans," I mused. "Copy something, but don't get it exactly right."

When Ronaldinho didn't show up the next morning, I ran to his hotel and woke him from a deep sleep. We rushed to the bus station in a panic! The bus was due to leave at seven thirty sharp. We got there just in time. However, in the typical Afghan manner, the bus didn't leave until nine o'clock. The bus "station" consisted of a huge bare muddy field where all ages of buses stood in various stages of arrival and departure. The gunning of the motors, the cries of the porters, the bleating of sheep as they were loaded on the top of the buses and the babble of the travelers, created a raucous din. The drivers shuffled around aimlessly, occasionally ejecting great green gobs of *nesswar* from their mouths. *Nesswar* is a close relative to our chewing tobacco. The majority of it is composed of ground green tobacco, lime, and chalk. Some claim it contains opium.

We boarded our bus, leftover from World War I, a gunmetal gray affair that emitted an occasional thick cloud of black smoke. It was then we discovered that having a ticket only guaranteed the opportunity to mount the bus. Individual seating was unheard of. Six people in seats for two were the rule. Some men squatted on top of the seats fingering their *tassbees* that symbolized the ninety-nine attributes of the Creator and served the same purpose as the Christian rosary. Women in *chadorees* (the veil) had infants and children on their laps and parcels with food surrounding them. Considering all that was going on, it was amazingly silent as people waited patiently for the bus to start.

Ronaldinho and I found two seats right behind the bus driver. These were the best seats since you had a clear view of the road ahead through the windscreen. Because we were foreigners, no one insisted on making our two seats into places for four or more.

As we waited for the bus to depart, I reflected on my time in Kabul and felt sadness wash over me at the knowledge that soon I would be returning to New York. Then I'd really miss Kabul and the kindness and hospitality of my Afghan friends. I'd miss the noise of the bazaars and the quiet hush of the cottages around Qargah Dam. I felt as if I could live here for the rest of my life.

CHAPTER TEN

Thė Khybėr Pȧṣṣ

"Hot spiced tea with cardamom, cloves, and cinnamon,
Boiled up in the fatty milk of black water buffaloes,
Cramped seats on Pakistani International Airlines,
The sickening, cloying smell of cheap jasmine hair oil,
Pak air hostesses with huge doe-like eyes,
Shimmering along in traditional outfits embroidered with mirrors,
Modern appliances tied up in old cloth bundles,
Lurching forward in the overhead racks,
Acrid sweat of the porters mingled with the pungent odor of diesel,
The smell of the perfumed earth after a rain,
The call to prayer,
Offal in the streets,
Hi-pitched songs blaring from static-y loudspeakers,
The primitive stares of the people,
Men's brown suede sandals fringed with colorful beads,
Adobe teahouses huddled on the side of the road,
Squatting figures in occasional murmurs of conversation,
Black silk turbans and bandoliers of bullets,
Gold teeth flashing, matching gold wristwatches and rings,
Two-foot high water pipes gurgling thoughtfully
As their stems are passed around."
The Author's poem on Pakistan

My thoughts were interrupted when the driver turned on his portable radio and popular songs blared out of the tinny loudspeakers. With that, the bus rolled forward.

Ronaldinho and I spent our time telling each other our histories as the bus lumbered gasping and belching from Kabul to Jalalabad. We began our descent to the plains of Pakistan through the Khyber Pass or the *Khaibar*, as the Afghans called it. An ominous spiky-toothed jagged range with gaunt cliffs cascading down for thousands of feet in long clean shattered curves loomed above us. Here the dirt track narrowed to barely accommodate two buses going in the opposite directions. As if this weren't enough, the Afghans drive on the right side of the road like the Americans and the Pakistanis on the left like the British! Despite our conversation, we feared for our lives. Since the "road" twisted like a corkscrew, it was necessary for the driver to incessantly lean on the horn to avoid an instant and hideous death.

The craggy mountains lent a sinister air to the dangerous trip. On several occasions, we saw the remains of animals, goods, and bus parts that littered the huge crevices like confetti from a ticker-tape parade. I shuddered knowing that with one wrong twist of the wheel, our fate would be sealed. Sensing the danger, the normal chatter on the bus ceased, even sounds from small children.

A gushing opaque khaki-colored river accompanied us as we drove into the Peshawar Valley, first across the Swat River and then the Indus River at Attock. At the border post of Landi Kotal, I remained on the bus as Ronaldinho took both of our passports and visas to the customs officials. The post was a sprinkling of adobe huts carved into the niches of the mountains with several charpoys for tea drinking as well as for smoking the huge three-foot-high water pipes. Six-foot-four Pakhtuns, as the Afghans are known in Pakistan, with eight yards of turban wound around their heads, were perched here and there calmly fingering their *tassbees*. But it was the mountain behind the Pakhtuns that caught and held my eye. There in the mountain niches were a plethora of colorful American Cadillacs from the nineteen fifties in different stages of repair with their big fins shining in the sun! I always wondered what happened to those cars.

We continued our journey into the city of Peshawar itself. Pakistan was another world. It was green palm trees, hot humid weather, dirt roads, polluted air, stinking sewage trenches, insanely congested traffic, and, compared to the Afghans I was soon to discover, replete with rude people. In contrast, Kabul was snowy mountains, gracious hospitality, sheepskin coats, high altitudes, crystal clear air, cold nights warmed by juniper and cedar fires, and hot dry days.

Peshawar was teeming with life in muggy sweltering heat at four o'clock in the afternoon. The heat seemed to have no effect upon the population. We stopped at a hotel in the main bazaar for two rupees (twenty cents) per night. The manager took us upstairs to a small, very dirty room whose sole window was just below the ceiling. To make matters worse, it had dirty linen on the two single beds and a communal water tank sitting on the terrace that ran around the courtyard. The only bathroom on that floor was a room with a hole in the floor. The water tank, we were told, was to be used to clean your body after toileting. The locks on the door were the cheap variety found in Afghanistan. Ronaldinho made and won the same bet with the hotel manager that he could open any lock in the hotel with the key he purchased in Afghanistan ... much to the surprise of this Pakistani. We decided to pay for the room and leave our bags there so we would be free to find something better.

Ronaldinho and I walked down the street with its unpaved roads, dodging piles of fresh animal dung from the horse-drawn carts, burden-bearing donkeys, and trains of aimless black water buffaloes wandering among the throng of people. The Pakistanis were very rude. Little boys made crude noises and the men's stares were hostile. "Shades of Iran," I thought.

Hungry, we stopped to buy some bananas. We bought two of them and when we asked how much they cost, the merchant held up two fingers. Ronaldinho gave him a ten-rupee note and he gave us eight *rupees* change. We then realized that he had meant two *annas*. There were one hundred *annas* to a *rupee* and twelve *rupees* to the dollar. So we argued for the change since two *rupees* put the price of bananas at the same rate as our hotel room. We got our change and, tired of people gawking, grabbed a *rickshaw*.

These tiny three-wheel vehicles looked as if they belonged in an amusement park. They were just big enough for two people to cram into the back on a high perch behind the driver. An iron bar separated us from him. The motor is the same as that of a motor scooter and there are no shock absorbers. After a short ride, my bones felt churned to butter! The entire little cart was decorated with mirrors, ribbons and colorful pieces of vinyl. The roof and doors were iron bars covered with the same vinyl pieces. We felt as if we were in a funhouse ride at a fair. The inside of the *rickshaws* had a collage of Pakistani film stars and clips from movie posters. It made interesting scenery as we jounced through the throng of humanity. The young Pak driver didn't understand English. We gathered the usual crowd around us and I kept repeating the word "hotel." A Pak in the crowd said "Jan's" and explained this to the driver. Away we sailed.

Jan's was a five-storey narrow building that looked brand new with rooms surrounding a courtyard. However, it was forty-five rupees per night and we felt that this was too much to pay for a hotel in Pakistan. The two Paks at the front desk spoke English and were kind enough to suggest another hotel down the road called the Shahzar that only cost ten *rupees*.

The Shahzar was to our liking. It was very clean with hot running water and its own restaurant. The manager was a polite middle-aged gentleman. We registered and then he came out to tell our driver to take us back to where we deposited our bags. We managed to get all of our gear stowed on the floor of the rickshaw next to the driver and he returned us to the Shahzar.

After checking in, we went to the Storyteller's Bazaar. It was a tangle of lanes with single-storey adobe shops spilling onto each other. There were pharmacies that displayed human skulls, *tassbee* shops where cripples strung the ninety-nine names of Allah, and shops containing essential oils. The shops leaned into the stalls of shoemakers, butchers, glass blowers, porters, basket makers, cloth sellers, jewelers, spice sellers, and potters. After delighting our senses, we returned to the Shahzar.

The only food we had eaten all day was oranges and bananas. Ravenous, we went downstairs to the restaurant. It was a large windowless room with white tablecloths on each of the twenty-odd tables. There was a television set that didn't work. It was the first set we had seen since Teheran. We ordered chicken curry and rice. The chicken was tough but tasty and the rice had a lovely saffron flavor. The meal came with a salad of tomatoes and onions dotted with chopped green chili peppers and some fragrant fresh-baked, whole-wheat round bread that the Paks call *roti*. After the meal we ordered tea. It was the same black tea that I had at Mr. Rao's home, boiled up with milk. Ronaldinho and I both preferred the lighter Afghan tea flavored with cardamom seeds. After our meal, exhausted, we went upstairs and fell asleep.

The next day, we took the bus to Lahore, the capital of the Punjab region of Pakistan. The bus was ancient with strings of colored lights inside that cheered us up. When the bus stopped, it shook like a dying elephant. The driver, who looked like Egyptian President Nasser, was too busy looking at me in the rearview mirror to keep his eyes on the road as we barreled along at close to one hundred miles an hour. Sometimes the driver inserted a cassette into his tape player for our entertainment. These popular Pak songs with women's high falsetto voices against an instrumental background were interspersed with raucous sounds made by modern pop music. It was a grating experience ... an assault on the senses.

Since this was the direct bus to Lahore, it only stopped two dozen times. At each stop, the windows were pried open by dozens of food vendors. They shoved trays of fried turnovers stuffed with meat or vegetables, sweets, fruits, and candies into the bus while setting up a cacophonous din on the merits and cost of their wares. The majority of these vendors were children under the age of twelve jockeying for position. Nearest to us was a boy of seven whose tray held wonderful spicy *samosas and pakoras*, deep-fried meat turnovers and vegetable fritters. We picked out a half dozen of each, gave him a *rupee* and he was swallowed up by the crowd. The food was delicious, redolent with fragrant spices and just the right amount of hot pepper.

We made a stop in Rawalpindi around two o'clock and the bus pulled off the road into a small bazaar area. The mud was ankle deep and the noise deafening as buses roared in and out and the drivers screamed out their destinations, pushing us around to get our attention. The hostility and frustration on these peoples' faces made me angry and afraid at the same time. Surrounding the buses were small kebab stands and fruit and soda shops. We just had time to grab some fruit and two bottles of "Tops," the Pak equivalent of Seven-Up, when we saw "Nasser" board the bus.

As we approached our seats, my heart sank. I had left my pack on the seat and now a blank space stared up at me. Everything I had heard from other travelers about Pakistan was true. Leave something for a minute and it disappears. Ronaldinho and I got out of the bus and refused to board until my pack was found. Two Pakistanis who were already on the bus bristled with anger and insisted that we board. Just as angry, we refused to budge. I motioned that either this was the wrong bus or someone had stolen my pack. The two Paks were gesticulating and demanding in Urdu that we board and kept pointing to our seats. When we did board, I saw my pack. Someone had placed it under my seat for safe keeping. Sheepishly, I apologized to the two Paks and the driver for holding up the bus.

At the next stop, there were no food vendors and Ronaldinho and I wanted some bananas from the nearby stalls. I drew a picture of a banana and motioned "food" by putting my hand to my mouth and gave the picture to one of the passengers. He immediately got off the bus and returned with two bunches of bananas. We thanked him and tried to reimburse him but he insisted on treating us since we "were guests in his country." This was more like Afghan hospitality. I handed out bananas to him, "Nasser" and his replacement driver. "Nasser" came up to us, shook our hands and bid us "Selam Aleikum" as he strode off the bus.

A young Pak boarded and took the aisle seat next to Ronaldinho. He and Ronaldinho were busy exchanging and lighting each other's brands of cigarettes. I gave him one of our oranges. He spoke some English and he started asking us the usual questions about where we were from and where we were going and how we liked Pakistan. At the next stop, he got off the bus and returned with some apples and walnuts. I thought that he was being hospitable until I felt his hand on my shoulder. He had stretched his arm over the back of the seat behind Ronaldinho. I told Ronaldinho and he asked the Pak to remove his arm. The Pak was mortified! He had made the mistake of thinking that an unveiled foreigner was fair game. He put his head in his hands and remained that way for the rest of the trip to Lahore. I felt sorry for him.

We had a twenty-minute rest stop at Jhelum that night and were invited to dinner by an eighteen-year-old named Gulraez who was on his way to business school in Lahore. The restaurant was adobe and had eight, raw-wood tables with matching chairs in the room. The table tops were covered with pieces of linoleum and the usual bare light bulb hung from the ceiling, giving off its dim aura. It was jammed with Pakistani men who immediately started smiling when we entered. There was no menu and I told Gulraez that I wanted to see the food myself instead of letting him choose.

The kitchen contained two adobe embankments, one of which turned out to be the stove and oven combination. Two men squatted on the other embankment. One doled out food from the huge pots half buried in the adobe stove and the other was in charge of grilling kebabs over an open fire. They smiled at Ronaldinho and me as I pointed to a perfumed spicy rice dish studded with chunks of lamb, and a ground meat and green peas stew. They motioned for us to go back and sit down and brought our food with *roti* and Pak style tea. Now the men in the restaurant started laughing. I couldn't figure out what the joke was until Ronaldinho and I tasted the ground meat and peas stew. It was so hot that the tears rolled down our faces but so delicious we kept eating to the amazement of the rest of the diners! Gulraez insisted on treating us as guests in his country. I began to feel that the Paks were not such bad people after all.

We arrived in Lahore at ten o'clock at night. Basing hotel prices on Peshawar's, we chose a fifteen-rupee hotel. That got us a filthy room with a smelly bathroom and no water for cleaning ourselves. Of course, there was no toilet paper either. The linen was equally dirty and when we complained to the manager, he said that the laundry man was sick. We waved goodbye and the manager suddenly brought clean linen.

The next morning we ordered hot water for a shower and were presented with a filthy slimy bucket with tepid water and a grimy plastic cup floating around inside the bucket. We made do with the cold water tap.

On our way out to explore the city, one of the clerks gave us our "hot water" bill. Ronaldinho laughed and tore it to shreds. The bug-eyed clerk ran for the manager. When he arrived, we explained why and he laughed too. We all shook hands and left.

Ronaldinho and I headed for the American Express office where we were informed that the Youth Hostel and the Auto Association were the places to camp. We settled on the latter that was run by a charming elderly Pak gentleman, whom we addressed as *Chachaji* (Respected Paternal Uncle). He spoke some English and his thin, almost gaunt, but tall frame bore loose traditional clothing the color of the khaki dust of the desert. His merry brown eyes sparkled and his grizzled gray head was topped by a makeshift turban of a black and white checked cloth that doubled sometimes as a shawl. We set up Ronaldinho's tent, and for twenty cents a night, we lived in this wonderfully manicured garden with its eight foot high green hedges as a border. Bushes of roses scented the air and at dusk, the old man came out with his water pipe and had a smoke and a chat with us. He was retired from the Pak army and had many children and grandchildren. He held this job to supplement his pension.

I pointed to his clothing and said, *"Peeran tambon."*

He smiled and said, *"Shelwar kamiz,"* the Urdu word for traditional clothes.We had a little conversation where I picked up some more Urdu words.

We rarely left this sanctuary except to make periodic trips to the bazaar for food and supplies. These experiences were always nerve-wracking. No matter that I wore a long tunic, jeans, and boots, men surrounded us, made rude noises, and threw objects at me because I was an unveiled foreign woman. Or, they asked one hundred and one questions regarding what we thought of Pakistan. Ronaldinho wound up hurling bodies around just so we could get the simplest shopping done.

We walked off to find the Italian Consulate for Ronaldinho's Indian visa. The Italian Consulate accommodated Italians, Spaniards, and the Portuguese.

Lahore is a very graceful old city where the British erected beautiful malls and parks with old Victorian buildings on the main streets. It had a rather strange effect on me. The Pakistanis tended careful gardens around their bungalows with pots of bright flowers on the verandas. This was a definite contrast to the adobe homes of the Afghans that blended into the barren mountains where spring flowers riotously bloomed in every direction in unimaginable color. It wasn't until two years later, when I was in England, that I realized that the houses and gardens I saw in Pakistan were a leftover from the British presence. All of the English houses outside of the London metropolitan area had those same gardens with flower pots around the front of the house.

Just behind the broad tree-lined boulevards, were small rutted-beaten earth lanes, with open sewage trenches flowing by red adobe homes that emitted the acrid smell of burning cow dung. The hostile primitive stares of the people gave me a claustrophobic feeling.

Blackwater buffaloes roamed without hindrance around the traffic of pedestrians, bicyclists, *tongas* (horse-drawn carts) and an occasional Mercedes. Motor scooters were driven by young men in western clothes with veiled women clinging side-saddle on the back. Their westernized high heel sandals stuck out below traditional cuffed pantaloons while several children nestled in their arms. The veil here is called the *burkha*. It is a long black coat that falls to the wrists and ankles. The head is covered in what we'd consider a nun's veil with a sheer black face veil that starts at the hairline and ends at the base of the neck. Like Afghanistan, where the women wore the *chadoree,* the Pak women wore the *burkha* to observe *purdah* (veiling) in the presence of strange men.

Rickshaws careened in and out of this sea of traffic. Ringing bells, tooting horns, and lowing buffaloes, produced a discordant symphony of unabated noise and made me feel that I had truly reached the subcontinent. Gone was the hush of the wild barren plains where serenity reigned even among the throngs of humanity who strolled the bazaars.

The stink of dung, mingled with the stench of the carbon monoxide from the scooters and rickshaws, created an impenetrable wall of pollution in the humid air.

My Portuguese friend and I went back along the mall and viewed the various fabric and antique shops with their openly-advertised high prices for tourists. We stopped a Pak man in western clothing to ask about the Italian Embassy.

He had black curly hair, thick eyebrows, and mustache, complete with a swarthy complexion and a piercing stare. This was relieved when he smiled at us and explained that the consulate was across the street, but closed for the day. It was one o'clock in the afternoon. He asked where we were from and I told him. Ronaldinho had said, "No Eeenglish," in reply to his question.

Then this "gentleman" turned his full "charm" on me and asked me to allow him to take us to lunch as guests in his country. Using the behavior of the Afghans as my yard stick, Ronaldinho and I agreed to accept his invitation. He introduced himself to us as Imtiaz, and we all shook hands as we walked across the Mall to an elegant looking restaurant called "Lord's." It was dim and cool with slow-moving ceiling fans and snow-white tablecloths. After the one hundred and five degree heat with its eighty percent humidity, this was a welcome change.

Imtiaz called for menus and encouraged us to order whatever we liked at his expense. Never ones to impose on a host, we both ordered several inexpensive dishes. While waiting for the food, Imtiaz began his barrage of questions that would become so familiar to me that I became an expert at cutting them off immediately. Since this was my first experience with Pak men, I was sincere and honest in my answers.

Imtiaz asked, "What do you think of Pakistan?"

"It is very lovely."

"Do you like our food?" asked Imtiaz.

"Oh yes, very much!" I exclaimed.

"Are you and Ronaldinho married?" he asked.

"No, we are just friends traveling together," I responded.

"I too am not married. Where are you staying? May I come to see you sometime?"

"We are staying at the Auto Association; you may call on us if you like."

"Perhaps you would like to stay in my house; I live with my two brothers. You could have your own room. We have a big house. My brothers and I would like to sleep with you. You are very beautiful," he said with his back turned to Ronaldinho and all his intensity concentrated on me. Rage shot through me at the nerve of this man talking so casually about sleeping with me in a public restaurant as if he were discussing the weather.

"Please say that you will come with me today," Imtiaz urged as he gripped my hands.

Indignant, I quickly pulled away and said, "Absolutely not! And if I tell Ronaldinho what you just said, there will be a big fight."

Ronaldinho saw that something was wrong and got up from his chair. I told him that Imtiaz was just asking about America and he sat down but on full alert.

Imtiaz got up from his place and said, "Very good, Madam. Good day."

He walked out of the restaurant. Realizing that if Ronaldinho knew that I had been insulted he would probably run after Imtiaz and beat him to a pulp, I explained to Ronaldinho that Imtiaz had forgotten a previous appointment. We were left to eat our food and pay a large bill. However, the food was so good that we even ordered mango ice cream for dessert and this was a real treat.

CHAPTER ELEVEN

Propositions

"The law of asylum must be granted,
Even if the person who grants asylum loses their life in doing so.
In Afghanistan, our word is our bond."
The second great law of the Afghans, *nanawatai*

Beggars were another problem. *Chachaji* (Respected Uncle), our caretaker explained that begging was generational. If a child is born disabled, the parents consider this fortunate because they are assured of a lifetime income. They set the baby out immediately in a little cart with a begging bowl. Some poor parents purposely maim their children at birth. Beggar children become very insistent for money and gleefully wave their stumps and diseased body parts in the faces of foreigners. Some even become vicious and attack in groups.

One time when Ronaldinho and I refused to give money, we found ourselves racing down the street with running, squirming, crawling, limping, filthy, maimed children in hot pursuit. It was revolting to me as a germ-conscious American and the word, "unclean" ran through my head. I felt like this was a past life experience where I was one of these children preying on people as they were preying on me.

Pakistan was in some ways more primitive than Afghanistan. It was a created Muslim state in 1948 by the British who ruled India. British colonization left its peculiar mark upon their psyches. On one hand, many people spoke English and all road and street signs were in English making it very easy to travel here. On the other hand, there was a basic distrust and hostility towards foreigners.

Now I had the additional burden of men who spoke English propositioning me to sleep with them if they paid for my meal. When I refused, they left the table like Imtiaz, I quickly learned. In Afghanistan, I was never accosted.

We spent the rest of the day in our retreat, talking to the caretaker. Ronaldinho insisted on staying with me until I could get my Afghan visa and leave Pakistan. *Chachaji* said not to worry. He assigned his tall well-built sixteen-year-old grandson as my chaperone so Ronaldinho could be on his way.

Ronaldinho and I had several more encounters with Pak men before I realized that these were not chance, but the behavior of "westernized" Pak men towards western women. I became so expert in sensing what was going to happen that when I spotted some man looking in my direction, I'd look directly into his eyes and emphatically shake my head, "No!"

I hated Pakistan! The men in traditional clothing, who were too shy to proposition me, stood in groups and stared, made rude remarks or tried to get close enough to touch my face or hair. At least they hadn't gotten around to the bottom-pinching of the Turks yet, but it was sufficient for a woman to be touched or remarked on in public to mark her as "up for grabs."

Ronaldinho and I discussed the absence of westernized Pak women in dresses or jeans on the streets. Unlike Afghanistan, the few women I saw here wore traditional clothing covered with the *burkha,* the Pak veil. Even these women were a rarity. The entire country seemed to house only boys and men plus an occasional school girl. I was very uncomfortable in this atmosphere and both of us were always on the alert against verbal or physical harassment with an absolute mistrust of everyone we met.

One day Ronaldinho and I decided to walk over to the Anarkali bazaar. It was named after a beautiful dancing girl called "Black Pomegranate." The legend said that she was buried alive by an emperor because she was unfaithful to him. Anarkali consisted of several main connected streets jammed on either side with shops surrounded by open sewage trenches. To avoid falling into these trenches, it was necessary to step up into the shops. The bazaar was very crowded with men walking, riding bicycles, or driving cars with their wives and families nestled inside.

As usual, the men made vulgar gestures, and Ronaldinho had to kick a few of them for throwing pebbles at me or trying to run me down. We bought some crispy *pakoras* (vegetable fritters). As we munched, browsing past the booksellers and cloth merchants, we wound up in a hardware store and bought a one-burner stove. This enabled us to cut down on going out.

At the vegetable market, an old man with brightly hennaed hair and mustache, sold us carrots, peas, cauliflower, tomatoes, and some curry spices to prepare our own meals. We spent the rest of the day in our retreat, talking to the caretaker.

Before Ronaldinho left for India, he had established himself as my protector. His size and willingness to knock around those who got too close allowed me some personal space in the streets. I soon realized that the role of the imperious "*memsahib*" (mistress of the manor), was the only one I could play to protect myself. This was a lonely choice because no relationships could be established on any level. I confined myself to using my ears and eyes and speaking only to give an order, in a grave tone. Although I can carry this off easily, I prefer being open and kind but in Pakistan this was impossible. It was only in the company of Chachaji's grandson that I was able to apply for an Afghan visa without being jostled, touched, pushed or grabbed.

After a few days, I decided to spend time in Peshawar awaiting my Afghan visa. I checked into Jan's Hotel. The clerk at the desk greeted me with a smile. Happy to see a friendly face at last, I smiled and returned his greeting. He gave me a room key and personally insisted on carrying my bags. I went to tip him but he refused with a laugh. I laughed too feeling relaxed again since Peshawar was the land of the Pakhtuns, cousins to the Afghan Pashtuns. I felt their courtesy and hospitality surround me.

Later I went out for a while. When I returned the clerk inquired as to how I was feeling. Puzzled I said I was fine, just a little tired from the trip from Lahore.

He asked, "Can I come to your room?"

"What for?"

"To see you."

"What do you mean 'to see me'?" A nasty dread insinuated itself into my solar plexus.

"Oh please let me come to your room!" he begged.

Aggravated, I yelled, "NO! You may not come to my room!"

As my visa would not be ready for several weeks, I left Peshawar and found respite in Rawalpindi a city between Peshawar and Lahore. Here, the people were less ignorant and I had some freedom.

I chose an inexpensive motel whose rooms were little bungalows with a living room, bedroom, and bath. It was owned by two Pakhtun brothers and their wives who lived on the premises. The older brother, Happiness, in his thirties, liked me right away and adopted the position of a brother, protector, and friend. He was six-feet tall, with dark brown curly hair, light brown eyes, and a jovial manner. His wife, Queenie, was fair, medium height, slim, and very beautiful with large black eyes and long black hair worn in a thick braid. She was in her late twenties, was very kind and always ready to laugh. We three became great friends in no time at all.

In their living room, I met a politician who had spent the last three years in London with his family. Returning to Pakistan, they found it very hard to adjust to life here. His wife never observed *purdah* (veiling) and was used to driving. When his relatives heard this, they threatened to kill him if he ever set foot in their district. So he and his wife moved to Islamabad, the then twenty-year-old modern capital that housed embassy officials and other foreign personnel working in Pakistan.

I was sitting on the front porch of my motel room reading when I heard some noise from the bungalow next door. Two Pakhtuns and a woman came out on the porch. The men were attired in western suits with shoulder holsters. Curved knives protruded from their belts. They were tall and had black piercing eyes, hawk-like noses, black curly hair and black brush-like mustaches typical of the Pakhtuns. We started talking and they told me they were cousins.

The woman was medium height, extremely attractive with a lot of makeup, long nails and pounds of bracelets, rings, earrings, and necklaces over her traditional clothing. Since they didn't introduce her, I knew she was a prostitute. She had black flashing eyes and a regal bearing.

One man said, "I have two wives, and they always fight. But they are good women. They observe strict *purdah*. If anyone saw them I would have to kill them," and he pulled out his revolver for emphasis.

"Good thing I am not married to him! I could never be veiled," I thought.

Just then a car pulled up with another Pakhtun and they all vanished inside the bungalow. I was curious because I always saw three men and one prostitute in various hotels. I asked my friend Queenie about this.

She said, "This is because one woman can please three men at the same time. She has three pleasure orifices in her body."

I remembered Imtiaz, the Pakistani who accosted me in the restaurant in Lahore. He stated that he had two brothers and the three of them would like to sleep with me. I was outraged at the time visualizing each one taking turns. Now I had a different vision of all three at once!

When my visa was ready, Happiness and Queenie drove me to Peshawar in their car. I spent several weeks in the company of these good-hearted people who reminded me so much of my dearly loved Afghans. Queenie and I cried when it was time for me to leave. With their love and good wishes surrounding me, visa in hand, I took an uneventful bus ride back through the Khaibar to Afghanistan.

*   *   *

It was an early Kabul morning. I was just beginning to feel hungry, thinking about a breakfast of *naan* and *chai*, when there was a discreet knock on the white wooden door of my hotel room.

"Who art thou?" I called in Dari.

"A policeman, Oh Khanum," came the reply.

I opened the door and asked, *"What is thy business with me?"*

"Thou must be guided by me to the police quarters."

"And what may be thy reason?"

"This request comes from my superior."

"And what may be his reason?"

"W'Allah (by God), *it hath not reached my ears."*

Behind this giant of a Hazara with his flat moon face and almond eyes stood the hotel manager, my Tajik friend, Glory-of-the-Faith who spoke tolerable English. I declared that I had no intention of going anywhere. Glory-of-the-Faith translated this to the policeman.

He looked at me amazed and said, *"But I <u>must</u> bring thee!"*

"Nay, I shalt not go with thee."

"Yay, thou wilt," and he made a grab for my arm.

I felt the blood rush to my face. Glory-of-the-Faith forestalled the imminent explosion by stepping between us. But before he could say anything my mind snapped at an idea.

I countered with, *"I shalt first attire myself for thy illustrious superior and then I shalt follow thee."*

Mollified, the policeman said, *"I shalt come for thee in a while."*

I closed and locked the door. Then I sat on the simple cot with its rough, brown army blanket. I pulled on a clean, red Afghan shirt, with mirrored embroidery on the yolk, over my jeans and belted the shirt with a red petit-point embroidered belt. Next, I got into my wool socks and black suede knee-high boots made for me by my hashish-befuddled boot maker. I attached my brown leather pouch containing my passport and Afghan and American currency to my belt and grabbed my embroidered lambskin vest.

Turning the half-moon silver-colored metal doorknob of my room, I was faced with the policeman, wearing his faded patched threadbare violet-colored uniform, belted at the waist with a thick, black worn leather belt. His trousers were stuffed into calf-length, dusty black leather boots and his face resembled a Persian miniature painting. He stood aside to let me go down the smooth stone steps to the street.

The day had become gray and cold as I walked with purpose towards King's shop. King's servant gave me the *"Selam"* and the policeman waited outside. King was in his usual spot behind the old wooden desk in the back room of the shop facing the front door. King rose, smiled and started towards me. I went to him with my right hand extended and gripped his large hand in mine as we gave each other the greeting. He led me to the part of the sofa nearest him and returned to his chair as he called Mohammed to make tea. Then he asked how he may serve me. I told him about the policeman and that I wouldn't go unless I knew what it was all about.

King picked up the ancient telephone, dialed four digits, and shouted into it. When he was connected to the right person there followed a quick, wrathful barrage of Dari. Most of it I couldn't follow. He hung up, took out a Marlboro cigarette and offered one to me. I watched him take short, furious puffs while gazing into space. In the silence that ensued, I ventured to ask him what happened but he motioned for silence.

I sat watching King's large hands. One was occupied with the cigarette, and the other hand, whose thumb bore a huge silver ring with a carved carnelian stone, was twisting his big, black mustache. His large bulging brown eyes were at half-mast showing him to be engaged in some intricate scheme. His thick, wavy ebony hair fell below the collar of his tan suit. His six-foot-five frame rippled as the telephone jarred the room with its high-pitched scream. He let it ring three times before he answered in his deep voice. A torrent of words too rapid for me to understand gushed forth and the phone was replaced.

Then he turned to me and said in Dari: "*Oh Catee-jon, thou must go now to the police. A taxi has been procured for thy convenience and he hath been given my command to await thy return.*"

I was frozen to the spot! King Protecting Friend was a nobleman. On previous occasions, he made phone calls on my behalf. By uttering one or two sentences, he had my visa extended for several months without my having to travel to Pakistan to renew it like most tourists and assigned someone to represent me at customs, among other things. Fear climbed up from the pit of my stomach as I wondered what crime I had committed that he couldn't solve?

I exclaimed in Dari, "*Oh King-jon, canst thou not take the ear of the Chief of Police? What crime dost they hold against me?*"

"*W'Allah,* (By God) *thou hath committed no crime and I have set all things to right. All that is needed of thee is to put thy mark upon a paper.*"

Trusting King's word, I took the old, dusty black and white Russian taxi waiting outside of the shop. I sat down in the back of the cab and sunk to such depths in the broken-down seat that I could barely see out of the windows.

The driver gave me a stiff "*Selam*" and I returned it along with the traditional greeting in Dari.

His face lit up with a smile and he asked, "*And from where hath thou taken knowledge of Dari?*"

"*From Kabul,*" I replied.

We had a pleasant conversation all the way to the police station. When we arrived, I attempted to pay him the customary fifteen cents but he refused, saying he had already been paid and would wait for me.

I got out into the muddy streets of the old section of the city. The police station was a building of stone blocks sitting on the right side of the street. I walked into an alley and turned left to go up some old stone steps that must have been constructed for giants. At the top of the second landing was a door covered by a light-blue piece of cotton material. The policeman who had come to my hotel was waiting outside the door and went in before me. He presented himself to his superior, bowing from the waist with his right hand over his heart, announcing that he had carried out his instructions.

The police chief was a tall man in his early fifties. His skull was completely shaved. He had turquoise eyes, a black brush mustache and a copper-colored complexion with typical Mediterranean features. He came around from his desk. It stood alone in the bare cement room with the exception of two wood and glass cabinets standing on either side of the one window. A picture of the king was on the wall. He smiled and greeted me in English and I returned his greeting in Dari. A flush of pleasure suffused his face. We spent a few minutes exchanging niceties.

He opened a door and out came Betty and Bobbie, the English couple whom I had first met in the Khyber Restaurant. Both of them looked tired and shaken but very glad to see me. They took turns telling me what happened.

They had met a man from Turkey in the Khyber Restaurant who was hitchhiking. He was going all the way to Indonesia like Betty and Bobbie. They offered him a ride in return for sharing expenses. After dinner, they brought him to their hotel where he took a room next to theirs. They invited him to smoke a *chillum*, a cylindrical clay pipe, filled with hashish together with them and some other tourists. While they were smoking, some Americans brought out comic books like "Superman" and "Archie". Everyone was high from the hashish and laughing at the comics. The Turk, who didn't speak English, assumed that the pictures must be "dirty" or "wrong." He excused himself and left. This Turk, who had never smoked hashish before, became paranoid and went to the police. He said that Betty and Bobbie "sullied his reputation as a good Muslim" by showing him indecent pictures. Bobbie and Betty were immediately taken to this police station where they spent a sleepless night being cross-examined. In the morning, instead of the promised release, their passports were confiscated. They panicked and contacted the only person they knew in Kabul ... me. I could feel my anger rising as I addressed the police chief in Dari.

"Why oh Good Sir, hath their passports been taken from them?"

"They hath not been taken, oh Khanum, freedom awaits these ones."

"Take your passports," I said to Bobbie pointing to the desk.

Just as Bobbie moved forward, the police chief stepped between him and the desk.

"Before freedom canst be gotten, these ones must sign a paper saying that they art sorry for what hath been done."

"And what hath been done, oh Good Sir?"

"Oh Khanum, these ones hath shown unclean books to a Muslim."

At this stupidity, I lost my temper, grabbed a ledger on his desk and thrust it at him.

"Oh Good Sir, tell me this, in this ledger art things which hath not reached my understanding, or that of my companions. If I were to tell them that what is written within is 'unclean' or 'unlawful' wouldst that be truth?"

"Nay-", he started to reply but I gave him no room.

"Yay, my Good Sir, then how canst this Turk who canst not read our tongue know what is written within our books? Hath the truth been spoken?"

"Yay, Oh Khanum, thou hath said right. But Khanum, he is a good Muslim so if thou wouldst consent to make a paper telling all that hath happened in the company of thy friends and to put thy mark upon it, 'twouldst be well."

I consulted my English friends who were only too glad to do anything to get out of there and told the police chief that we agreed. He brought out several pieces of unlined, white paper and some cheap plastic ballpoint pens and told us to go into the next room, one at a time and begin. I went first. The room contained a dilapidated brown sofa and a small window covered with a cheap flower print curtain situated high upon the wall. I put the paper on my money pouch and began to write. At that moment, the police chief entered the room and sat down beside me.

All formality gone, he said in English with a quavering voice, glistening eyes and moist lips, "Oh you are ve-e-e-ry nice! Will you go with me for food this evening?"

I looked at him with utmost seriousness and replied, "Of course." Wanting nothing to do with him, I edged farther away on the sofa. At that point, the policeman entered the room. They spoke for a few minutes and left. I finished my account and returned to the main office.

While I waited, Bobbie and Betty wrote their versions of last night and signed them.

When we were all together again, the policeman appeared with the Turk. We all stiffened a little as the chief came out from behind his desk and presented him our "confessions." It amused me to see the Turk "reading" them at a glance and handing them back to the police chief with a satisfied air.

Then the police chief said in English, "I want all of you to shake hands."

With great reluctance, Bobbie and Betty shook the Turk's hand and then it was my turn. I extended my hand and when the Turk did the same, I withdrew mine turned on my heel and spat on the floor.

"Oh dog and son of a dog! Oh unfertilized egg of a jackass! Son of a noseless mother!" I ranted in Dari.

This last reference was to women who are caught committing adultery and have their noses cut off. All were grave insults to any Muslim.

Whether the enraged Turk understood Dari was a moot point. He could tell from my demeanor that he was being insulted. He tried to leap upon me but was restrained by four policemen galvanized by the police chief's shout. I retrieved my friends' passports, bid the amazed police chief good day and stalked out of the office. Once outside we all got into the waiting taxi and headed for King's shop.

Betty and Bobbie were only too happy to leave Afghanistan and decided to go as soon as possible. I, too, was ready to head home and took an Ariana Afghan Airlines flight to Frankfurt Germany where I caught a Pan American flight to New York.

CHAPTER TWELVE

The Prostitutes

"I was ten.
The landlord married me and kept me in his house
As his concubine until I was fifteen.
One day I spilled tea on his papers ..."
Leila, a prostitute

Homecoming was a complete culture shock to me. Gone was the silence of Kabul, the kind smiles of welcome, the fresh air perfumed with cedar-wood smoke. Instead, I was faced with buses, garbage collection trucks, and cars that roared by all hours of the day and night. The air was "perfumed" with the fumes of diesel, gasoline, dog waste and restaurant garbage. No one looked at each other on the streets; they just hurried along tending to their own affairs. I barricaded myself in my apartment for a week before I could venture out. My own family and friends seemed strange to me, their conversations trivial. They had little interest in where I had been and what I had seen and done. I felt like Marco Polo who had the same experience when he returned from the East to Italy.

I immediately began planning my return to Kabul. I went around to some avant-garde clothing boutiques and showed them what I had brought back as samples of Afghan handicrafts. The shops were interested and I took some orders.

Elated, I went to Bloomingdale's and secured more orders. I was becoming an exporter of fashions from Afghanistan. They all wanted the orders instantly and I had to explain to them that I was a one-woman show and must spend time in Afghanistan overseeing the quality of the work. When I described how people lived there with few telephones and fewer faxes, they showed mercy and gave me several months to fulfill the orders.

After I arrived at home and settled myself, I was invited by two Hindu friends to see a woman perform a traditional, classical Indian dance. The woman looked like all of the pictures I had ever seen of Hindu temple carvings. She was tiny, less than five feet tall but muscular, with high, round breasts and long, black hair that cascaded in blackish blue waves down to her feet. Her large, black eyes, accented with "Cleopatra" make up, commanded her face, above a strong nose and full, ruby colored lips. She was dressed in red and gold, the color of brides with a short top that exposed her midriff and a very simple sari-like skirt without the voluminous folds. She had clusters of brass bells around each ankle that jingled like sleigh bells as she danced. She was Lakshmi Devi, a very famous classical dancer. Her final performance was on a brass platter where she moved from side to side, playing both male and female roles while simultaneously revolving the platter around the stage. I was enthralled! I had never seen anything like this before.

Afterward, my friends asked if I wished to meet her.

"Yes," I breathlessly replied.

Lakshmi Devi's dressing room was packed. Resembling a queen on a throne, she sat at the far end of this tiny cubicle. The minute I entered, she beckoned to me. I turned about feeling sure she was calling my two friends whom she knew. I turned back to her and she beckoned again. Doubting, I pointed to myself with a questioning look. She nodded in the affirmative. The only Westerner in the room, I made my way through her throng of Hindu admirers.

Suddenly this tiny, powerful woman demanded in an imperious voice, accenting each word, "Do you dance?"

I stood there dumbstruck.

She repeated the same thing only louder.

I stammered, "Y-y-you mean like you?"

"Yes! You have the body and the carriage of a dancer. Come and take tea with me tomorrow at three-thirty."

Humbled, to be summoned by this extraordinary woman, I made my way to her Manhattan apartment the following day.

She said, "I have only sons. I wish to pass my craft to someone, and I feel that it is you. Will you become my disciple?"

I protested in shame that I had two left feet, and she said never mind ... I would learn. As we were drinking spiced Indian tea, words that I have never spoken to a living soul spilled from my lips.

"Who is Sonali Dass Gupta?" I asked.

She looked at me as if I had asked about the weather and replied, "Sonali was a daughter of the Gupta clan in the fifteenth century in Assam, my home in northeastern India. She was a fabulous dancer, and dedicated to the god Indra as a temple dancer, where she served in fame and fortune throughout her life."

I said, "I have been saying Sonali Dass Gupta, Sonali Dass Gupta over and over in my mind since I was eleven years old."

"It is obvious that you are the reincarnation of Sonali Dass Gupta," pronounced Lakshmi Devi in a matter of fact tone.

We made an appointment to start my lessons the following week. Three days later, she called to say her husband had died, and she must return to India for the mourning ceremonies. Easterners mourn for at least forty days. By the time she returned, I was in Afghanistan. When I returned six months later, she had moved away. I never saw her again.

The purpose of our meeting was only for me to know about the name going around in my mind all these years. Now I knew why the Afghans said that I danced like a Hindu temple dancer even though I have never seen a Hindu temple dancer dance. The name Sonali Dass Gupta, Sonali Dass Gupta continued to echo in the corridors of my mind.

*　*　*

As my Ariana Afghan Airlines flight made its descent among the purplish-brown mountains my heart soared to be once again in Afghanistan!

The air was crystal clear, the sky periwinkle blue in contrast to the brilliant golden October sun that warmed my face. I walked across the landing field, surrounded by planes ready for takeoff. The stench of diesel spewed into the air as men loaded baggage, yelling above the roar of the engines.

I entered the cool stone and marble customs hall. With a few words of greeting in Dari, to the amazed and then delighted officials, I breezed right through.

There were several taxis waiting and the drivers called *"Taxi, Mistaarr!"*

A warm flush of pleasure suffused my being to hear that old familiar phrase. I chose a cab and got in the back with my luggage. I told the driver, "Shar-ee-Now."

He rumbled down the paved road away from the airport. Suddenly the pavement ended and with it the noise of civilization. We were plunged into a deep silence, parked in the powder-fine, ocher-color dust with nothing but a few trees and the mountains in the distance. We waited while a caravan of nomads with their camels crossed our path. The only sound was the soft ching-ching of the occasional camel bell as they plodded by. While we waited, I silently thanked God for allowing me to see the beauty of this land once again.

When I arrived in Shar-ee-Now, I paid the driver, took my luggage and walked down the street to the Mustafa Hotel. I clambered up the one flight of steps to the office. Glory-of-the-Faith, the manager, looked at me and grinned. He put his right six-fingered hand over his heart and we greeted one another with joy and gladness. It was like seeing an old friend again.

With pride, he pointed to a piece of paper on the wall that gave the prices of the rooms in English. My face registered shock as I saw rooms for a dollar twenty-five to one-fifty per night, where nine months ago, all were twenty-five cents!

Seeing that I was upset, Glory-of-the-Faith said, *"Parwa nist"* (Never mind).

He took his pen and crossed off the prices.

Then he said, "For you, only thirty cents per night."

We both laughed as I thought ... *In Afghanistan, once a friend, always a friend.*

The room was small but very clean. On the two single beds were thin mattress with clean homemade sheets and pillowcases. There was also a sign that hot water was available twice a day for showers. This was an improvement over showers from six to ten in the morning only. I could see now why they raised their prices. They had to use more wood to keep the water hot.

After I got settled, had a shower and change of clothes, I locked my door and skipped down the two blocks to King's shop. My best friend was very excited to see me. He gave me the Afghan kiss on the right, left, and right sides of the face along with the traditional greeting. After we poured sweet sayings on each other, he asked his servant to bring *chai*.

King aged ten years in the space of nine months. Strands of gray nestled among his once jet black hair. The lines in his face were more pronounced and he had gained fifteen pounds. His huge brown eyes were tainted with sadness.

King started singing one of his compositions *"Tu nominee, tu nomadee, tu nomadee, behar omad, tu nomadee"* (You didn't come back, spring has come back but not you).

He used the familiar form of "you" that is spoken to family members, lovers, and those called *"dost"* or intimate friends.

Then in true Afghan fashion, he said in English, "I wait and wait and you no come. You have brought me sorrow for long time and now I return it in full measure."

And we both laughed, knowing the third great law of the Afghans is *badal* or revenge! Then he handed me a beautiful white silk embroidered Kandahari man's wedding shirt on very soft white Afghan cotton.

"This for you, Catee-jon."

I gasped in ecstasy at the beautiful symmetry of the geometric embroidery so perfect that it was impossible to tell inside from out, and squeezed my dear friend's hands.

He looked at me and said, "Welcome to Afghanistan. Come Catee-jon, I show you my new restaurant."

We jumped into his Mercedes and traveled the busy streets to the Cherai Hajji Yacub crossing. There my eyes were assaulted by this two-storey, orange-colored, jagged stone-topped building, blistered by raw chunks of multicolor glass. The windows, like bulging eyeballs, protruded in various places on the façade! King called this creation "City of Lamentations," after a place in northern Afghanistan that was destroyed by Genghis Khan.

I asked him in Dari, *"Oh King-jon why didst thou choose this name for thy new club?"*

He replied, *"Too many family and business problems, Catee-jon. If this club fails, it is better that people remember it as the destruction of Genghis Khan instead of a failure of mine!"*

Hysterical laughter burst out from both of us, but his heart was heavy.

The interior of the place was massive with huge arches marking the different rooms. All had domed ceilings. Rough cut polished marble slabs were low to the ground table tops on burnished, cut, tree-trunk bases. Antique Nouristani chairs, with their flowery, carved wooden backs and animal gut seats six inches off the ground, crowded the rough-edged tables. King told me, with no small amount of pride, that one room would be done in traditional Afghan style with only carpets, soft sofas, bolsters, and cushions.

Jet lag plus the two thousand foot altitude made me very tired, so King drove me back to the hotel and said he would take me to a party that evening.

"Please invite any friends you want," he said.

I slept for the rest of the day, showered, and dressed in jeans and the shirt King gave me. I invited some tourists. There was a woman from New Zealand, and two American men. Excitement mounted as we walked to King's shop. None of them knew any Afghans on a personal basis. Their only interactions with Afghans were the merchants in the bazaar.

The Seer was there and, in contrast to King, looked ten years younger! He was wearing his black hair short. It was cut close on the sides with a shock of hair at the top. The only signs of aging were the deepening lines on his forehead.

The Seer as always tried to impress me. He rushed to be the first to greet me with the Afghan kiss. I gave him a perfunctory greeting and went to King's side. I sat on the sofa near his desk. The Seer was always teasing both of us about being lovers. When I told him I had no lover, he would try to cozy up to me. He simply didn't understand that my lover was my choice and had nothing to do with gifts or words.

Introductions were made and we all drank the obligatory three cups of black tea. The beet sugar, emulating clear crystals floating in a maroon sea, half-filled the tea bowls. Then King announced that it was time to go to the party. We all crammed into the car and drove down Chicken Street to one of many houses surrounded by nine-foot-high adobe walls.

We passed through the garden, went up three stone steps and removed our shoes. Off the hall was a carpeted room that had bolsters, sofas, and cushions along the walls and a crowd of about sixty people. They rose as one and bowed, not only to King and the Seer but also to me and my friends as honored guests. I was amazed and humbled by this gesture. Then we went from person to person, giving and receiving the greeting as is the custom.

My friends and I found a place along the wall. I was next to a young Afghan woman who spoke French. Waseema told me that she had lived in Paris for several years. She was exceptionally beautiful with olive color skin, huge eyes with ultra-thick eyebrows and eyelashes, a small nose, and a pretty mouth. Her thick black hair had been cut in a modern shoulder-length style. She wore a European black, calf-length skirt, a short-sleeved, black pullover sweater and sheer black stockings. Compared to her, my friends and I resembled construction workers in jeans, work shirts, sheepskin vests, and socks! The only fancy thing I wore was the gift that King had given me.

Waseema was the wife of a Minister. Afghans never feel it necessary to reveal their status. You are an honored guest in their homes and they are bound by their law of hospitality: as they do for the guest, Allah will do for them in paradise.

I later heard from King that the governor of Herat, the Minister of Finance, and the Head of Criminal Law were there. They all came for King who was a great musician and composer, something I heard from others, never from King.

He simply said, "*I write, I play, I sing.*"

Our position in society meant nothing to the Afghans. They saw into your heart in a matter of seconds and you were either their friend for whom they would do anything or their enemy to whom they would do everything.

King took his customary place in the center of the room with his harmonium and a man with two *tablas* sat down next to him. While they were tuning their instruments, King joked and everybody talked and laughed. I reveled in their energy and joy.

Several women came out with enormous flat, woven baskets. On each was piled groups of dried fruits and raw shelled nuts making a beautiful four-color mountain. There were long green raisins, black raisins round and plump, shelled almonds and shelled walnuts.

Waseema told me that the green color was for the trees, the black for the hair of the people, the brown almonds represented the mountains, and the yellowish meat of the walnut was the earth.

There were also several bottles of Johnny Walker Red, besides Afghan brandy, and of course, the best hashish. We all began drinking, eating, and smoking as King played and sang his compositions and people praised him with *"Voh, voh!"* (Bravo!), while applauding different passages.

The Afghans all pressed me to dance to their music. When I did, they remarked that I danced like a Hindu temple dancer and it reminded me of Lakshmi Devi.

I noticed this very pretty Afghan woman who started to cry. Every time she looked my way her sobs grew louder. Everyone tried to console her.

I said in Dari, *"Oh Waseema-jon what ails this one when she looks upon my face?"*

"Oh, that is Maryam, Catee-jon. Come with me, thou must hear her story."

Maryam heard me and motioned us near. Then she burst into fresh sobs and said in Dari, *"Oh Catee-jon, a thousand pardons I beg of thee. When I see thy face, I am reminded of what I once was before my life was cruelly taken from me. I was much like thee, beautiful, kind, intelligent, and trusting. Now in human eyes, I am less than khak-ay-sarak* (the filth of the streets). *I shalt relate to thee my history."*

I sat next to her on the sofa and took her hand.

"My family hath much of wealth. Good fortune was given to me, praise be to Allah, to attend the university. After graduating I worked as a doctor in the women's hospital. I met a man in the university and we loved each other with one thousand lives. His family did not possess the same position as mine. My parents withheld permission for marriage. We could not abandon each other and we met in secret to drive to the outskirts of the city in his car.

"One night of horror, misfortune visited us, and we were set upon by eight bandits. They didst what no man wants, to my lover and then made him watch while they took me violently and vilely again and again. My valiant lover fought as well as he couldst to no avail, and the light fled from his eyes. The voice of a woman screaming filled my ears and t'was not until all went black before my eyes that I knew this woman was me.

"They abandoned my lover, tied with his belt, his pants down at his ankles. They stole his car and we drove for a long time. The dawn hath just shown her face whence we came upon a house in another city where several women lived."

Maryam started sobbing all over again as she said, "*The women told me that now I am one who sells the body for money like they do. One of the girls, Leila, told her history.*"

'*I was ten years old, the youngest of four sisters, and my parents sold me to a wealthy landlord when they no longer could find sustenance for all ten of us. The landlord married me and kept me in his house as his concubine until I was fifteen. One day I spilled tea on his papers. He sold me to this house. I am eighteen now. Because I was married at such an age, I cannot conceive. It is a blessing from Allah.*'

"Another girl, Sitara said to me," '*The mullahs who act as scouts go to the caravanserais to wait for the men. They find out who wants a woman. The scout hath a paper that he calls the short marriage paper. He writes one of our names on this paper. The man writes his name and then comes to claim us as his wife after paying the mullah. The mullah brings one of us to the serai and then we must do all the duties of a wife for this man until he is satisfied. Some of the men use us very hard and many times in one night. Sometimes we art so tired we can scarcely make the tea in the morning.*

'*Some husbands art kind. When the husband wishes to go, the paper is burnt, and we wait in this house to be taken to the serai for the next husband.*'

"Jamila then told me her story." '*I hath eight or nine years when I was engaged to my cousin. He was twenty-five years older. We were married when I was eleven. My husband deflowered me. I was too young. I never was able to grow as a woman and hath many problems. We lived in a small village in Pakistan. My children wouldst not come and I was sure that my life was over from all the blood from the children passing through my body. When I hath taken the age of thirteen, my daughter was born. My husband was so angry that his child was not a son that he returned me to my parents' house for one year. My parents felt shame so they brought me back to my husband after much talking. I was with child again, but the child came out of me and again my husband returned me to my parents' house. My parents talked much with my husband so he wouldst not divorce me. My father couldst not return the bride price. It was long spent. When I reached the age of sixteen, my son was born. The following year, another child came out of me and I was very sick for a long time. I was sure that I wouldst die. My husband returned me to my parents and* told them he wanted a divorce. My son was taken from me and nursed by my husband's married sister. My husband bought himself a second wife of fourteen, who was able to have sons. I was content to remain in my father's house but my parents wouldst not hear of it saying they wouldst be disgraced. They approached my husband and he agreed to take me back but only as a cook and housekeeper.

My husband and his family were cruel. They gave me very little food and struck me for everything. They told my son to strike me, they told him that I was only a beggar that they found on the street. He was three years and I was happy when he tried to strike me. This was the only time they allowed him to be near me. They told that my husband's sister was his mother. I thought to end my life, but the rope broke on the tree. My husband's family sent me out on the streets because of the dishonor I hath brought to them. I sold my body. Then I was "married" to a caravaneer. When he came to Afghanistan, he sold me to this house.'"

Maryam continued, "I was in this house for several months until I was sold to a caravaneer and taken on a trek near Kabul. I was able, by my talk, to cajole my 'husband' to agree to my going to the hammam (public baths) to further beautify myself for him. I told my tale to the women in the hammam and they gave me another color chadoree (the veil) than the one I hath. I made my escape amongst the women who went out at the same time. By day, I made my way to Kabul hiding in caves at night and praying I wouldst not be set upon again. I couldst not approach my family due to the shame that I hath brought upon them. My lover, because of the thing done to him, wouldst not want me as I am a reminder of his shame. I went in an old chadoree to the women's hospital and one of my unmarried female colleagues took me to her apartment so I could recover. This is my last night here with my friends. Oh, Catee-jon. Tomorrow I go in the chadoree with my friend's brother to find my life in Pakistan."

Drying my own tears, I wished her good fortune and called down the blessings of Allah upon her as we kissed and hugged.

"Oh where in Pakistan wilt thou go, Maryam-jon?" I asked.

"To Karachi. Hath thou seen Karachi, Catee-jon?

"Yay, 'tis a very modern city."

"My colleague hath a cousin, a doctor in the women's hospital. I bear a letter to her."

Just then, the hostess announced, "The food is ready."

My friends and I got up off the carpets and were led to a room that contained nothing but a gigantic table with just enough space for all of us to walk single file around it. It was loaded with every kind of rice, meat and vegetable dishes, meatballs, eggplants, potatoes, spinach, chicken, stuffed cabbage rolls, and salads. We looked at the food and then at each other. Without a word, we threw caution to the winds regarding contracting dysentery and piled our plates to overflowing. The food was fantastic, wonderful seasonings tantalized my mouth and nose. The flavor and tenderness of the meats and vegetables transported us to heaven. Through all this, King continued to play, sing, and joke and we all enjoyed each other's company. This was the first of many dinner parties welcoming me to Afghanistan.

Hours later, desserts were served. Rose water and cardamom-scented puddings and flaky pastries filled the entire table. Some of the pastries were deep fried and perfumed with musk, and of course, the ever-present *chai*. No longer able to move, King drove us back to the hotel and we slept like the dead.

CHAPTER THIRTEEN

Great Lion

"Why art thou just tasting the food? Eat it!"
Said after the author refused a second huge portion

Several days later, I was awakened at dawn by the call to prayer. I went out to sit on the balcony of my room that was perched over a group of assorted small shops. The dawn sky captured the gentle essence of the cedar-wood smoke that was winding its way out of the *bokharees* from the first fires of the day. I watched this through the bare branches of a tree in front of the hotel. The sun crept around the mountains, turning their usual violet-brown color a soft peach- rose.

One of the gray dilapidated Russian army leftovers from WWI that passed for Kabul's bus service lumbered to a stop halfway down the road and opened its doors with a groan to disgorge a handful of men and women in traditional clothing. Industrious souls, they were already about the day's business. The bus conductor, a young man in his late teens dressed in a brown tunic with pantaloons, rode on the back stairs of the bus and jumped off when it stopped. Matching an auctioneer's pace, he announced the various destinations. When he was sure that the bus was boarded to its breaking point, he shouted, "Go with good news," to the bus driver and ran alongside until the bus picked up speed. Then he grabbed onto the still open back doors and hung there until the next stop.

I sat on the balcony in the thirty-five-degree air watching the street scene below me. The cook from the kebab stand across the road came from behind the restaurant and threw something into the *jooey* in front of his shop. *Jooeys* were the water trenches that crisscrossed Kabul. These conduits on both sides of the road are kept scrupulously clean in Iran, and twice a day when the water exits from the city's reservoirs, people came out to wash their dishes. However, in Kabul, they are in a polluted and stagnant state. Since Kabul is woven with underground springs ideal for indoor plumbing, the neglected *jooey* (drainage ditch) is now used as a garbage disposal. Sometimes children play in this filthy water.

I decided that today I would visit my friend, Great Lion's carpet shop. By Kabul standards, it was a big shop consisting of two floors. The ground floor contained piles of rolled up carpets and *ghelams*, the flat weave Afghan rugs; groups of antique rifles called *jezails* made of wood inlaid with brass and mother of pearl; old carved metal household utensils; antique clothing from various areas of Afghanistan; antique wall hangings; and embroidered pieces.

The shop floor was completely covered in traditional black and red Turkmen carpets. Great Lion sat in the back of the shop in the right-hand corner, behind an old wooden desk. Lion, as most people affectionately called him, was a chubby man of five-feet-two with huge, round, brown eyes. He had a small nose and a Cupid's bow mouth that was partially hidden by a sparse mustache and goatee outlined his chubby rosy cheeks. He looked like a mischievous cherub and was always laughing and happy. From a large important Tajik family and the youngest of five sons and six daughters, Lion was his father's favorite. Two of his brothers, Ali and Ahmad, were math instructors in a boys' middle school and only worked in the shop part-time. The other two brothers managed their father's shop in Mazar-i-Sharif in northern Afghanistan. His sisters, with one exception, were all married and lived with their husbands' families.

The room on the second floor of the shop was identical to the one below plus a balcony. It was here that Lion's father held court. He was an old rascal who loved to give pretty girls the eye. Anyone who was good-looking was taken upstairs to meet him. He was five-feet-four and pudgy with a full head of snow white hair. His brown eyes twinkled above a Roman nose and a nicely formed mouth over slightly buck teeth. He sat in his café-au-lait colored suit that matched his skin tone as opposed to Lion's shiny worn navy blue suit. *Awgha* (Sir), as I called him, sat at his desk like a pasha with a dark brown *karakul* cap that rakishly clung diagonally to his head. When I greeted him in Dari, he was delighted and had me sit at his right hand ... a mark of honor. He ordered his servant to bring me a Coca-Cola thinking that I'd be more pleased with my own drink than Afghan tea.

He questioned me as to how I learned his language, how I liked Kabul and about my family. In no time at all, "Dad" and I became fast friends. When he discovered that my mother was Polish he regaled me with rapturous Polish love songs accompanied by much eye-rolling guaranteeing my laughter every time. He said that he had been on several business trips to Poland and had gotten to know the Polish people well. I thought about his children and how Great Lion looked very European. I wondered to myself if he had a Polish wife as well as an Afghan one.

Talking with Dad, I smelled some wonderful aromas percolating in the hall below. When I first entered the shop, I noticed a servant tending a pot on a hotplate on the floor in the corner of the hallway. Around one o'clock in the afternoon, Lion called out that lunch was ready.

Dad and I went downstairs just as a servant was unrolling a huge piece of tanned leather in the middle of the carpeted floor. Next, he doled out a large freshly baked oblong *naan* at each place setting. Meanwhile, Lion, his brothers, father, and I plus whoever happened to be in the shop at the time, lined up to wash our hands. It was a very tiny bathroom with a one-spigot cold water tap in a tiny sink and a worn cake of pink, Cameo-brand soap. There was a filthy hand towel hanging from a nail that I avoided and dried my hands on my jeans.

Then we all sat cross-legged on the carpets around the "table" and had a fabulous lunch of lamb and vegetable soup with *naan*.

When I sat back satiated, Dad reached over, chucked me under the chin and said in Dari, *"Why art thou just tasting the food? Eat it!"*

And he reached into the tureen to pull out more vegetables and soaked bread for me. Everyone laughed.

After the meal ended, the servant came around with a gracefully carved, goose-neck metal water pitcher that stood in its own large carved tureen. He poured rose-scented water over our right hands and gave us a clean cloth to dry ourselves. The piece of leather that had served as a tablecloth was taken outside the shop, shaken free of crumbs and bits of food into the *jooey* (the drainage ditch) and stored for the next day. After the servant took his portion, leftovers were rolled up in the bread and given to anyone who was hungry and came to ask. About twenty minutes later, we would all be back in the *saloon* as the servant brought *chai*.

Of course, Lion and Dad both insisted that I come to live with them as a guest in their home. Lion's living compound looked the same as any other dwelling on the outskirts of the city. It was a huge adobe fortress where Lion, his wife, Full Moon, and their children lived with his parents. Their four older sons with their families and one unmarried daughter resided with them. This is a typical family arrangement. It benefited the women by freeing them from constant food preparation and childcare. They were able to do handicrafts or pursue leisure activities such as visiting friends or their own parents and siblings. The children were raised and cared for by many adults as well as having ample opportunity to suckle any nearby breast. This created strong matriarchal bonds needed for the children's upbringing and future marriage partners since the women alone made these choices.

I was given a guest room at the end of Lion's apartment within the fortress. His parents and other family members had their own apartments as well. All the rooms in the house were alike. Carpets covered the beaten earth floors, and embroidered materials hung on the walls giving the rooms a festive and cozy air. *Toshaks* (cotton stuffed pallets), big bolsters and pillows were strewn around the base of the walls. Bedding consisted of colorful thick hand sewn patchwork quilts that are rolled up and put in a corner during the day.

All of the food preparation was done in the communal courtyard and then brought to the adobe kitchen to be cooked. Women stirred huge vats of rice and stews. They baked simple *chapatti*-like bread over cast-iron ovals on the adobe stove, but the popular oblong *naan* was always purchased from a baker.

The bathroom was a large windowless room whose floor was built on a slant towards a hole in one corner of the room. There was a slatted footstool and several bowls and basins on the floor. A *bokharee,* (wood-burning stove) stood in one corner and was fed with wood to heat both the room and the water. The lone faucet on the sink then provided hot water that was poured into the basins. Bowls were used to scoop water over yourself as you squatted on the stool to "bathe."

* * *

On a follow-up visit to Afghanistan, the hideous hand of "progress" had shown itself. I was led, with great pride, into the bathroom where a reeking modern toilet, filled to the brim, sat alone on the floor unconnected to any plumbing. I was urged to make use of this "modern convenience" assured that it was emptied once a day by a servant. If I weren't so revolted, I would've laughed! I continued using the squatter in the adobe hut in the corner of the garden.

Next, I was ushered into the *saloon* (living room). As I peered at Great Lion and his wife's beaming faces, I viewed the black imitation leather couches that replaced the beautifully embroidered cushions and bolsters and the colorful pallets. Full Moon was a short, chubby, very pretty woman who smiled with every part of her face. I was expected to congratulate them on their new possessions and I did ... with a false jubilance and a sinking heart. I felt it would not be long before Kabul was flooded with cheap Western products and the streets glowing with neon signs. But these "Western delights" did not end here.

Lion informed me that now I no longer had to sleep on a pallet on the carpet as they did. He threw open the door to my room and there sat a *charpoy* (a four-legged rope bed). Lion had put a pallet on the bed and a cushion for my head. He was so pleased to provide this for me that I did not have the heart to tell him that I preferred the carpet.

I spent a most miserable night lying on this creaky hammock of a bed and awoke to find my body covered in welts from the small mites residing in the ropes. When Lion's servant brought my morning tea, his eyes widened at the sight of my red swollen arms. He alerted Lion and Full Moon who were very concerned about me. They examined the welts and applied some homemade ointment and then went to check the bed. There was much talking and gesticulating between them. That evening when I returned to my room, the offending bed had been removed, replaced by one of their own *toshaks* (pallets).

A few days later when I went into the bathroom, I noticed that the toilet too had been removed. I am sure they thought me very strange for not wanting to use familiar western conveniences.

One morning, I motioned to Full Moon that I wanted to wash my hair. She smiled and left the room to return with some white marbled burnt sienna colored rocks in a tin washbasin. She poured boiling water over the rocks from the metal teapot that was simmering on top of the *bokharee*.

The rocks began to effervesce and disappeared into a liquid before my eyes. She then poured this opaque liquid into another pan, pointed to it and to my hair.

I said in Dari, "*Oh Full Moon-jon, what may I ask is this?*"

"*Oh Catee-jon, 'tis gel-ay-sashoy* (Afghan shampoo)."

"*Oh, Full Moon-jon, in what manner must I use this?*"

With this Full Moon smiled and made a motion of washing her hair. She pointed to her head and put my hand on her hair. It was very thick, black and somewhat coarse with a slight auburn tinge. I thought to myself that I liked my fine but full hair well enough, and didn't really want to change its consistency.

But before I voiced any thoughts, Full Moon declared in Dari, "*All Afghans use gel-ay-sashoy, Catee-jon. But thou must wash it well from thy hair.*"

So saying, she brought a six-inch-high wooden stool for me to squat on, tilted my head downwards, and began to wet my hair with the *gel-ay-sashoy*. She rubbed my scalp and hair vigorously for several minutes until it tingled, and when she was satisfied that I was properly shampooed, rinsed my hair with warm water until it ran clean. After my hair dried I noticed that it was thick with body and had an auburn tinge but wasn't coarse like Full Moon's.

I asked Full Moon in Dari where to get *gel-ay-sashoy*.

"*In the bazaar, Oh Catee-jon,*" she reported in Dari

"*And what hath they told is the price of this?*"

"*W'Allah, for this priceless thing they ask one cent per kilogram. Assuredly 'tis worth the asking price, isn't it?*"

"*Thou hath spoken the truth, Oh Full Moon. 'Tis worth this and much more.*"

From then on, I only washed my hair with *gel-ay-sashoy*.

CHAPTER FOURTEEN

Ṫhẹ Prọspẹctivẹ Bridẹ

"May thou walk on my eyes"
Words of the groom to the bride

In the middle of twelfth-century Afghanistan, I discovered a discotheque. The owner, Exalted, was a member of the nobility who had attended a university in the States and got his disco ideas from there. At first, the *mullahs* vehemently protested and forbade anyone called Muslim to enter a place where liquor was served and men and women, not related by blood or marriage, consorted in public.

Unmarried men and women were culturally prohibited from being in each other's company. Sex before marriage was also prohibited; the woman should be a virgin and technically, so should the man. Among the educated class, sex sometimes took place before the marriage. Marriages, usually to first paternal cousins if possible, are social and economic contracts arranged by mothers. Should the couple happen to love each other, so much the better. Parents consult astrologers when matchmaking to ensure harmony between the couple and the girl is asked if she would like to marry so and so. She usually agrees because of family pressure even though she may have only met him once in the presence of their women relatives. She has no choice because there is no opportunity to meet men outside of the home. She must rely on the judgment of her women relatives. A young woman may request that her husband be tall or have green eyes etc. Respect, financial support, conjugal duty, and kindness are prized in male marriage partners.

Westernized Afghan men, tourists, and businessmen came to Kabul and frequented Exalted's club. Through bribes to local officials and promises of contained decorum, Exalted managed to keep the club open. It didn't hurt that he was a relative of the King.

Exalted was looking for true love. He expressed interest in every foreign woman who passed through his doors, and I was no exception. I found him too immature for my taste, a true "King of the Discotheque". In between his tight-lipped orders to his staff, Exalted fell over himself trying to impress women tourists. I watched as he drifted from one affair to another. Then he expressed interest in me. I told him he wasn't my type, but we could be friends. He jumped at the chance and promptly invited me to his home. He lived as a bachelor in a new section of Kabul that was still under construction. His house was decorated in a westernized manner. The *saloon* contained a pseudo-leather couch with a Formica coffee table. I marveled. I have seen this in various countries in the world who want to copy American taste unfortunately not our better taste. We sat down, and he offered me some wine. I talked to him as an older sister. I explained about the negative impression his behavior made on women.

He put his head in his hands, cried and said, "I am so confused, trying to be Afghan and Western at the same time. My parents chose an Afghan woman for me. She is a cousin, but I don't want to marry her. I like Western women. You know, I never got over Mary Lee."

"Wasn't she that American girl you were dating when I first arrived in Kabul several years ago?"

"Yes, I really loved her, but she didn't want to marry me. Catee-*jon*, please keep our conversation private, I wouldn't want anyone else to know this."

"Don't worry," I said with a grin, "if I ever tell what I know about most Afghans, one-half of Kabul would be divorced, and the other half murdered. Relax, don't try so hard. You will meet someone," I told him as I rubbed his shoulders.

Exalted half-laughed and hugged me. We pledged our friendship, and after that, he stopped trying to impress me, and I ceased looking down on him.

I told Exalted that I wanted to rent a house, and he offered me one of his apartments until I could find one. It was ultra-modern and I hated it, but it was better than living in one of the hippie hotels.

I was there about three weeks when I met Brian, an American who came back and forth to Afghanistan exporting and selling carpets in the States. Brian and I liked each other instantly. He was living with a French couple in the center of town. We spent several days there, and then I invited him to my place. He was due to arrive at seven o'clock. Seven o'clock came and went with no sign of Brian. Since neither of us had a phone, I just assumed that he couldn't make it and put aside my disappointment.

The next day I went around to his place. The French couple was about to leave but said I could wait there for him. I went into his room and sat on the bed looking at all his scattered papers. Brian arrived and was delighted to see me. He asked what happened last night.

"Nothing" I replied, "you never showed up."

His eyebrows flew up and he said, "When I arrived at your place, the watchman told me you weren't home."

Since Brian spoke fluent Dari there could have been no mistake. *So I thought, even though I wasn't dating Exalted, I was still under his protection (nanawatai) as a guest and off limits to "strange men". Now that I thought of it, the only man to ever visit me was Exalted, ostensibly to "see if I needed anything."* All this flew through my mind as I explained about Exalted, my landlord. Brian understood immediately.

Then I remembered another friend of mine who was leaving for the States. He said he would come over to give me his cassettes tapes, so I would have something besides Afghan music to occupy me. Sean never appeared either. As I related this to Brian, we concluded that I would have to find my own house fast.

When I was in New York, Exalted had married his dream girl, an American tourist. Jennifer was a tall, attractive, slim blonde whom Exalted had made a big play for. She was the typical California surfer girl who wore no makeup and whose tawny hair was streaked platinum from the sun. Every tourist and Afghan in Kabul was talking about their wedding. When I met them, they seemed truly in love with each other. He had finally found his mate. He looked confident and she looked radiant and I was happy for them. Perhaps now, I could slip out from under his "protection" since his wife would occupy him.

One bright November morning, Exalted came out of a nearby house accompanied by another man. After exchanging the greeting with Exalted, the other man, Excellent, put his right hand over his heart bowed and exchanged the greeting with me.

Excellent stood there in his shiny, second-hand American suit, both eyes devouring me. His gaze was a mixture of desire and curiosity. Turning my attention to Exalted, I told him that I still wanted to rent a house and he put Excellent in charge of this duty.

Excellent was six-feet-tall, bulky with thinning black hair, a square, tan face, large black eyes, and a thick brush-like mustache over rows of gleaming white teeth. He informed me that he was twenty-nine, but he looked middle-aged already. He addressed me as Catee-*jon* in imitation of his boss, Exalted.

Excellent did everything he could to ingratiate himself to me with surreptitious looks of controlled smoldering passion. He figured out that my relationship to Exalted was only friendship. With each subsequent meeting, he came closer and closer to me with a beseeching look in his eyes. His speech progressed to flowery, using the term *"May thou walk on my eyes"* to every slight request I made. As distasteful as his ardor was to me, I knew that alienating him would cause him to lose face with his employer thus creating a spiteful enemy. Excellent himself provided me with a way out of this dilemma. The next time we met, he was bold enough to grasp my fingertips and press them to his lips with murmurs of endearments.

Seizing my chance, I said in Dari, *"It is my desire to see thy mother."*

Since mothers handle all marriage arrangements, Excellent was ecstatic, thinking that I accepted his suit. He was also relieved that all matters would now be taken from his hands.

He dazzled me with his teeth and replied, *"Sheh"* (Good) in Pashto.

Excellent went about making the arrangements in a state of ecstasy. I, too, was overjoyed and relieved because now that he knew I understood his intentions, he no longer felt the need to expose me to his ardor. Several days later, Excellent informed me that he would be *"as the dust under my feet,"* the phrase that indicated the behavior of the husband to his future wife. He said he'd take me to his home in Kandahar.

Excellent and I set out in Exalted's dark green Land Rover on the four hour trip to Kandahar. Excellent could not do enough for his "future wife" on the drive, stopping in village bazaars for pomegranates and oranges to "quench my thirst" and at a local teahouse for a brunch of kebabs and *chai.*

We reached the biblical city of Kandahar and drove into one of its many *chowks*, concentric circles around which restaurants and shops huddled. It was at one of these *chowks* that we left the car in front of a handicraft shop owned by one of Excellent's friends. We wended our way on foot behind the *chowk* into the narrow, twisting, stony lanes showing only the blank adobe walls of the sides of the houses, with an occasional solid wooden door niched into these walls. The lane was filled with piles of refuse of all kinds. Little hills of bloody rags, orange peels, meat bones, vegetable scraps, human excrement, and bits of cloth dotted the landscape. Around these piles, fruit and vegetable sellers, crying out the merits of their wares, paraded by with donkeys dwarfed by their loads. We hopscotched the sewage trench, the hills of rubble, and the existing livestock between these adobe fortresses, to arrive at Excellent's house. A broken-down, faded-green wooden door with peeling paint, hung with its mouth agape. Excellent stepped over the six-inch-high sill and held the door for me to enter the tiny square, dun-colored vestibule. A similar door to the left was padlocked with a chain. Its thick nail passed through an iron ring. Curious, I asked Excellent where his mother and sisters were and he replied that they were in the house. I was confused regarding the padlock. Excellent explained that this was done to protect the women when there is no man about. The latched door discouraged any would-be male visitors. Breaking and entering was unthinkable in places where neighbors were vigilant and knew one another.

We were suddenly in a large rectangular courtyard with a small adobe fountain in its center. One of the rooms off the courtyard had a flower print cloth covering the door.

This led to a carpeted sitting room where Excellent's three enormously fat unmarried sisters waited. They were in their late teens and early twenties and were delighted to meet me. Greetings were exchanged. Since Excellent was the oldest unmarried brother, and his father had died, he was responsible for looking after his sisters until a suitable match could be found. Like all Afghans, he lived with his family when he was not working in Kabul.

His sisters were dressed in identical empire-style, flower-print dresses, and traditional plain pastel cotton *tambon*. They were barefoot with white cotton cloths draped loosely over their heads and shoulders. The sisters were dark-skinned and resembled Excellent. They had

131

blackened their eyes with kohl in the prescribed manner. The effect made their eyes appear even smaller than they were. The palms of their hands and soles of their feet were red from the henna they had used to prepare for my arrival as that of the prospective bride.

After several minutes of their picking at my clothing, touching my hair and face, chattering in Pashto and laughing, their mother entered the room. Excellent was an exact replica of his mother. She was an indomitable soul with a perceiving eye. Through the midst of greetings, we took a fair appraisal of each other and reached a tacit understanding.

She sat down on the carpet and offered me her water pipe. In it, she had a bit of rough-cut tobacco and a tiny piece of hashish. I took a draught from its amber tip stem and passed it back to her. She let me know with approving grunts, in response to my carefully prepared Pashto, that I was very welcome in her home.

I spent the rest of the afternoon sitting with the women in this windowless adobe room conversing with Excellent's help. As the guest of honor, I was fed by his mother's own hand. There was a delicious spicy *chalow*, colored a medium pink from tomato sauce with whole baby eggplants buried inside along with meatballs stuffed with prunes in a brown sauce. This was served with fresh fruit, raw pine nuts, and long green raisins. We all drank many cups of sweetened green tea with crushed cardamom seeds. The afternoon slipped away and soon it was time to leave.

All of a sudden, a tiny brown-skinned woman with pure white hair entered the room and sat down on the pallet next to me. She was followed by Excellent's brother, his wife, and several of their neighbors who were curious to see Excellent's "foreign fiancée." The little woman was Excellent's paternal grandmother. I took her tiny birdlike hand in mine and looked into her soul so present in her large brown eyes.

I said in Dari, *"Oh mother may thou experience long life, thou art truly beautiful."*

She replied *"Oh Sweet Soul of Life, truly the beauty is in thine eyes,"* while she beamed into my face.

I laid my head on her knee in such utter peace and contentment as she gently caressed my hair murmuring motherly endearments. The entire group gave little cries of admiration and appreciation, praising God that a foreigner could be so like them.

Grandmother looked up at them and said in Pashto, *"Why art thou surprised? She hath belief in the Holy Book, an Isawee* (believer in Jesus), *not an infidel. Besides did not Allah in His wisdom fashion us all in the same way?"*

They mumbled assent among themselves as we said our goodbyes. Excellent was very quiet on the drive back to Kabul. He was almost docile now that his mother had met me and he need only wait for her verdict. I had no doubt in my mind as to what that'd be. In an instant, she knew I had no desire to marry her son but that I was pleased to meet her and allow her to make the choice, saving face on all sides. When Excellent next returned to visit, she would look at him and say the equivalent of "She is not for you," and this would be the end of my problem. All marriage negotiations are done by mothers. Their verdicts are final and without question. The "no" that his mother was bound to give would not be too hard on Excellent because I was a foreigner and the chance that his mother would approve, was slight.

For my part, I had accomplished several aims. I let Excellent down in a gentle manner so I could still claim his assistance. I had the opportunity of visiting an Afghan family as a prospective bride and I would ever remain the beloved "daughter" welcome in their midst at any time.

CHAPTER FIFTEEN

Mowlowdaut and Sabera

"The dawn's pink cedar wood smoke
Embroidered the violet skirt
Of the ermine capped mountains."
The Author

It was a typical, crystal-clear, cold winter day with the sun blazing in the bright, royal-blue sky. The dry, desert mountain air still toasted my skin but I shivered in the shade. Excellent, true to his pledge, found a rental house in Shar-ee-Now near the mosque. It cost fifteen dollars per month and was built of stone and wood in the style made popular by King Amanullah who when abroad, fell in love with European architecture.

The wall of the living room that faced the front yard was round like a turret and had floor to ceiling windows. The ceiling was polished wooden planks set in a geometric design. There were five other rooms, plus a bathroom and a kitchen. The bathroom was done in gray stone with an old marble bathtub, a copper *bokharee* (wood burning stove), and an old toilet that worked on occasion, minus its seat. The kitchen was a bare room except for some wooden wall cupboards and a metal water tank.

As I was standing in the kitchen I heard the cry in Dari, "*Sak Oooooow!*" "Water!" and knew that this announced the water-carrier's rounds. I ran down the front steps, and out of the wooden gate that was perched in the adobe wall surrounding my house, to intercept him.

He was a grizzled Hazara of indeterminable age. An ancient gray rag was twisted around his shaved skull. The cow skin, full of water, left wet marks on his gray, one size too big, western suit jacket. His *tambon* (pantaloons) were halfway up his calves identifying him as a manual laborer. His feet were encased in broken down, once brown, leather sandals now tan from his thousands of daily footsteps in Afghanistan's talcum powder, fine dust.

I stood just outside the gate in my black wool turtleneck sweater and black gabardine slacks, looking like any other upper-class Kabuli woman. I extended my arm, flipped my hand upwards from my wrist crying, "*Come here!*" in Dari.

Shouldering his cow skin, he turned his steps in my direction. As he came into the gate, I greeted him in Dari, "*May peace be upon thee.*"

He returned the greeting, "*And may peace be upon thee, Oh Khanum.*"

I slipped the gate's bolt into place and led him up the stone steps into the house and to the kitchen. He removed the top from the water tank, put one end of the sweating cow skin inside it, and pulled out the wooden plug. Cool, sweet water from Kabul's underground springs trickled into the tank. Always interested to know more about the Afghans, I continued our conversation in Dari.

"*Where art thou from?*"

"*The Hazarajat.*"

"*By what name art thou called?*"

"*Ali, after the son-in-law of the Prophet, may God's Peace be upon him. "Excuse me, Khanum, is thy honorable self a Tajik?*"

I was pleased by this question. My Dari accent was good enough to be taken for an Afghan. The Tajiks are mostly European-Irani stock and some are fairer than I am.

"*Nay, my brother, 'tis the will of Allah that I am an American.*"

"*By the Holy Quran, thou art very knowledgeable of our tongue!*" he exclaimed.

"*Nay by God, I am only a student of thy speech,*" I replied.

"*Naaaay, Khanum.*" He paused and then continued, "*Yay, thy country Amrika (America) hath goodness.*"

"*Hath thine eyes seen it my brother?*" I knew full well that he had never even seen all of Kabul.

"*Nay, but these honorable ones art building a road in the Hazarajat and art a very kind people.*"

"'*Tis given to me to understand that the Russians art also building a road,*" I prodded, curious to see his reaction.

"Yay, these godless devils art about. May their fathers roast in hell!" he exclaimed as he hawked and spat.

Ali went on to tell me that the Russians were barbarians who conquered the ancient Mongol *Khanates* (areas that were northern Afghanistan ruled by *khans*) of Khiva, Kokand, and Bokhara in the seventeen and eighteen hundreds. Creating Soviet Socialist Republics, the Russians suppressed the Afghans' religious beliefs and obliterated their great culture. These *khanates* had been centers of learning in Central Asia where fine silk and fabulous jewelry were made. Many of the people in this area: Uzbeks, Tajiks, Turkmen, Kirghiz, and Kazakhs fled south into Afghanistan to retain their customs.

I also knew of the enmity between the minority Shiite and the Sunni majority. The people of the Hazarajat are Shiites. I wanted to see Ali's reaction to this schism. I knew that Ali would not speak with such force to a foreigner against his own countrymen.

I pursued the conversation further in Dari, *"Oh brother, soon I shalt visit our neighbors the Pakistanis. Art they as kind as my brothers in Afghanistan?"* I innocently inquired.

"Oh those unfertilized eggs of jackasses!" he cried. *"These ones art so stupid, they canst not find their own mother's breast!"*

I laughed out loud at this witticism as Ali removed the deflated cow skin from my tank.

"And how much paisa (money) *wilt thou take?"*

"No thing Khanum," he said with a grin.

I knew that he would seek to be paid at a later time. Before I could say anything more he took a stubby piece of white chalk from his pocket and wrote "two *afghanis*" in Dari above the tank on the green pastel colored wall. This was the Afghan equivalent of the credit card. If Afghans know their business with you will be repetitive like that of the water carrier, they mark what you owe in chalk on your kitchen wall and collect money once a month.

I bowed, placed my right hand over my heart and said, *"I thank thee, Mister Ali."*

And in the same stance, he replied, *"There is nothing to thank me for, Oh Khanum. Welcome to Afghanistan. Walk in the Peace of Allah."*

And with that he retraced his steps out of the house, calling as he reached the yard, *"Sak Oooooow!"*

I was very pleased with my house. With the help of my merchant friends, I set about covering the floors with carpets, and *ghelams* (flat weave rugs), as well as bolsters, pillows, *charpoys*, cotton pallets, quilts, and mats that make the Afghan home so comfortable. On the morning of the fourth day, there was a banging on the gate. I opened it and was faced with a man who had a bundle of possessions wrapped in a shawl at his feet. He was five-foot-three, medium build, with copper-colored skin, black eyes, close-cropped black hair, and the usual black brush-like mustache.

He put his right hand over his heart, bowed and said in Dari, *"Selam Aleikum, Khanum, How art thou? Is everything all right? What is happening? I trust thou art not tired. May thy life be long."*

I returned his greeting and then he said, *"Excuse me, Khanum, I am Mowlowdowt . . . . . "*

Before he could finish his sentence, Azim appeared and we both began the greeting. Azim was my friend, Sally's servant. She was a tall, blonde Canadian from Toronto who exported carpets and *ghelams* ... one of a handful of foreigners doing handicrafts exports. I met her at Exalted's club. She told me she rented a house, had a servant, and invited me to her home. Nestling in an alley behind a garden with rose bushes, the Afghans' favorite flower, was a small, adobe house with four rooms plus a tiny bathroom. Azim answered the gate and welcomed me.

I walked into Sally's hallway carpeted with straw matting. On both sides of the hall, were two small rooms, one occupied by Azim and the other stored with Sally's merchandise,-waiting to be shipped to Canada. At the other end of the hall lay a rectangular room, its walls covered with *dussmol*, the embroidered handkerchiefs given by the bride's family to the groom's when his suit is accepted. Sally had hung the best of her collection, along with some colorful posters depicting various Muslim saints embellished with their appropriate supplications. Large cushions made out of carpeting or *ghelam* material stood on the floor in the corners of the room. This was Sally's showroom. Behind this was a large, square room housing a queen size bed with small prayer carpets on the floor. Several wooden, hand-carved cabinets from Nuristan stood around the walls. One wall was completely taken up with a built-in wall cupboard painted pastel green, the most common color seen in Afghan homes. On the wall above the head of the bed, was a large, yellow silk wall hanging with a profusion of colorful embroidered flowers strewn all over it. Other hangings of various colors adorned the room. I told Sally that I was looking for a house and a servant, and she assured me that Azim was trustworthy and would find me a good person.

All this coursed through my mind as I was brought back to the present when Azim said in Dari, "*This one is a cousin of mine*," looking at Mowlowdowt. "*He is also from Panjshir Valley and wishes to work for thee. I hath told him of thy goodness, Oh Catee Khanum.*"

Mowlowdowt beamed at me. I replied in Dari with a laugh, "*And how much didst thou tell him I wouldst pay him, Oh Azim?*" knowing that when compliments start, prices rise.

Azim smiled and shook his head from side to side indicating that he had said nothing. Mowlowdowt smiled also. I made a quick trip into my mental file marked "servants' pay" and knew it was five to eight dollars per month plus room and board with gifts of clothing and foodstuffs on holidays. Some wealthy Kabulis paid ten dollars. Because I was a foreigner, I resolved to pay him fifteen dollars.

I said in Dari, "*Oh Azim, this year I regret to inform thee that I am very poor and canst only give ten dollars per month.*"

Azim replied, "*Thirty dollars wouldst be proper, Khanum.*"

"*How so Azim, when the usual rate is five to eight dollars?*"

"*Thou hath said right, Oh Khanum but that was last year and you know that things art more expensive now.*"

While chuckling inside at "inflation," I pretended to deeply consider this matter and finally said, "*Well Mowlowdowt, what dost thou think?*"

Mowlowdowt replied with the traditional Afghan saying of trust and respect, "*As thy heart desires Khanum Sahib* (Noble Lady)."

"By the Holy Quran, Mowlowdowt, at this time I canst only pay thee ten."

Azim broke in with "*Oh Khanum, this is good but this cousin of mine wishes to marry soon. Twenty-five if you please.*"

I understood at once. Azim, who worked for foreigners, wanted to help his cousin to get a similar job so Mowlowdowt could get married. In order to marry, an Afghan man must first repay his parents for his upbringing, and then raise money for the bride price. This is achieved by working his father's lands, as a farmer or in his father's shop in the city, as a merchant. If he's a clever trader, and what Afghan isn't, he will accomplish this before he's thirty-five. Besides his mother may have money put aside for just such an occasion in the form of a piece of land or some jewelry so she can have a bargaining chip with the bride's parents. Landless peasants wishing to marry hire themselves out to rich Kabuli families or to foreigners as servants in order that they may accumulate the bride price or *shir baha* quicker. The money the bride commands, *shir baha* (money for her mothers' milk that nurtured her) is the woman's way of repaying her parents for her education in embroidery or rug making plus cooking, dancing, and singing, as well as her beauty. The more beautiful and talented she is, the higher the bride price. As an income-producing member of her family, some of her income goes into the family pot, and the rest is for her dowry. Since her parents will lose this income when she moves to her husband's home, *shir baha* is their "social security."

A servant is part of the family. He or she must be sheltered, fed and clothed in addition to receiving a salary. Servants act as confidants as well as news bearers from the bazaars.

Again I pretended to hesitate on such a "weighty decision" and said in Dari with a sigh, *"All right Azim, because he is thy cousin, even though his skills art untested with me, I shalt give him fifteen dollars per month."*

Azim smiled, held out his hand American style, and shook mine as they both thanked me, feeling sure that they had made a terrific deal. I always let the Afghans have a little more than the going rate since that endeared them to me and they stood by me as protectors and navigators in the intricate world of Afghan culture.

Since servants were members of the household, sometimes since childhood, they played an integral part in the daily life of the family. Mowlowdowt was not only my servant but my advisor and confidant. In his open, sincere, and loyal way, he became my instructor in the habits and customs of Afghan society. I didn't dream of making a move without first consulting him on protocol.

Mowlowdowt and I took to each other instantly. He soon settled into the routine of the household. Afghans are hardworking people, and his only complaint was that I never gave him enough to do. He rarely had to cook because I was often invited to my Afghan friends' homes or I ate in restaurants. Since I was only one person, the housekeeping was light. Most of the time, my home was filled with the sound of his melodious voice singing verses from the Quran, praising God as he went about his chores.

He rose before dawn with the call to prayer, made his ablutions, prayed and then fed the bathroom stove with cedar wood to heat the water. At seven o'clock, he tapped on my door, and I ran through the cold dining room, with its *ghelims* (flat weave rugs) covering the stone floor, to the warmth of the bathroom and a hot bath.

By the time I finished, Mowlowdowt brought *chai* and *naan* with sweet Danish butter to my room for breakfast and stirred the embers in the *bokharee* to ignite a new fire. I watched him light the stove, so I could repeat it when necessary. He placed a huge chunk of wood in the belly of the stove, surrounded it with kindling and paper, and then judiciously used the flue to create a roaring fire from one match. At its maximum, the stove turned a reddish color, and zinged and pinged as the flames consumed the wood.

I coaxed him to eat with me but he refused three times as custom dictated. The fourth time, he gave in but only drank tea. He felt it was not proper to eat in my presence since I was his employer and in his mind, superior to him.

After breakfast, I was ready to walk to the bazaars for a day of buying. If I needed anything from the market, I told Mowlowdowt. He locked up the house and went to the bazaar where he gossiped with his peers, bought my items, and learned the latest news. I spent the entire day outside the house and returned at dusk to have tea with Mowlowdowt. I showed him my purchases and talked with him as he shared the daily bazaar gossip. Then I changed and went out for the evening.

It was a cold, dreary day towards the end of winter. Melting snow made the roads and lanes a muddy morass, ceasing all but the most necessary traffic. A hushed silence laid like a quilt over the city, pierced only by the wail of the call to prayer. The enormous bulk of the mountains that ringed Kabul wore majestic cloaks of snow.

I had just finished my breakfast when I heard a banging on the gate. Several minutes later, there was a discreet tap on my bedroom door. When I responded, a little girl of eleven years old entered my room after removing her plastic blue sandals. She stood before me with her bare toes red from the cold. She had light brown hair, red cheeks, and beautiful, turquoise eyes. Her lips were the color of a pastel pink rose in bloom in her grave little face. She gave me the traditional greeting. While I returned it, there was another tap on the door, and this time Azim's smiling face appeared. He told me that this was his sister, Sabera (Patience). I was delighted to be with a little girl, to see the culture through her eyes.

Sabera spent several hours with me that day. She dusted my room, even though Mowlowdowt saw to it that there was never a speck of dust in the house. She also straightened my clothes and books. Since we both had limited knowledge of each other's language, we spent time watching each other and smiling. The first thing I decided to do was to get her some proper shoes and socks for the winter. She was dressed in a pastel, floral print dress, faded, royal-blue drawstring pants, a baby-blue cotton, western jacket, the blue plastic sandals, and a stained, yellow, cotton head covering.

Mowlowdowt entered the room to inform me that he had a family problem, and must return to his home in the Panj Shir (Five Lions) Valley for a week. To Afghan thinking, when Mowlowdowt had to return home, it was incumbent upon him to provide me with a substitute servant. First, I paid him monthly and second, I was a woman alone in his country and he was bound by the second great law of *nanawatai,* protection.

That was why Azim brought Sabera to keep me company and also assigned his elderly father to watch the house. Azim's father entered the room and we both greeted each other. The old man had a grizzled gray beard and a shaved head. He was dressed in a worn but clean, gray *peeran tambon* (traditional outfit) with a dark-green, western vest, a faded, embroidered skullcap, and a gray, cloth turban.

Later, as the sky threatened more snow, Sabera and I ventured out into the cold, wet, gray air. The earth smelled of clay from the mix of the air's moisture and dust that poured out of the cracked adobe walls. We trudged to the main road, and then on to the bootmaker's shop.

After the obligatory three cups of sweetened black tea, I picked out a pair of ready-made, black leather, calf-high boots and had Sabera try them on. She smiled up at me with delight. I paid Sayeed ten dollars and, with many goodbyes and blessings on his part, we left. Next, Sabera and I went to a small, westernized store near one of the tourist hotels, and I purchased a pair of socks to go with the boots. She sat on the floor of the shop and pulled off the boots that had already started to blister her feet. Afterward, she gave me a grateful smile. On our way back home, we passed the cloth bazaar and I bought a piece of dark-green velvet as a head covering for her. She was especially pleased and thanked me for her gifts.

Several days later, Sabera appeared in her usual blue plastic sandals. Surprised, I asked in Dari, *"Where art thy socks and boots? Hath thou lost them?"*

She replied, *"Oh Lady Catee, my sister hath need of them."*

I said nothing but resolved to visit her home, see what they needed and supply it to them.

Sabera's father was good at keeping the stoves burning and answering the gate. Regarding housekeeping, he had no clue whatsoever. Scouring the tub and pouring buckets of water into the toilet to "flush it" was beyond him.

In time, Sabera and I began to communicate more and more with each other. She became comfortable in my presence, and her grave little face lapsed into occasional smiles at my humor. One day, I felt it was time to go shopping with her, curious to see how much the merchants were overcharging me as a foreigner.

We left the house, walked to the main road and took a taxi. This was a first for Sabera. I watched her staring in astonishment as people and animals "whizzed by" at the great speed of ten miles an hour. We arrived at the cloth bazaar in Jad-ee-Maiwand, a bunch of stalls run by Sikhs. I paid the driver and we got down to browse. I made several inquiries as to prices and watched Sabera's expression from the corner of my eye. With downcast eyes, she held her breath, and I could tell from this, the merchant had quoted me a "first price" that was way too high. At the third stall, Sabera breathed easily at "first price." I chose fabrics of different colors and designs while I asked prices, and haggled over them. The choice was narrowed down to a yellow cotton print with tiny, red flowers or a plain but brilliant, turquoise one that matched Sabera's eyes. I turned to her and asked which one she liked.

"This one," she said in Dari touching the turquoise cloth.

I smiled at the merchant, bought one meter of the fabric and handed it to Sabera, telling her it was a head covering for her. She smiled and thanked me but she still wore the old, yellow one perhaps saving the new one from too much wear and tear. She sometimes wore the turquoise one to please me ... to show me that she honored my gift.

On the way back to the house, the taffy-like mud slowed people, animals, and vehicles to the extent that our normal fifteen-minute taxi ride turned into forty-five.

Once home, Sabera's father greeted me and started to call down blessings for hiring his nephew as my servant. I smiled at him and addressed him as "Father dear," a common way of addressing older men with affection.

The following day, both Azim and Mowlowdowt arrived. Sabera proudly showed them her new gift, and they both called down blessings upon me. Later when we were alone, I told Azim that his father did not take care of the house as I had wished. He apologized to me, and the matter was dropped.

Several days later, I decided it was time to try to get Sabera another pair of boots. Off we went to Sayeed's shop. With bleary eyes and slurred speech, he greeted me in his usual joyful manner as he tried out his sparse English on me and ordered tea.

After the amenities were over, I told him I wanted him to make a pair of boots for Sabera. He called one of his myriad assistants to bring paper and pencil and proceeded to trace her foot. We chose a black piece of leather for the boots and I dissuaded him from his first price of twenty dollars. We agreed on twelve. He said the boots would be ready in five days.

Sabera was delighted and showered me with one of her rare smiles, complete with dimples. We spent the rest of that cold day in the bedroom, by the warm crackling *bokharee*, talking while Sabera folded my handicrafts for shipment. I taught her a few words in English that thrilled her to no end. By the following week, she was running to the door to answer it.

She'd proclaim to my non-Afghan visitors, "Catee is here" or "Catee is not here," followed by, "What is your name?"

A week later, Sabera and I went to collect the boots only to discover that they were too small. I told Sayeed, and he brought out the tracing of Sabera's feet and placed the offending boots on it to show me a perfect fit. I told him that I did not care what the tracing said, the boots were too small. Agitated, Sayeed swore by the Holy Quran that he had measured accurately and it was Sabera's feet that were the wrong size!

Then it dawned on me what was afoot. Sayeed used the tracing as the outer instead of the inner measurement for the boots. I settled the problem by drawing Sabera's footprints myself on a clean piece of paper only two inches bigger. This ensured the correct make of the boots with an inch of growth to spare.

When we returned several days later, to my delight, Sayeed had seized on my knowledge and had made the boots a half size bigger instead of his usual half size smaller. Sabera was very pleased with her boots but reserved in front of the shoemaker. I praised and thanked Sayeed for his wonderful work as Sabera put on the boots, and we walked home. Once there, I gave her a new pair of socks. With a joyful look, she put them on and tramped around the house all day in her new footwear.

The following morning, Sabera again appeared with the same sandals and red toes. Surprised a second time, I asked her where the boots were only to be met with the same reply in Dari.

"My sister hath need of them."

While I pondered this, Sabera in the next breath told me that her mother wanted to meet me. I willingly agreed, looking forward to becoming acquainted with another Afghan family. Late in the afternoon, Sabera and I set out.

Mowlowdowt farewelled us with, *"Go in the Peace of God, Khanum."*

Sabera and I walked out of the house into the desolate Afghan winter. The snow descended like soft lace and buried the world in its milk-white cloak. Even the vast mountains became indistinguishable from the plains. Life ebbed all around us. People had retreated into their homes, and the air was a redolent, pinkish haze of cedar-wood smoke from the stoves. The hardiest souls were the shopkeepers who remained open until the harsh winds and the absence of even the most regular customers, forced them to reluctantly close.

The Afghans wrapped themselves in layer upon layer of clothing topped with thick, quilted, cotton coats called *chapans* or army greatcoats from European world wars. Some wore these coats hung upon their turbaned heads. Their hands cradled small charcoal braziers near their chests, as they stamped up and down in the muddy snow in front of their tiny shops trying to keep warm. Even the afternoon sun could not pierce the wet, gray air.

We were greeted by a silent city except for some minor movements around the kabob shops. No buses, horses, pedestrians, taxis, or cars were to be seen on the deserted streets.

The last merchant in the line of shops came out, with the tail end of his turban pulled across his nose and mouth. His quilted *chapan* sleeves hung ten inches beyond his fingers and acted like mittens for his already numb hands. He pulled his sleeves back and struggled with the ancient, pockmarked, battered, wooden shutters as they stood fast in frozen defiance, resisting all motion. A shriek of icy wind snarled around the corner and ripped the shutters from his tenuous grasp. They groaned in their newfound freedom before they cracked against the frozen adobe walls, rattling like the bones of fragile skeletons. The merchant grasped the shutters, pushed them into place and threaded a short but heavy chain through an iron ring. He eyed the empty bazaar, nodded to us, and stumped his way home through the mud and snow.

Sabera and I kept walking. Only the produce and meat bazaars allowed me to believe that I had not entered a ghost town. Even these shopkeepers were immobilized by the dismal, dripping dampness. Instead of smiling and crying out the wonders of their wares, they sat silently behind their geometrical mounds of fruits and vegetables. Sabera and I plodded past the boot maker's shop to an open road that ran along a huge mountain shorn of its summer hair. It was studded with tiny, adobe hovels; some perched on top of each other. A cemetery with craggy-toothed headstones that punctured the horizon nestled at the foot of the slate gray sky. I looked at the mountain and then at Sabera with a question mark on my face and she nodded assent.

We began to climb. The twisted rocky lanes that passed for access roads were a morass of very thick, sticky mud. The trail was almost vertical. It was an arduous climb at best. Children ran and played in the mud while a sprinkling of adults went about their tasks.

About thirty minutes later, Sabera turned into an even narrower lane. We came to a battered, broken, wooden door that she pulled open into a small, bare, dark room. We left our shoes here, and then Sabera pushed aside a quilt that exposed a doorway into a larger room lit only by several candles. The entire family: father, mother, sisters, and brothers burst into the traditional greeting. They were all sitting on a tile platform that had a charcoal brazier underneath it. A huge quilt was shared by all, covering their bodies from the waist down to trap the warmth.

Sabera's mother rose with a cry of joy. Tariqa (Divinity) *"Selamed"* me and kissed my hands as a mark of gratitude and respect. When a guest enters a home, they are given the place of honor, the best place, nearest the wood burning stove if it is cold. This gesture fulfills the first great law of hospitality to the guest.

She thanked me for the kindness I had shown to her daughter. Tariqa then led me to her own place, the place of honor on the platform, and wrapped the quilt around my waist. The charcoal brazier did its job admirably, and it was very comfortable sitting on this warm platform after climbing the mountain in the raw damp air.

Sabera went to one edge of the platform where some used tea glasses stood. She took one of them and emptied its contents in one corner of the room onto the beaten, earth floor. She gave the glass to her mother who poured a little tea from a cracked teapot into the glass, swirled it around the rim, and threw its contents away, "cleaning" the glass. Then Sabera's mother poured a full glass of *chai*, with huge, black tea leaves that resembled a newborn infant's open palms and made a gracious offering to me. They were too poor to even afford sugar.

While this was going on, Sabera's siblings crowded around me and thanked me for my kindness to Sabera. We chatted about the market prices for foodstuff and clothing. All of us agreed that Kabul was more expensive than their mountain valley home in Panj Shir. Azim told me with pride that he had earned so much money working for Sally last year, he's now in a position to get married, having paid his rearing debt to his parents. Their other two sons also have hired themselves out as servants, and soon hope to be in the same position so that the family can return to their beloved valley.

I took several sips of the scalding tea and put the glass down to look around. This was Sabera's home, a one-room, adobe hovel with no plumbing, no electricity, and no furniture. There was a communal outhouse down the lane and a trip to the public baths every two weeks if they could afford it. Tea was boiled on top of a small gas ring and only a few candles lit the windowless room. The parents with two of their sons and three daughters all slept, ate and lived on this platform.

The friendship and love of these extremely poor people overwhelmed me. I remembered my annoyance with Sabera's father for not cleaning the house to my liking. White hot shame rose to my throat in a sour knot while tears stung my eyes. I was grateful that the room was dim. It was obvious that none of these people except Azim, Mowlowdowt, and Sabera had ever even seen a modern house much less knew how to clean one.

Tariqa told me they were forced to leave their valley so their children could find work to support themselves and their aging parents. Gone were the blue skies, neatly terraced green fields, and the beautiful orchards. Now there was only this squalid dwelling. No matter how poor, the law of hospitality to the guest still ruled. I guessed Tariqa was probably in her late forties. She was fifteen years younger than her husband.

Watching me look around, she smiled at me with glowing, faded turquoise eyes and said in Dari, *"My home is poor, but thou may sit in the light of my eyes."*

And shining indeed they were. I left amid many blessings and protestations that my visit was too short.

CHAPTER SIXTEEN

The Master Teacher

"Hath Ahmad Shah died
that there is no justice in this land?"
Afghan saying

I gratefully remained in my house in front of the crackling stove that was kept fed with cedar logs. Mowlowdowt brought tea, and I stared out of the window into the mortified garden, embarrassed to be shorn of her summer flowers and fruits. We marked time by the call to prayer. There were no parties to attend, and no one came to visit. Even Sabera had stopped coming. I had my servant, my dog, and my diary for company. It was a time of writing letters to America and pondering the world and its mysteries. I felt shut away from all life, as frozen as the earth in her annual sleep. Days passed and even the dog slept most of the time. My servant became mute, exhausted of conversation.

My dog was a beige color stray from the street. She looked part golden retriever but was smaller like a spaniel. She followed me home and I named her Lady. She was pretty scared at first and only came close to me on her belly. Eventually, we became friends.

One morning, weeks later, the sun showed a weak face, and I ventured outside of the walled garden. A vast silence greeted me, and I looked in awe at a ghost-like world. The distant mountain tops were hidden by gray vapors. I felt like the first person on earth. The wind was bitter. Ice crystals formed in my nostrils. The peace was incredible, and I welcomed it. A strange feeling surged through me, and I smiled in the face of winter's caustic breath. Flashes of the dream about my foreign husband in a strange country flew through my mind as if to show me that the time to meet him was near. The cold penetrated my suede pants and leather boots. The upper part of my body, ensconced in the depths of my sheepskin coat, felt only intense warmth. The smell of the burning cedar logs was intoxicating, and I started to feel lightheaded. I turned and headed back to the house, grateful for this small respite from winter's incarceration. I was greeted by Mowlowdowt with a tureen of lamb, noodles, beans, and vegetables swimming in yoghurt, and heavily seasoned with cayenne pepper. He informed me, with a grin, that this is the way Afghans dealt with winter.

After the weather cleared, Sabera continued to visit me on a regular basis. I always supplied her with things for her family, a new teapot, sugar, some more tea glasses, and some *kulcha* (hard biscuits).

Winter subsided and crawled towards spring. I met Hillary, a tall, slim bosomy Scottish girl with dark red, curly hair that hung down to her shoulder blades. She had piercing blue eyes. A nurse by trade, she had worked in New Zealand for two years and was now traveling overland back to her own country. We met in the Khyber Restaurant and became friends. Hillary and I shopped the bazaars, roomed and partied together. As two foreign women in a country of maybe 10, it was great fun to room and adventure together with someone who spoke English.

We loved to stroll along the streets of Shar-ee-Now. I saw Exhalted park his car and go around to open the passenger door for his wife, Jennifer. Excited to see them again and to introduce them to Hillary, I stopped short when I saw Jennifer's two black eyes and swollen lip. Open mouthed, I couldn't utter a word but saw the fear in her eyes. Exalted was tight-lipped and brushed by me. I told Hillary their romantic story and went to the Club. There I saw Exalted's brother, who was getting ready to open the club for the evening. He was alone and I spoke to him about Jennifer's bruises. He laughed and assured me that it was only a misunderstanding between Jennifer and Exalted and nothing to worry about. When I pressed him he quickly told me to stop because I was interfering in their marriage. I left the club and went straight to the American Embassy where I tried to convince them to do something since an American citizen was being abused. Their response was the same. They said that unless Jennifer herself made a complaint and even then, she was married to a foreigner living in his country so there was not much they could do. I couldn't figure out what else to do so, I caught up with Hillary.

After I introduced her to my Afghan friends, we became inseparable. Mornings we sat in King's shop, drinking tea and meeting his friends who dropped by.

One day we were introduced to Master Teacher by the Seer. He was a short, middle-aged man with a solid build. He had large eyes possessed by most Afghans, close-cropped, black and gray hair and a thick mustache. After several of these meetings in King's shop, he suggested that Hillary and I accompany him to Kandahar, his hometown. He agreed to show us around. Excited to be able to see that city with a local, we made plans. I asked King what he thought of this idea but he was noncommittal.

Hillary and I went on our merry way in Master Teacher's car with his two sons, Beloved, age six, and Special, age four. His friend Mighty, and Mighty's American business partner, Richard, who were also going to Kandahar, came along. Hailing from Pennsylvania, Richard was tall, broad-shouldered, and blonde with bright blue eyes. He met Mighty and decided to export Afghan carpets to the States.

We stopped to visit the mausoleum at Kandahar of Ahmad Shah *Baba*, the first king also dubbed "Father of modern Afghanistan." He was the founder of present-day Afghanistan and Teacher and Mighty took turns relating the following history.

"The King of Persia, Nadir Shah, was assassinated by Mohammed Khan Qajar, who founded the Qajar dynasty of Iran in 1747. A band of Afghans, headed by one Ahmed Khan, fled to Kandahar. At that time, the area around Herat, bordering Iran, was under the Persian Empire called Khorasan. Herat was named the 'pearl of Khorassan' by the Persians. Chiefs from various tribes in Afghanistan went to Kandahar to form their own independent government. Each one had one oral vote that he used for himself.

"When Ahmad Khan's turn came, he remained silent. A holy man called King Patience came forward and placed a stalk of wheat on Ahmad Khan's head. He declared him king because he was the only one to 'show wisdom in silence.' Today's coins have three stalks of wheat on one side of them. Ahmad Khan, a Pashtun of the Abdali tribe, now became Ahmad Shah (King) and founded the first Afghan dynasty, called the Abdali Dynasty. He later renamed it the Durrani (Pearl) Dynasty due to his love of pearls and added the title 'Pearl of Pearls' to his own name. Ahmad

Shah extended the borders of Afghanistan from the western capital of Herat and the Mongol Khanates in Central Asia to include all of Pakistan (at that time India) and Kashmir. Known for his humanity and justice, he was called 'father' by all. A common saying among the people who felt that they received unfair treatment was, 'Hath Ahmad Shah died that there is no justice in this land?'"

It was close to one o'clock, and we were hungry. There was nothing for miles around. We drove up to an adobe dwelling. At first, the solid adobe fortress squatting among the trees looked forbidding. As we got out of the car and started up the dirt road, excited children ran out to pull us in by our clothes and welcome us to their home. The walls were three feet thick. They held heat in the winter and were cool in the summer. With its crumbling façade and rifle slits for windows to discourage enemies, no one knew of the beauty inside. No matter how poor, hand embroidered and woven textiles abounded on the floors and the walls.

I asked Master Teacher, "Do you know these people?"

"No, it is one of the three great customs of Afghanistan that anyone can knock at any door and must be fed and cared for by the owner of the house for three days. After this time, the person thanks the host and leaves or states any business he wishes to conduct."

An old man in his seventies came out of the house. He was six-feet-tall and lean with a long, white beard. He wore a pale blue *peeran tambon* with a dark blue vest, and a white cotton turban wrapped around a hand-embroidered faded multi-colored skullcap. His tan face was etched with fine lines of kindness like many who spend their lives close to the land. He had blue eyes.

After greeting us, he ushered us into the house. We bowed our heads and lifted our feet to step up into the window-like cutout that served as the main door. Richard had never seen anything like this. He stepped up while ignoring the upper portion of the door, and received a severe blow to his forehead causing him to trip and fall to his hands and knees right into the house. Abdullah Jan and his sons, plus Teacher and Mighty uttered soothing words while helping Richard to his feet. I could almost read their minds.

"These barbarians have no idea how to enter a civilized home."

Perhaps the other thought that crossed their minds was that Richard was drunk because of Western people's known consumption of alcohol.

When he recovered, Richard asked Mighty, "Why is the doorway like this?"

Mighty replied, "Here, outside of the city, it discourages the entrance of snakes and scorpions and it is to show respect for the home to bow as you enter."

The ceiling of the *saloon* (living room) had young tree trunks for beams that were stripped of their bark. Their truncated ends stuck outside the walls of the house. The room was windowless but opened out onto the courtyard where all the household duties were performed. The floor of the room was beaten earth covered with *satrangees*, the woven multi-color, cotton runners of the poor. The usual assortment of huge pillows and bolsters graced the floors. Adobe shelves stuck out from one wall where the family's dishes and utensils were kept. Their bedding consisted of patchwork quilts that were rolled up in one corner of the room like those at Lion's house.

We were made welcome, and Abdullah Jan served us *qawa* green tea. He lived with his wife, two sons, and their young wives and children. His daughters were already married and living with their in-laws. When it was time to eat, Abdullah Jan spread a worn, cotton cloth on the floor, and brought out a platter of plain steamed rice, two small bowls of cooked spinach, a bowl of yoghurt, and some *naan*. He apologized to us for the meagerness of the fare while we, in turn, thanked him and swore that "by God" it was too much. The women remained in the kitchen since there were strange men in the house. Abdullah Jan and his two sons, Master Teacher and his two little boys, Mighty, Richard, Hillary, and I sat down to eat.

Richard, Hillary, and I took very little as did the family, but Master Teacher, Mighty, and the children fell to it with a relish. The old man eyed the three of us. He urged food on us, serving us with his own hand, showing honor to the guests. He insisted that we eat.

Master Teacher said in English, "It is a great insult for a guest to refuse food, even if the host is starving. This is our law of *melmastia* (hospitality)."

That relaxed Richard, Hillary, and I enough to take more but we contented ourselves with some rice and yoghurt.

When we left, Master Teacher, his sons, Mighty, and Richard went on ahead. The women and children came out of the house, cried, and walked a half mile down the road with Hillary and me "to lighten the steps of our journey."

Master Teacher drove around the bazaars where he gifted us with fruits and nuts that we shared with the boys. He dropped Mighty and Richard off and then told us that we would be staying in the house of his friend, Sincerity. We were thankful for this kind treatment that allowed us to stay with a family instead of one of the two existing tourist hotels.

Dusk draped its bluish cloak around us when we arrived at Sincerity's house. It was a recently whitewashed adobe, in a narrow street, surrounded by a high wall. In front of the wall was a small, snake-like, water trench, silent and furtive as it slid around piles of refuse.

Sincerity's servant, Shakur, a boy of fourteen, greeted us and ushered us into the living room. The floor was thick with rich carpets, and hand-tooled, leather cushions with raised designs in gold.

A minute later, a clean-shaven, burly man with thick, black, curly hair and a big paunch burst into the room with his arms outstretched. His small, pointed eyes, broad nose, and full mouth were stretched in the utmost joy as he and Master Teacher embraced, backslapped, and greeted each other in Pashto. He then turned his attention to Hillary and me, bowing and greeting us in Dari. He went on to explain that he was divorced so there were no other family members present. I thought this a bit strange that Master Teacher, knowing this, would arrange for us to stay here. I passed it off to our being Westerners and these things held no scandal for us.

We were led into a room that had a cheap, plastic imitation, black, leather sofa with several black, plastic armchairs. I groaned to myself. I wondered why the Afghans felt it necessary to mimic our worst habits.

Because we were Westerners, Hillary and I were expected to admire this room, and we did so while moaning inwardly, bringing a flush of pleasure to Sincerity's face. We were invited to sit in this room that felt odd to me since I was used to sitting on pallets and carpets.

Shakur served *qawa*, perfumed with crushed cardamom seeds, and a delicious chicken and rice dish, accompanied by *naan*, green grapes, mangoes, and more tea.

After the meal, sprinkled with many reminiscences in Pashto of the last meeting that he and Master Teacher had, Sincerity started to play some Kandahari music that he said he'd recorded on his cassette player, just for us. Settled with tea, he told us his story in Dari.

"Oh Catee Khanum, thou must know that my cousin Jelal and I, upon the urging of our parents, both married each other's sisters. My cousin Jelal was besotted with another cousin Jahan. But he was married to my sister Jamila. My wife was his sister, Majooba. Jelal was helpless in his love for Jahan. My sister Jamila frequented my home in sorrow because she could not capture the love of her husband.

"First warm and then hot words flew between Jelal and me but to no avail. Jelal divorced my sister and ran away with Jahan. This brought much shame to my family's honor, and so it was incumbent upon me to divorce my good wife, Majooba. This is the reason that my home is bereft of my relatives."

I translated this history for Hillary and we expressed sympathy for Sincerity. The Afghan custom of divorcing your wife if your cousin divorces your sister is to save face for the family. *"If thou bring shame to me, I shalt bring shame to thee."* Divorce is considered a disgrace in Afghanistan and is always the woman's fault.

By this time, we were so tired from our journey, we begged to be excused, with thoughts of preparing for sightseeing tomorrow.

Sincerity called Shakur to show us to the women's quarters and said that some of his friends would be coming later on and he would call us when they arrived.

The bedroom was pleasant enough, with two cots, clean linens, blankets, and quilts. An armoire was built into the wall and a small night table stood between the beds. The usual light bulb dangled from the ceiling. Hillary and I were asleep in an instant.

Several hours later, we were awakened by a tapping on the door. In reply to my sleepy response, Master Teacher asked in Dari, *"Oh Catee-jon, wouldst thou and thy companion grace these honored guests with thy presence?"*

"I pray thee excuse us for the sleep wilt not leave our eyes. May Sincerity's face be made white by the presence of such illustrious persons."

As the night wore on, the sound of men's voices became louder and the more liquor these so-called "westernized" Afghans consumed, the closer they got to the door. Unable to sleep, Hillary and I both sat up and wondered what the outcome of our little outing would be. We were two foreign women alone in a strange city with a bunch of drunken Afghans.

Our thoughts were shattered by a pounding on the door and shouting for us to come out. Fear fluttered our hearts. Easterners do not drink socially but drink to get drunk, abandoning all principles. Escape was impossible. The room had no windows and just that one door. After nearly ten minutes more of laughing, shouting and pounding, my mounting terror turned to fury at the feeling of being trapped.

I whipped on my clothes and made for the door, much to Hillary's speechless horror. I threw it open with a bang, standing there in a cascading rage. Silence descended on the room like a shroud. Every man was in a fixed position, frozen in time. A drink was halfway to the lips, a hand of cards was suspended midway to the table, and a lighter was poised at the end of a cigarette.

My rage boiled over as I bellowed at them in Dari, "*Why hath my sleep been disturbed by the voices of strange men? Do these Kandaharis bring shame to the great law of melmastia* (hospitality)? *The quarters of the women art inviolate! What wouldst thou do if thy sisters and mothers went abroad and were received in this manner by their hosts?*"

I ended my tirade by thrusting the quotation regarding Ahmad Shah back into my hosts' faces, "*Hath Ahmad Shah died that there is no justice in this land?*"

Without waiting for an answer, I slammed and bolted the door. Hillary and I could've heard a pin drop. We listened to the hushed sounds of movement as the men left one-by-one. The dry click of the door settling into its frame on an empty room revealed that they were gone. Hillary and I hugged each other and went back to sleep.

Now I realized why King wouldn't give me a clear-cut answer as to whether or not I should go on this trip. If he said no, I could have interpreted it as jealousy toward the honor of entertaining a guest, and as a restraint on my freedom. If on the other hand, he agreed and something happened, people would reproach him as *namak haram* (unfaithful to his salt) a grievous offense that meant he did not protect his guest.

The following morning a sheepish and apologetic Master Teacher drove us back to Kabul. Sincerity never made another appearance. The house was empty as we packed to leave.

However, things did not quite end there. It seemed that The Seer, who was always jealous of my relationship with King, had seen Master Teacher's wife during our absence. He asked her what she thought of our going to Kandahar alone with her husband. She believed that her husband was in the company of her sons and Mighty and lost no time in giving her husband hell upon his return. When we saw him several days later, he was too ashamed to look us in the face and spoke only when we addressed him.

Not content with this, Master Teacher's wife put in a call to her sister whose husband, Rasul was the head of the tourist visa police. She wanted to "ensure that those prostitutes" would not have their visas extended. Rasul's fear of his wife's and her sister's vituperative personalities and their powerful family connections was common knowledge.

When Hillary and I went to have our visas renewed, we were turned down. Puzzled, we went to a restaurant to have lunch and think things over. The Seer was there, and he appeared very nervous. We pressed him for an explanation as to the visa situation. He blurted out that the reason they were not extended is because someone said that we were prostitutes. Hillary and I almost fell off our chairs in shock! We further pushed him to reveal this person's identity.

He replied, "King Protecting Friend."

My stomach fell to the floor and twisted into a knot! I considered King my dearest friend! Of course, I failed to take into consideration the third great Afghan law of *badal* (revenge).

King and The Seer were good friends. When I first met The Seer, he made a big play for me. When he saw that I preferred King, he switched his attention to Hillary. Rebuffed a second time, King's "good friend" became his enemy. He thought to ruin my friendship with King in the ignorant hope that I would turn to him.

The Seer had been educated in America and believed that he understood western women. He brought up the concept of "free love" several times. His understanding of this much-abused term was that he may choose any western woman he wished and she would have sex with him without money or marriage. It never occurred to him that a woman could refuse or have any say in the matter whatsoever. Therefore, he was dumbfounded by my attitude towards him and never ceased to attempt to blackball me with my Afghan friends. Even after he had been caught lying, he remained obstinate in his tales, though he became the joke of Kabul..."Oh, there goes The Seer, cooking up some story about Catee-*jon* again."

Upon hearing The Seer say that King had called Hillary and me prostitutes, I lost no time in racing down to his shop to confront him. He was sitting behind his desk as usual when I burst in and began shouting and gesticulating in English.

He jumped up, grabbed me by the shoulders and shouted back "No E -e-e-glish!" and ran from the shop.

After a few minutes, he returned, and I was able to calm down enough to speak Dari and to explain what the Seer had said. He shook his head, and swore, "by his eyes," that he was innocent, and vowed to question the Seer who, when confronted, denied everything of course.

The following morning, Hillary and I appeared in King's shop where he helped us compose a letter to Rasul's superior, Adil Shah, the military governor of Kabul. This letter stated that Hillary and I were awaiting money routed through Delhi that was held up due to the Indo-Pakistani war. Therefore we needed an extension of our visas. He then made a brief phone call and informed us that we had an appointment with Adil Shah immediately and sent his servant for a taxi.

Adil Shah's office was a white, wooden house with dark green shutters in the midst of a copse of shade trees surrounded by an adobe wall. We entered the compound, and crossed the dusty unpaved courtyard, mounting a flight of steps to Adil Shah's office. An adjutant in military dress took us down a dim hallway. We passed the closed doors of many offices until finally, at the end of the passage, he tapped on the last door on the left. A man's voice responded and we entered the room.

Adil Shah was tall, over six feet, slim with iron-gray hair, thick, black eyebrows, black, piercing eyes, a Roman nose, and a tender mouth that belied his grave countenance. After the customary greeting was finished, he asked us to sit down. We perched on the edge of our chairs as befitted supplicants. I presented him with our letter, and while he was occupied, I made note of the surroundings.

It was a large room with a huge window and a window seat that overlooked a garden where trees threw their shadowy light upon Adil Shah's back. The room itself was bare of everything except for a large, rich, Turkmen carpet where Adil Shah's mahogany desk and armchair were arranged. There were also the two straight back chairs that we sat on in front of the desk. His writing materials were encrusted with gold and had intricate designs. There was a hand-painted cigarette box from Kashmir. The usual pile of documents and papers were in neat stacks on his desk.

After Adil Shah read the letter, he asked in Dari, *"Hath thou informed thy superiors at the embassy of Amrika of this matter?"*

"Nay, Oh Noble Governor, we deemed it prudent to take thy ear first."

A slight smile at the knowledge that he would not lose face with either his superiors or the Americans, relieved the gravity of his features. I could tell that I had found the correct approach.

Then he picked up his pen and wrote that we could remain in Afghanistan for another month. He signed it with a flourish and placed his signature seal upon the note. We rose together, and with our right hands over our hearts and many expressions of thanks and long life, we backed out of the room.

Hillary and I practically flew to Rasul's office. But it was closed for lunch. We made ourselves comfortable sitting on the ground in the courtyard. A dry, cold, winter smell wafted from the earth and its adobe dust. We filed our nails and waited. Outside the whitewashed walls, the barren plains led to winter's bald-headed mountains.

After thirty minutes, we stood in front of Rasul who gave off a cunning smile and refused to grant our visas even upon his superior's orders. With the same cunning look and polite phrases, I asked if the room could be cleared of his minions so I may "take his ear alone."

A gleam of hope that I would offer myself to him lightened his face as he gave the order. I proceeded to explain to him in a very polite way, that if he would not extend our visas, I would be greatly saddened to return to Adil Shah Sahib and forced to inform him that the second great law, *nanawatai*, protection was transgressed by one of his subordinates. I would also tell Adil Shah that this same subordinate threatened the chastity of guests in his country when they looked to him for the performance of his duty. The color drained from his face and he sat motionless for several seconds.

A broken man, he reached for the necessary implements and Hillary and I listened contentedly to the scratch of the quill pen and the thump of the stamps upon our passports. At the door, turning to thank him, and bid him goodbye so he would not lose face with his subordinates who were peering into his office, I was silenced by the look of pure venom on Rasul's face. Hillary and I left and did not vent our joy until we reached King's shop, where the three of us danced around laughing and hugging each other.

CHAPTER SEVENTEEN

Șervánt óf thė Crėáțòr

"Oh Am-shir-jon, 'tis good that thou come
to my home in Kandahar and sit amongst us.
My mother and sisters-in-law wilt prepare
thy food with their own hands.
We shalt give thee smiles of welcome
that wilt put the sun to shame and
our tears on thy departure wilt be as the spring rain,
Oh Am-shir-jon."
Servant of the Creator

There was a man, his soul cried unto mine. I called him brother. His name was Servant-of-the-Creator. He was a short Pashtun from a merchant family in the city of Kandahar. The youngest of six brothers and four older sisters, his mother decided that he should come to Kabul to start a shop selling the embroidery work of his sisters.

Mothers decide what upbringing the child will have, what schooling, what profession and whom the child will marry. Women start their trousseau as infants with jewelry, land, and animals that are used to help themselves and their future children. Occupations are embroidery and rug making that the men of her family sell in the bazaars so she can save some of her income for her dowry while the rest goes into the family pot.

Like most Afghans, Creator never went to school. He was one of the first merchants to have a shop on Chicken Street.

Creator had dark skin with a bluish cast as do most southern Afghans, Pakistanis, and Hindus. The northern people in these countries are tall with fair or copper-colored complexions. Creator had black liquid eyes, a prominent nose, and medium size lips surrounded by a black mustache and short beard. His *peeran tambon* (traditional outfit) varied from charcoal gray to tan, the business "suit" of the merchant class. He

161

wore a crocheted white skull cap and several yards of black silk for a turban. His sandals were brown leather slip-ons with pointed toes that curled upwards.

The first time I went to Creator's shop to purchase some embroidery, I tried to remove my boots to respect local custom but he stopped me, gesturing that it wasn't necessary.

I thanked him with a smile with my right hand over my heart but pulled my boots off anyway before entering in my Afghan wool socks. I felt an immediate kinship with this man, and I could sense that he felt the same about me. He pointed to a small pile of carpets for me to sit on and left the shop with a steaming teapot and glass. He emptied the *chai* from his own glass onto the street. Then he ran some boiling tea around the rim. He returned to the shop and poured me a full glass of *chai*. He presented me with a tiny dish of sugared-coated almonds to hold in my mouth to sweeten the tea. With gestures and words in Dari, Pashto, and English, we told each other our names and something about our lives.

After the obligatory three cups, Creator pulled out a pile of embroideries. I liked what I saw but nothing really interested me. Then he brought out a pile of "white on white" Kandahari men's wedding shirts. Creator reiterated what I had heard from Bob in his brownstone in Brooklyn that these are lovingly made for the groom by his mother and sisters to wear at his wedding. The groom wears white signifying purity and the bride wears red for happiness, fertility, and blood indicating her virginity. Although fascinated by this information, I already visualized the wedding shirts as short bodice blouses with balloon sleeves. I spent more than I intended and offered to run to the money bazaar to return with local currency.

Creator said in Dari, *"Take thy goods and thy money and inshallah, tomorrow thou wilt bring me the total."*

"But," I countered, *"What if I must leave for Amrika for two seasons?"*

He smiled, *"Go in the peace of Allah."*

I was astounded that this merchant should have such trust in a total stranger and a foreigner at that!

When I related this to my Afghan friends, they looked at me and said in Dari, *"Thou gave thy word to him didst thou not? He is now bound to thee and wilt remain bound providing thee with food and if necessary shelter until thou pay him and set him free from this duty."*

Since Creator's first language was Pashto and mine English, we both learned Dari from living in Kabul. The merchants and their families were my instructors. So he with his Pashto accent and I with my New York one happily mutilated both Dari and English together. Creator was responsible for some of the Dari and most of the Pashto that I learned. We had intense conversations on every subject under the sun with body language and gestures thrown in. When we came to a point in conversation where all language and gesture failed, Creator removed his turban and stroked his shaved skull as if to coax an answer from his brain. We spent many happy hours sitting in his shop, eating *qabili pullow*, the national dish of rice and lamb, and drinking endless cups of *qawa*, sweetened with beet sugar.

Culturally forbidden the company of women not related to him, Creator was thrilled with my companionship. It was socially acceptable because I was a foreigner and a customer to boot. Homesick for Kandahar, we had many conversations about the life of women in western countries. For my part, I was fascinated by anyone or anything Afghan and welcomed the opportunity to gain any kind of first-hand knowledge of this culture.

After our midday meal, I stepped outside the shop to see what the rest of the world was doing. The sun fondled my face with her fiery fingers. Other merchants were busy dozing cross-legged outside their shops. Their two cup teapots and tiny tea bowls rested by their side as their fingers gently wore away their amber or coral prayer beads.

Creator ate, slept, and conducted business in this small shop. The back room was an alcove where he kept extra goods. He made himself a bed by putting a small carpet over bales of embroidered cloth and arranged a few embroidered pillows for comfort. It made a very comfortable sofa.

Drawn to the Kandahari wedding shirts, I spent hours studying their geometric embroidery and asking questions. After several visits, Creator presented me with an exquisite piece of white cotton with a minute version of this type of geometric embroidery.

"If it be pleasing to thee, I shalt have a garment made for thee," he said in Dari.

I was standing before the small mirror near his carpet bed in the back room and when he said that I turned to thank him. Our eyes met and I saw my brother's love for me. He opened his arms and I went to him and embraced him, resting my head on his shoulder in absolute peace and trust. We stayed in that position for a few minutes and then we looked into each other's eyes again and smiled. Our hearts burst from the wonder and joy of having discovered each other. From that moment on, Creator called me "*Amshir-jon* (The One Who Shares My Mother's Milk or sister)."

One Thursday, Creator and I had just finished lunch. It was siesta time. He put some *nesswar* (similar to chewing tobacco), under his tongue and leaned back on the piles of embroidery.

His nephew cleared away the leather cloth and the remnants of bread that had served as plates for our *pullow*. There was only a tiny teapot and two small glasses full of sugar left in front of us.

Creator began our usual afternoon conversation regarding the weather, his family, my family, and business. Although he had no formal schooling, except memorizing the Quran taught by a *mullah* (interpreter of the Quran), Creator was a shrewd businessman.

A woman in a pale blue *chadoree* (the veil) greeted us. She put the tips of the closed fingers of her right hand to where her mouth was and said something. Creator reached into his vest pocket and pulled out a coin and handed it to her with blessings. She, in turn, called down blessings upon both of us.

Curious, I asked in Dari, "*Oh my brother, dost thou know this woman?*"

"*Nay my sister. 'Tis our custom on Thursday afternoons to give alms to all who ask in the name of Allah.*"

"*What significance hath this day?*"

"*This day is before Friday, a very sacred day to all Muslims. We close our shops and businesses and sit amongst our families and pray in the masjid (the mosque). This alms giving is so that all may be in joy with their relatives and have food to share.*"

"*Oh my brother, what significance hath the chadoree?*"

"*My dear sister, the chadoree hath the significance of protection for our womenfolk from the eyes of strangers. The faces of our mothers, sisters, and wives art sacred to us and should only be viewed with respect by those who love them. For all women, the chadoree shows that they art of an age to marry.*"

"*Dost all of the womenfolk wear the chadoree?*"

"Nay my sister, the nomadic women, the nobly born, and the women who work the land dost not. If the women who work the land come into the city, then they hath the chadoree. Our women of the cities take pleasure in the chadoree because it marks them as women who dost not work at manual labor. They hath the leisure to visit the bazaar and talk with their relations and friends."

"So my brother, the chadoree is only worn outside of the home?"

"Yay my sister, no women need protection from their own relations."

Creator, taking up his teacup said, *"So my sister, when wilt thou take a husband?"*

"I am awaiting thy betrothal, brother dear," I replied with a laugh.

"Nay, nay, nay!" he exclaimed. *"I shalt take a wife after thou take a husband. By my eyes, Oh Am-shir-jon,"* he said as his face grew serious, *"if thou art first, I shalt attend thy wedding and if my marriage is first thou must attend mine. Hath the truth been spoken?"*

"Yay my brother, thou hath spoken the truth." And we clasped hands to seal the bargain.

* * *

After I sold all of my costumes and jewelry in New York, I returned to Kabul. I threw my bags into one of the rooms of the Mustafa Hotel, took a shower, and changed my clothes. I was elated to be here at last. The staff from the manager down to the *chai* boys gave me a jubilant welcome. There were many *"Selams"* and "Where have you been?" Of course, they insisted that I at least take tea with them, and recount my adventures since "their eyes were last brightened by my presence." When we were caught up, I headed down Chicken Street to see Creator.

He sprang up from his pallet and we exchanged the Afghan embrace while greeting each other. He asked me to sit down and called his nephew, who was now fourteen, to go for tea and food. Janan ran to a nearby restaurant and returned with a platter of *qabili pullow* accompanied by a small bowl of stewed spinach and *chai*. After we ate, I paid Creator his money and he responded with, *"Good I am free,"* and we both laughed.

Knowing the answer beforehand, I still couldn't help but ask if this meant that I could no longer eat with him since his obligation to me was discharged.

He lovingly replied in Dari, *"Oh Am-shir-jon 'tis good that thou come to my home in Kandahar and sit amongst us. My mother and sisters-in-law wilt prepare thy food with their own hands. We shalt give thee smiles of welcome that wilt put the sun to shame and our tears on thy departure wilt be as the spring rain, Oh Am-shir-jon."*

I felt my heart open and join his as I bowed to him in respect. We sat in peace gazing into each other's eyes. Later that day, we walked across town to the bus depot and mounted an ancient, wheezing, wreck, belching black smoke on its six-hour drive to Kandahar. Creator brought thick anise-flavored bread and sweet juicy tangerines for our journey. When the men stopped for the afternoon prayer, two little ten-year-old girls ran up to the window where I sat, to show off their silk dresses interwoven with silver threads. Creator explained that it was the three-day feast of Eide ul Fitr that followed the month of fasting called Ramazan. Everyone got new clothing and two and a half percent of your wealth must be distributed to the poor.

Dusk was creeping on cat-like feet, as we reached the outskirts of Kandahar. There was a boy in pink pastel clothing with a multi-colored, mirrored embroidered skullcap surrounded by a white turban. He was leading a donkey loaded with freshly kilned jugs and stopped by the side of the road to pray. The color of the sky was orange turning to mauve and then blue. The dying rays of the setting sun splashed the powder fine, ocher color earth. The boy spread his turban cloth, faced west towards Mecca, and began his prostrations.

Knowing my penchant for purchases, Creator directed our steps to the covered bazaar. A quick afternoon downpour had turned the dirt into mud. I made my way through the maze of lanes, a hundred tiny shops on each side, until I came to the stall of the hat merchant. Serene, he sat, a timelessness etched upon his features while I studied the different varieties of skullcaps and hats. All hand embroidered, there were ones with red and yellow floral designs on thick cotton backing and others beaded in a black and white star pattern. But my favorites were the caps whose threads were dipped in liquid gold or silver and embroidered in geometric designs. After choosing several of each kind, Creator paid the merchant so there would be no haggling and we walked into the main square.

Creator raised his right hand and a horse-drawn cart approached us. For fifteen cents we were clip-clopped across town.

CHAPTER EIGHTEEN

Mǎry ǎnd Jěṣṳ̣ṣ

"When thou hath a child he is thy son,
after thou raise that child,
he is thy servant, beholden to thee for the rest of his life
because he owes thee more than the gift of life itself."
An Afghan Mother

The fading sun drenched the dun-colored fortresses, forcing them to cast oblique, dark shadows on the rock-strewn, khaki-color dirt lane. Creator and I side-stepped passersby and heaps of festering refuse where litters of kittens and puppies prowled, their mewing and yipping setting up a din as they foraged for food. After fifteen minutes, we came to an ancient, peeling, ragged, faded green, wooden door in an adobe wall, no different from any others in this lane. The Afghans keep the outside of the houses as plain and poor-looking as possible to discourage unwanted entry. This, of course, belies the richly decorated interior of the home. Creator pushed the gate open. We stepped over the twelve-inch-high door sill into a tiny vestibule of a courtyard to face two sturdy, wooden doors in a less faded green.

We walked into a large, rectangular courtyard where a small, peaceful fountain bubbled. The house that surrounded the courtyard had whitewashed walls and the various doors were painted a pastel blue. The second storey was belted with a fabulous veranda of hand-carved sandstone. Graceful, pale green pillars supported it. Multi-color, hand-painted flowers burst into bloom on the walls of the upper storey. With no small amount of pride, Creator told me that it took him and his brothers three years to build this house for their parents.

He brought me to his mother who was squatting barefoot on one side of the courtyard, her shoes nearby. She was removing pebbles and bits of straw from a pan of dry rice. She remained in this position and smiled up at me in an open and friendly manner as we gave each other the *Selam*. Creator's mother wore the traditional white city *tambon* (elephant-leg pantaloons), cuffed in white lace, with a dark brown, calf-length paisley print western dress over it. A long, tan piece of cotton material was draped over her black and gray hair. Creator told me his mother was in her eighties but to me, she looked no older than early sixties.

Creator's Mother and Father

In a shady corner, not far away, her husband sat cross-legged picking through a bunch of fresh cilantro. He resembled the typical, old patriarch with a white cotton turban, long flowing white beard and tan-color clothing. Creator told me that his father was in his late nineties and blind. The old man gripped my hand with surprising strength.

After greeting each other he said in Pashto, *"Oh my daughter, thy illustrious presence brings light and honor to this poor home."*

I replied, *"May Allah grant thy desires, oh father dear, for indeed it is thy son who is illustrious whilst I hath the privilege to sit in his shade."*

The old man smiled at my words. Then he touched his forehead, his lips, and his heart in a gesture of respect and went back to his task.

I asked Creator what this gesture meant and he replied, "May my thoughts, my words and my feelings be as one."

Creator's mother gestured to me and I squatted next to her. She marveled that I could do this because the only westerners she had seen were in magazines and seated on chairs. She thought that they'd forgotten how to use their legs!

I exclaimed at the beauty of her home. She replied in Pashto, *"The beauty resides in thine eyes, my daughter."* Then she smiled, touched my cheek and chattered away in Pashto.

One of Creator's sisters, Rose, who is married to Creator's cousin, Great, came into the courtyard. She squatted next to me and smiled. She asked Creator to translate for her and told me her story.

She and her husband had five sons: the oldest is twenty-eight and the youngest twelve. Rose got married at sixteen. She was now forty-four years old with very beautiful Greek-Irani features and thick, long black hair. Mercy, her sister, came out to see me. She was only thirty-eight but looked ten years older. She had been married since she was nineteen. In her eighteen years of marriage, she had not been able to conceive, even though she'd been to many doctors. The doctors didn't know if the problem was hers or her husband Freedom's.

Rose gave her second son to her sister Mercy to raise and care for so that she and her husband would have someone to look after them in their old age. They named the son *Issa* (Jesus) and Mercy changed her name to Mary (Maryam). Muslims believe in Mary's virgin birth and that Jesus is just as great a Prophet as Moses and Mohammad.

Maryam said in Dari, *"When thou hath a child he is thy son, after thou raise that child, he is thy servant, beholden to thee for the rest of his life because he owes thee more than the gift of life itself."*

A child is beholden to his parents, particularly his mother for his education, his career, and his marriage partner.

The children addressed their parents as "Dear Mistress" and "Dear Master." They also had a very affectionate name for their mothers such as "My Heart, My Life, and Queen of Roses." The children were very polite and solicitous, asking after my welfare and bringing sweetened *qawa*.

I was surprised that both sisters wore solid-colored materials for their clothing. When I questioned them about the beautiful floral cotton prints that many women wore, they uttered curses and said that these prints were from Russia whom they consider a godless nation. Then they brought me into a room for a massage after the long journey from Kabul. They made me lay face down on a pallet while they sat on either side of me pulling the skin along my spine. This was deeply relaxing. Rose commented that I was not wearing a brassiere under my sweater. When I asked if they wore them, they both pulled up their dresses to exhibit Victoria's Secret bras!

Rose asked me in Pashto, *"How many languages dost thou speak?"*

"English, some French, Italian, Dari, Pashto, Urdu and may Allah forgive me, Russian."

Pah! Russian dogs! May their fathers roast in hell!" They spat and cursed in Pashto as they adjusted their headscarves. The Afghans considered the Russians godless barbarians since they "ate" the ancient khanates of Kiva, Kokand, and Bokhara that were once a part of the Afghan empire turning them into Soviet Socialist Republics.

When they saw that I was serious, their eyebrows flew up in surprise. *"Hath thou really learned Russian?"* Maryam asked.

"Yay, I studied Russian in the university in Amrika."

"Tis well," they conceded, *"as long as thou dost not speak it amongst us!"* We all laughed.

The third sister, Gift, a divorced woman in her early fifties, was also visiting. She cried and said that she no longer wished to live because she cannot get along with her new daughter-in-law. A divorced wife is expected to live with her adult son or, if she has no children, with her parents. If they are deceased, then she is expected to live with her brother.

When Gift was married, they moved to Kabul where she learned Dari. They had only one son, the Mentor. When she didn't conceive again, her husband divorced her and married someone else with whom he had six children. Gift and the Mentor lived isolated lives, unheard of in this culture. Now that he was married, according to tradition, the mother of the groom lives with the couple. But because of disagreements, Gift has moved in with her brother who is bound by duty to care for her. Gift viewed this as a disgrace. She asked me to talk to her son on her behalf to "make his wife behave in the proper way towards her." I promised to meet him.

After I returned to Kabul, I called the Mentor. He said he was going crazy. "This is my third attempt at marriage. I have married two women before from other countries and these marriages ended in divorce. Can you find a job for my wife, Queen of the Castle, so she has something to do and will be in a better frame of mind?"

I told him I would see what I could do and asked him to arrange a meeting with his wife.

She was a blonde, blue-eyed Hungarian. I spent a whole afternoon listening to her woes. She said, "My husband is very unsanitary in his personal habits. He keeps his clean clothes in the same place as his dirty ones. He never showers or cleans his teeth unless I tell him that he cannot come to bed!"

"My mother-in-law," she continued, "wants to be the ruler of the house. Whenever the Mentor and I have an argument, she tries to hit me over the head with her shoes. I am not used to being treated like this! I have always expressed my opinions in my father's house and was not beaten for it."

"The second time my mother-in-law tried to hit me, I pushed her and she fell on the coffee table and broke it. I ran out of the house, called some Hungarian friends here and explained that I wanted to stay with them. After a few days, I called the Mentor. I told him that I wanted to pick up my clothes, but he said that I couldn't have them. So I called the police and went with a very high Hungarian official to his house. My husband was shocked that I would involve someone outside the family in our dispute. He started shouting to the police that I was a prostitute! The police did not know what to do so we all had to go to see the Chief of Police. After two hours, the Chief of Police told my husband to let me have my things."

"And another thing, he doesn't know how to act in bed."

"You must teach him," I said.

"He said it is because he's never been married or had girlfriends."

"He's been married and divorced twice before!" I blurted out.

Queen looked at me with tears in her eyes, and I could see that what I had revealed was news to her. I put my hand over my mouth and apologized.

Queen replied through her tears, "No, it is good you told me. Now I feel you're my friend."

She said that she would never have married him had she known this.

I said, "Even though someone is my friend, I could never side with them if they're wrong."

"Now I'm sure that the Mentor will be even more adamant when I ask him for a divorce," she said wiping her eyes.

I told her to let things cool down for a while, and then let me talk to him first.

Queen said he was a tourist in her country and they knew each other only ten days. She had quarreled with her boyfriend and thought that the best revenge would be to marry another.

She looked at me and said with sarcasm, "Nice revenge! My government investigated the Mentor for a year before they allowed our marriage. He had to sign a paper for them stating that he was never married before. He lied! He also told me that if I do not live with him for two years, I'll be deported, and probably go to jail!"

"I think he is trying to scare you into staying with him, Queen," I said.

Queen said, "Oh you do not know my government! They will make me live in exile in my own country because I left. Already my relatives write that they are having problems."

"Maybe the government will not recognize your marriage because the Mentor lied about his previous marriages," I said.

"The Mentor also never told me we would be living in an extended family. And he is not honest with money. He gave me a thousand dollar check for my wedding present. I cashed it at my friend's bank. My husband was very angry and told me to give the check back or the bank will close his account."

"Perhaps this was the marriage portion that a wife receives upon the death of her spouse," I told her. "In that case, he did not lie, this is Afghan custom."

Queen is the only child of divorced parents, similar to the Mentor's background. The Afghan custom of never allowing a family member or guest to be alone, plus the constant coming and going of company drove her crazy. To make things worse, most of the Mentor's friends and relatives did not speak English let alone Hungarian, and she did not speak Dari. She and her husband communicated in English. Queen surmised that the Mentor, age thirty-one, married a twenty-two-year-old girl who was intelligent, attractive, and he thought, young enough to bend to his ways. Therefore, the Mentor played up the "good life" in Afghanistan versus her life in a communist country.

"So what do I do now? Stay with my husband or go back into exile? Which is worse?" she asked me. I couldn't answer.

* * *

I was back in New York again. I had forgotten about the conversation Creator and I had regarding each other's weddings. Creator could not read and write, so he paid a university student to write a letter to me in English, saying that his parents had found a match and according to our agreement, he expected me at his wedding. He was to be married towards the end of March, the Afghan New Year, *Nowroz* (that takes place on the vernal equinox March 21st ... a propitious time when many marriages occur).

Given the fact that Afghan mail at its best took one to two months to arrive, and only if the postal worker didn't take the stamp for his collection, it is not surprising that I never received the letter. My normal journey was first to Afghanistan, then to Pakistan to renew my visa and then back to Afghanistan. However, I received a large order from a New York department store for scarves from Pakistan. I figured that this would take two weeks and then I would be off to Afghanistan.

While waiting for my shipment, I met an Australian couple on their way to Kabul. Ignorant of Creator's impending wedding, I told them to drop in on my brother to tell him that I would arrive at the end of March. Creator later told me that he was elated to get this message.

As it happened, Lahore was out of scarves and they had to be made in Karachi, eight hundred miles further south. This meant an indefinite delay while I went to Karachi, and *baksheeshed* (in this case, 'bribed') my way into having the mill go into production for a few hundred bolts of material when the minimum order was five thousand. My efforts, what with the wining and dining plus the spreading of Pakistani rupees, were finally rewarded towards the middle of April. All that remained was the cutting, tailoring, and shipping of the scarves which took another four weeks. At last, having seen the goods off to the States, I grabbed an ancient, Afghan bus through the Khaibar, and landed in Kabul in the middle of May.

It was around seven o'clock at night, and I made straight for King's shop but it was closed. So I turned my steps to Creator's expecting the usual embraces and greetings. I burst into the shop with a grin. Creator looked up with a shocked expression on his face. He jumped up from where he sat, tore his turban off his head and hurled it to the floor, cursing all the while. I stood there wide-eyed with my mouth hanging open.

He shouted in Dari, *"I am supposed to be married! Ba' Quran, it was told to me by those Australians that thou were coming in two weeks! I told my parents and the bride's parents that I shalt not marry unless Catee is at my wedding! They made an agreement to await the first of April. The tenth of May hath passed! W'Allah my parents art angry with me, the bride's parents think that my purpose is to disgrace their daughter by my hesitation and thou-"*

I cut him off, *"This news hath not reached my ears! I beg forgiveness for any difficulty caused."*

"When didst thou receive my letter?"

I threw him a blank look and said in English, "What letter?"

He was so amazed by this question that he took a step backward, his eyes big as two full moons. I could just see the Afghan postman keeping the stamp to sell to someone else and discarding the letter. I began to laugh.

He continued in Dari, *"Why art thou laughing? This is very bad. My face hath become black at my own wedding!"*

But I saw a smile start creeping around his mouth. After I pressed his right hand to my eyes and inclined my head, I heard him chuckle, and soon we were both roaring with laughter, at the thought of all the trouble we caused because my brother wouldn't break his word to me.

Creator and I rushed to a nearby shop and used the telephone to call Creator's family and give them the good news. His brother was delighted, and plans were made for Creator to leave for Kandahar immediately. After he replaced the receiver, Creator grabbed my hand and pressed it to his heart.

He said in Dari, *"Bring all those thou desire. My apprentice, Vali, wilt accompany thee on the bus to Kandahar. I must go to the baths where I shalt be prepared for my marriage."*

"What wilt occur at the baths?"

"I shalt be massaged, scrubbed, and shampooed. My beard wilt be trimmed and perfumed, my head shaved, and the soles of my feet wilt receive the henna."

"Thou wilt be a most becoming groom," I smiled.

Excited about Creator's wedding, I raced back to my hotel where I met some British and American friends and invited them to Creator's wedding. Some of them had done business with Creator and were ecstatic to accompany me to view a traditional Pashtun wedding.

The next morning, I packed a small bag with a fancy *shelwar kamiz* of lilac and black, collected my friends, and took an early taxi to the bus station at Kotee Sangee. We scrambled aboard a shiny, new, red bus bound for Kandahar. Vali handed the bus driver eight tickets that he had purchased with money Creator had given him. Vali also bought some sweet, round, buttery bread with nigella seeds that a young Hazara boy sold. After we were seated, the bus driver announced that only seven seats were available. Vali would have to take the next bus. He was crestfallen as he related this to me. I pushed Vali up to the driver and told him that either we all go or no one goes. Just then our Uzbek friend arrived to say that one of the Europeans couldn't make it. Vali's eyes lit up, and a huge grin almost split his face. He skipped off to the bazaar to buy some cucumbers to slake our thirst on the long trip.

It was noon when the bus driver stopped for prayer, and we all stretched our legs for fifteen minutes. Then we continued roaring down the dusty, barren road to Kandahar. By two o'clock all the snacks had been consumed and we were ravenous. We saw a teahouse in the distance and looked forward to having our stomachs filled. However, as the driver tore passed, our longings "entered the realm of dreams." Jolted into reality we set up a hue and cry in Dari, Pashto, Turkic, and English.

Surprised, the driver caromed into the soft shoulder of the road and eyed us, perplexed at the commotion. Since the driver spoke only Pashto, we elected Vali our spokesman. He made it very clear that our destination was that teahouse several hundred yards back. The rest of the Afghans sided with us, so the disgruntled bus driver had no choice but to turn around. I asked Vali why the driver was so upset at having to stop?

"To make their jobs more interesting, they make bets as to who can arrive first."

Appalled, I commented, "Yes, and they break every rule in the book to achieve this without any regard for the passengers." Visions of buses with scattered goods, people, and animals impaled in the spiky crevasses of the Khaiber flew through my mind.

We went into the two-storey teahouse and clambered up onto one of many, three-foot-high adobe embankments covered with multi-striped, cotton runners. Shoes off, we sat cross-legged while the *chai* boy distributed metal glasses of sweet cold water. The teahouse was dark and cool inside. In addition to the embankments, small raw wood tables and chairs lined the balcony that ran around the four sides of the room on the second storey. Carpets decorated the walls. On one of the embankments sat the *samowat* (the Afghan equivalent of the Russian samovar). It was a huge, copper urn, heated underneath by a wood fire, with a spigot that dispensed boiling water for tea.

Nearby were stacks of porcelain tea bowls and small teapots waiting to be pressed into service. Each teapot held sixteen ounces of tea, a veritable plethora after the tiny six-ounce teapots and their egg-size bowls.

The owner of the teahouse, a proud man with kind eyes came forward to serve us himself. With many apologies, he told us that the only food he had left from lunch was some hard-boiled eggs, bread, a yoghurt drink, tea and a few bottles of orange soda. We told him that we would enjoy whatever he had to offer, and he smiled and thanked us for "whitening his face."

After lunch, we returned to the bus and took off. The six-hour journey to Kandahar was pleasant enough, until the last two hours, when the heat of the plains descended upon us with a vengeance. We felt like poached eggs. Behind windows locked against the fine dust that seeped into our eyelids, our tongues lolled and our eyes rolled. We had finished the last of the juicy cucumbers hours ago.

After a searing eternity, we pulled into the bus depot. It was a rickety, wooden structure crammed between two equally rickety, two-storey shops on street level including living quarters above. As we got off the bus and stepped into the rock-strewn alley, the twelfth century closed over me like a shroud. Here, even veiled women were absent from the streets. The low buzz of men's voices in trade and the soft slap of sandaled feet in the dust made small dents in the total silence. In the oppressive airless heat of the late afternoon, we were surrounded by a sea of white turbans, with a sprinkling of gray and black ones.

CHAPTER NINETEEN

A Kándáhári Wëdding

"The tablecloth was decorated with multi-colored embroidered flowers with the word "welcome" in Dari upon its face. Huge slabs of fresh naan heaped with sweet rice, decorated with raisins, almonds, chicken, and orange peels, colored with saffron, arrived. A wheat pudding soaked in rose oil, and a sweet omelet fragrant with ground cardamom seeds, followed. All of these wedding feast foods had festive splashes of red, orange, and green food coloring."
The Author

I saw Creator striding towards the bus in his wedding clothes. He wore a beautiful white *peeran tambon* (traditional outfit). His turban, a cream-colored silk, with thin, gold stripes, graced his head. His eyes were kohled, and he had a new, polished pair of black leather sandals on his henna-soled feet. We joyously gave each other the greeting, and he welcomed us all. Then we walked over to a nearby hotel and Creator spoke to the manager and arranged rooms for all of us.

The hotel was built in 1973, at the height of Afghanistan's tourist trade. It was a series of double-occupancy bungalows clustered around a large rectangular swimming pool. Each bungalow had its own working, western bathroom ... a rarity and a privilege!

After settling in, we sat in the shady courtyard, drinking tea. I noticed a very tall, slim but muscular, good-looking man sitting by the pool in white swimming trunks that set off his dark complexion. He had a large, magnificent head with jet-black, shoulder-length, wavy hair, large, black eyes that were slightly slanted, a Roman nose, and full, dark, "bee-stung lips" (the Afghan term for those who have an extra little bulge of skin in the center of the upper lip). His mouth was surrounded by a black mustache and a short beard. He was six-feet-three inches tall, and in his late thirties. We gazed at each other and just as I was wondering how to get acquainted with him, Creator's cousin arrived to drive us to the wedding and gave Creator a large combination radio and cassette tape player for a wedding present. We all congratulated him on this beautiful gift and Creator beamed. As we were leaving, I looked back. The man remained at the edge of the pool dangling his feet in the water looking in another direction. At a later time, he would be very helpful to me.

While driving, Creator said in Dari, *"Bring the two women with thee to see the bride."*

When we arrived, I translated what Creator said for Rosalind and Maureen and they excitedly jumped up and down. We all laughed. They started to tease the guys restricted to the men's quarters in the courtyard next door. Creator, the women, and I walked through the narrow, rutted, rocky, refuse-filled lanes that separated the high adobe walls of the houses on either side. We came to a pale-green, chipped, wooden door that was ajar as if in welcome. We stepped over the twelve-inch high doorsill into the tiny courtyard and then into a much larger, rectangular one.

Suddenly pandemonium erupted as a horde of women and children, all talking and laughing, surrounded us. My friends were startled and a little frightened and almost stood on top of me. I smiled at the women and began a string of Pashtun greetings. They replied in kind and exclaimed at my Pashto. I let them know that they had just heard the beginning and the end of it. Now they moved even closer to us, and some of the women and older girls touched our faces and smoothed our hair exclaiming at its fineness while the younger girls sat close to our feet staring up into our faces. Just as we wondered if we were about to be undressed from sheer curiosity, Creator appeared, clapped his hands, told them to let us breathe and to bring us to see his bride. We were seized by the elbows and arms and propelled forward in the crush of women.

Off to the side of the courtyard, between two open, turquoise-painted doors, the bride sat on piles of embroidered cushions on top of a carpet. Creator avoided looking at his bride out of respect. They are only supposed to see each other for the first time on the third night of the wedding when a mirror is placed between them.

Honey Rose, I was informed, was twenty-two years old. She was five-feet-tall and chubby with thick, black hair cut short on the sides, a bush of bangs, and many braids hanging down her back. Her braids were tied with seven different colored ribbons. Honey Rose sat in silence with her heavily kohled eyes downcast as befits the bride. Her cheeks and rosebud mouth had rouge and lipstick. Her somewhat pockmarked face was whitened with powder. She wore the traditional bridal colors: a bright red silk tunic with a mirror-embroidered front and green silk pantaloons. A red silk shawl, embroidered with gold thread, was draped around her shoulders. She was covered from head to toe in jewelry: earrings, necklaces, wrist and ankle bracelets, finger and toe rings, and even a pearl nose jewel. When Honey Rose moved, her clothing gave off fragrant clouds of rose perfume.

I remarked on the rose scent to Creator and he displayed a tiny silver perfume holder and said in Dari, *"The souls of one thousand roses live in this bottle, Oh Amshir-jon."*

He put a dab on my wrist with the words, *"All of womankind love the scent of flowers, who art their sisters."*

I turned back to Honey Rose and congratulated her in Pashto telling her that Creator was a fine fellow. She solemnly thanked me without raising her eyes, showing modesty, as was the custom.

Creator pressed me with "Isn't she beautiful? Isn't she nice?"

I paused thinking that Honey Rose didn't fit the western idea of beauty but to see the joy in Creator's eyes was enough.

I replied in Dari, *"Yay, indeed, and thou wilt be very happy."*

He gushed on and on about her excellent family background and her phenomenal embroidery. He enthused that her white embroidered wedding shirts were without equal. I assured him that I'd be glad to use her embroideries in my clothing designs. His face was wreathed in smiles as he squeezed my hands and thanked me.

As we moved away, the women attached themselves to us again. I tried to take some pictures of them in their finery but it was impossible to get them to step back. When they saw my camera, a great roar went up, and they clung to me like glue, to be sure they'd get in the picture. Laughing, I gave up and allowed them to touch and stare at us to their hearts' content.

It was suffocating in the airless courtyard and Creator rescued us. He took us up to the second–storey of the house and served us cold sweetened green tea. We watched the women below as they danced and sang to a tambourine accompaniment. Their clothing made whirling splashes of red, green, violet, and yellow against the adobe courtyard.

Creator led us downstairs to a large, carpeted room where his parents, sisters, and sisters-in-law were busy putting food out in large trays to be carried by ten-year-old boys to the house next door where the men were grouped. The women rose from their squatting positions and greeted me with embraces and kind words. I went to his parents and put their right hands to my lips and eyes and congratulated them while Creator lit up like a beacon. I noticed that his sisters all wore the same outfits, same as our bridesmaids do. They wore black cotton *peerans* (tunics) with minute, bright-orange, geometric embroidery interwoven with silver threads, complemented by black cotton *tambons* (pantaloons). Marziah, one of Creator's older sisters, came forward and handed me a bundle of folded black cloth. I opened it to discover an identical outfit. Marziah saw my delight and said that since I was Creator's sister, I should be dressed like them.

Creator's family insisted we eat. Rosalind and Maureen took their cues from me and sat cross-legged on the carpet. Marziah brought a beautiful, white tablecloth and placed it in front of us. The tablecloth was decorated with multi-colored embroidered flowers with the word "welcome" in Dari upon its face. Huge slabs of fresh *naan* heaped with sweet rice, decorated with raisins, almonds, chicken, and orange peels, and colored with saffron, arrived. Dishes containing a lamb and potato stew and a spinach and lamb stew were passed around. A wheat pudding soaked in rose oil, and a sweet omelet fragrant with ground cardamom seeds followed. All of the food had festive splashes of red, orange, and green food coloring.

My friends watched me break off a piece of the bread, and use it as a utensil with my right hand as my left hand rested in my lap. I explained to them that the left hand was only used in the bathroom, and to use this

184

hand at the table is very rude. It was permitted for all to dip into the stew bowls with your individual piece of bread. After this repast, we went into the courtyard where a young boy brought a jug of water to wash our hands from the remnants of the meal.

Creator suggested he take the three of us next door where the men were celebrating. The odor of charcoal-grilled lamb and spicy pullows surrounded us with an intoxicating aura. The night was moonless. The one, naked light bulb hung over the carpeted platform where the musicians sat covered in garlands of roses. Their brilliant, white clothes, embroidered with silver threads, sparkled like diamonds against the black velvet sky. Their hair and beards were perfumed and they sat in intent but regal splendor, dispensing largesse through classical music. Rahim Baksh's rich baritone never faltered throughout the night as he played the harmonium and sang those romantic classical ballads for which he was renowned. He filled the air with poignant melodic sounds. The crowd murmured appreciation at appropriate moments, in between their mouthfuls of *pullow*, sips of tea or inhalations from the hashish pipes making the rounds.

We cut a path through the forest of turbans and climbed up onto the rooftop, where we found a small space with a good view of the courtyard below. Shoulder to shoulder we sat cross-legged with the men. One corner of the courtyard was taken up with gigantic vats of rice and trays of kebabs, all in various stages of steaming and grilling. A light breeze wafted the odors of the grilled meat with an overlay of hashish over us.

A man, who heard us speaking English, chimed in with a broken version of it. He told us he was a landlord from Lashkargah, west of Kandahar, and invited us to be his guests. We thanked him but said we had to return to Kabul. He inclined his head and passed the *chillum* (vertical handheld pipe). In the airless darkness, we listened to the plaintive cries of Rahim Baksh as he told of unrequited love. The hashish made us oblivious to language but allowed us to experience his great longing for his beloved.

After a while, Creator reappeared to escort us women back to the bride's house to view the *chubazi* (the sword dance). We arrived just in time to see Creator's nephew, Janan leading a group of men with wooden swords, in a circular dance. At intervals, they stopped dancing and engaged in mock swordplay. It was all very fluid and rhythmic. I marveled at Janan's maturity in just the past year. He seemed to spring up overnight from boy to man. He grew four inches and looked very stylish in his gray silk and gold striped turban, a sign that a boy had reached puberty.

We returned to the men's side just in time to see a transvestite perform. He had extremely long, curly, black hair, and false eyelashes that he batted as he wiggled his hips. He was dressed in women's clothing. The men gave a roar of approval and began to clap with a rhythmic beat, encouraging him to dance. The music began, and the transvestite, responding to the whistles and shouts of the men, enacted one of the most sinuous, graceful but lascivious dances I'd ever see. I felt the sexual tension in the air, and when he finished some men rushed to surround him. I asked the landlord what was going on, and he said that the men were making "appointments" to see him in private.

I turned to my friends. Ali, the Uzbek, together with Bob, Bill, and Steve were all staring straight ahead with glazed eyes and slack mouths. Afghanistan's first quality hashish had found its mark. Since it was well after midnight, I made some sounds about their returning to their hotel, and was met with dumb nods of agreement but no movement. Rosalind, Maureen and I were ready to leave. I waited for Creator to come back. He had spent the entire evening making the rounds amongst the men and the women to see if they needed anything. He never stopped for a moment. He made sure that the guests, musicians, family members and even the servants were all enjoying themselves and had their every wish fulfilled. The wedding would go on for two more nights with people coming and going in relays. Some slept right on the carpets spread in the courtyard; others availed themselves of the *masjid* down the street. Any Muslim can spend a night or two in a mosque when needed.

Afghan weddings are three nights long with much feasting, music, dancing, joking and general merrymaking. They are all alike except for different dances with a variation on the food served. In the more conservative families, the women and men are in separate quarters like this wedding. The more modern families have men and women participating together. The actual ceremony itself, no matter the social status of the family is a meeting between the male representatives of the two families and a mullah where a marriage document is signed by them.

I mentioned to Creator that he was working too hard at his own wedding, and he confided in me that when this was over, he will take a two-month honeymoon to recover while his nephew runs the shop in Kabul. He still had two more nights of the same to be the host and celebrate his wedding. It seemed more work than fun for him but no matter the first of the great Afghan laws, hospitality, must be satisfied.

When he saw the condition of my friends, he sent a boy for a taxi that appeared an hour later. Everyone attempted to reach a vertical state, and it was surprising that they made it to the outer courtyard. In the pitch blackness of the moonless night, Creator and I lead our little group through the treacherous, twisting lanes, back to the main road. I believe that Afghans see like cats and are as surefooted as goats. Due to Creator's careful guidance, not one intoxicated foreigner broke a limb or stepped into something too heinous to describe. I got hold of Creator's shirt tail, and followed him like a blind woman, feeling my way with my sandals and stopping every few yards. At long last, we reached the taxi and said our goodnights.

Hand in hand, Creator and I meandered back to the house, talking about the wedding. I asked him where he got that beautiful rose oil that he still wore, and he replied that our mutual friend, the landlord from Lashkargah, grew the roses and prepared the *attar* (essential oil) himself. He pulled out the small, metal flagon from his tunic pocket and opened it under my nose. My nostrils were filled with the delicate, sweet, perfumed scent of roses in full bloom. I inhaled deeply and the stench of the refuse heaps abated. I put a drop on my upper lip and floated the rest of the way back to the house. Creator took me to a small, carpeted room in the women's quarters with a pallet and pillows and bade me "Happy Night." I went to my dreams in a cloud of rose essence drifting off to the sounds of Rahim Baksh.

*   *   *

When I returned to Kabul, I noticed that my servant was unusually cheerful. I said in Dari, *"Oh Mowlowdowt, how art thou?"*

"Very well, Khanum. And how art thou?"

"Not bad. Why art thou smiling? What is thy news?"

"Oh Lady Mistress, soon after thy departure for thy home in Amrika, the ruyibar (matchmaker) came to my mother, and a sister of mine hath said that a bride hath been found."

For most families, the paternal, first cousin marriage is the preferred one. However, due to financial and other circumstances, sometimes it is necessary to employ a matchmaker to find a suitable spouse.

"Good, oh Mowlowdowt! Congratulations! When wilt thou marry?" I asked him in Dari as I thought of losing him already.

"W'Allah (By God), I do not know, Oh Khanum. God willing, one year hence."

The traditional one-year waiting period is from the time the matchmaker finds the bride until the actual wedding. The bride's mother cannot be seen to be in a rush to give up her treasured daughter.

"One year hence is a great amount of time, Oh Mowlowdowt! Why?" I continued in Dari.

"It is our custom Khanum that the bride cannot be given until the soles of my family's shoes are worn as thin as an onion skin from going to the house to ask for the bride."

"And what part hath the matchmaker?" I asked.

"She, Oh Khanum, first found a girl of my station. She took tea with the family to study them among themselves very well. When she was assured that they were equal to my family, she said to them that she knows a family that looks with interest upon their daughter. Then my family and the bride's family have relatives sent to each other's homes to determine if the ruyibar said the truth."

The groom's women act as spies either in the bazaars or at the home of the bride when they are invited to tea by the bride's family. They report to their families on the habits and demeanor of the bride.

There was a banging on the gate. Mowlowdowt rose from his cross-legged position in one graceful movement and left the room. When he returned, his cousin Sabera was with him. She had grown taller in these last few months and would soon reach puberty. Then she was considered ready for marriage. Like other Afghan children, Sabera knew all the household duties intimately, having started her adult life at five years of age. She had the bearing of a thirty-year-old woman. Sabera and I smiled and greeted one another. I asked her what she thought of Mowlowdowt's upcoming marriage.

She smiled with downcast eyes and replied in Dari, "W'allah (by God), *I dost not know.*"

She was always a little shy and deferential with me at first. Little by little, I would draw her out but even then, she only spoke to me after being asked a question.

Mowlowdowt was very happy that he had saved enough money by working for me, to ensure his happiness, especially through my financial generosity to him on holidays. Settled back on my cushions on the carpet, Mowlowdowt and Sabera regaled me with ancient, marital customs still observed by the more traditional people. I knew that King and others of the nobility had adopted more western customs.

Sabera revealed to me that negotiations begin with the bride price demanded by the bride's family from the groom's family referred to as *shir baha.*

Sabera continued to explain the ceremony of *labs giriftan* (the taking of the lips or the promise). The bride's women give a *qand,* an eighteen-inch-high cone of raw sugar that is eight inches at the base. This is presented on a silver tray with prayers etched into it for good luck to seal the bargain. It shows that the groom's suit has been accepted.

In addition, a beautiful, double-sided, embroidered handkerchief called *dussmol* showing the outer and inner worlds of men and women respectively is also given to the groom's family. The *dussmol* is later returned with the bride price. This is followed by the serving of *qaymak chai,* a very special, green tea made with the equivalent of the French *crème fraiche.*

Mowlowdowt asked permission to leave my service for three months to get married.

"*Three months!*" I gasped out in Dari.

"*Two months, Oh Khanum,*" he replied.

When he saw no change in my incredulous expression, he offered one month. I consented to this only if he could furnish me with a servant to replace him.

His face brightened and he said in English "Upon my eyes, oh My Lady."

My "new" servant turned out to be a combination of Sabera and Azim.

One day, I asked Sabera in Dari, *"Dost thou wish to be a bride, Oh Sabera?"*

"Yay, Catee Khanum. In several moons time, I shalt gain enough years to wear the chadorees (veil).*"*

"And this wilt make thee a bride?"

"Yay, Khanum, for it tells that I am old enough for marriage," she said as she turned to go home with Azim.

CHAPTER TWENTY

The Traveling Fiancé

"Every leaf on every tree in the garden knows
that I love my beloved,
My beloved knows it not,
But every leaf on every tree knows."
An Urdu love poem recited by Jamal to the Author

It was the morning after my fateful evening with Jamal, the man I'd seen in my childhood dreams who'd walked away from me just before the sun rose, still had my mind and heart reeling. But, life in my house went on. Mowlowdowt prepared my usual breakfast of oranges, *chai,* and *naan* with unsalted butter. When I left for the bazaar, Mowlowdowt was sweeping the house, airing the bedding and dusting everything in sight. Afghan New Year was upon us and Mowlowdowt cheerfully made preparations.

Religious feasts were a break in daily life in a country where there was no public form of amusement. Since most of the population was non-literate, visiting relatives and friends, kite flying, storytelling, dancing, playing music and singing were their leisure pursuits. Feast days cropped up so often that there were months when government offices were closed for fifteen days or more. This was why I lived in Afghanistan for six months at a time in order to finish my export work.

But I could not settle into the day's routine. Meeting Jamal had shifted something deep inside of me and in the few sleepless hours I had endured since then, I heard him whisper again, a hundred times, "Come with me now then, for tomorrow I leave for Pakistan." Sometime during the night, I had made up my mind to go to Pakistan with him. My tailors had enough work to keep them busy for at least two weeks and I could renew my visa in Pakistan instead of having to face Rasul with his slimy machinations again.

At eight o'clock in the morning, I called the hotel where Jamal and his retinue were staying. It took a good ten minutes before he came to the phone at the front desk. While waiting, the thought crossed my mind that he had already left since it takes all day to get to the Pakistani border that closes at dusk. Then I heard this very groggy voice, like someone who had been roused from a very sound sleep, saying, "Hallo?"

"Good morning, *Khan Sahib*?"

"Yes? Who are you?" he mumbled.

"I am the lady that-"

"Yes! Yes!" he exclaimed in a rush now wide awake.

I said in Dari, *"I called to tell thee that my desire is to accompany thee to Pakistan."*

"What?" he roared. "You dare to disturb my sleep to give me this news?"

"Nay Khan Sahib," I retorted with equal vehemence, *"Thy sleep hath been disturbed to command thee procure a Pakistani visa for me!"*

I heard several choking sounds, and then Jamal said evenly, "Very well."

Thirty minutes later, there was a banging at the gate. My servant Mowlowdowt tapped at my bedroom door. At my acknowledgment, he entered with bulging eyes to announce in Dari, *"Oh Khanum Sahib!* (My Noble Lady Mistress) *Sahibzada* (the Nobleman) *Jamal Mahmood Yusuf Khan desires admittance to thy presence."*

I nodded and asked him to bring tea. Jamal strode into the room and Mowlowdowt quietly closed the door behind him. We lunged into each other's arms, and he crushed me against him. He kissed and bit my lips like a beggar at a banquet, as they pulsated between pleasure and pain. Then he thrust me away from him at arms' length, stared into my eyes with a face as fierce as a panther's and said in Dari in a voice resounding with passion, *"I am come for thee!"*

I breathed, *"Yay, My Lord,"* having made up my mind to be with him as long as I could. A banging at the gate interrupted this cataclysm of passion. I heard the voice of my friend, Morrie, and Mowlowdowt's footsteps.

I quickly filled Jamal in, "Last night, I promised to teach Morrie the rudiments of Dari so he would be able to better bargain in the sheepskin coat bazaar."

We sat on the bed as my servant brought Morrie into the room, and disappeared to get tea and *kulcha*, the hard biscuits made to be dunked in sweetened tea.

Morrie and Jamal began talking, and Jamal gave him his business card and wrote something on the back. It was the name, address, and telephone number of one of the main coat dealers in Kabul. This man was a personal friend of Jamal's and would ensure Morrie got a fair deal. Morrie was elated and spent another hour socializing with us while he drank the obligatory three cups of tea.

When he left, Jamal growled, "It is now ten forty-five. I called Abbas, the Pakistani consul, before I came here and made an eleven o'clock appointment with him."

I smiled wryly, "This is the second time we must postpone our love-making. What sign is this?"

"It is a sign that we shall not postpone it again," he replied adamantly as he swung off the bed, and headed towards the door. We got into the Mercedes, and Sattar drove us to the Pak consulate in five minutes. There we were greeted by Consul Shah Abbas, an old friend of Jamal's family. Since it was Friday, Abbas wore traditional clothing instead of a western suit. He was almost as tall as Jamal, had a similar build, a clean-shaven face, and steel-gray hair over a kind, open expression.

"Please sit down," he said with a gentle smile. His servant appeared, and Abbas ordered tea Pak style with sugar and condensed milk. Its richness began to nauseate me. I drank only a quarter of a cup. Abbas expression was a question mark. I explained that I was not used to tea this rich, and he laughed.

"My dear Ms. Cath-ay, in Pakistan we take our tea boiled up with water buffalo milk ... now that is rich! In Afghanistan, I can only offer you condensed milk. Please accept my apologies for my lack of hospitality but you know it is Friday and I only keep one servant this day."

"I assure you that your hospitality is most gracious. Thank you for letting us intrude on your day off," I said.

Jamal and Abbas talked for a few minutes in Urdu while Abbas stamped my passport. What arrived next was a fantastic assortment of fried turnovers, stuffed with every imaginable highly seasoned meat, poultry, or vegetables accompanied by three pungent sauces that were sweet, sour, and hot. As if this wasn't enough, a velvety-smooth dessert of fresh mango slices bathing in condensed milk, perfumed with crushed cardamom seeds, was served with more Pak tea. When I couldn't eat another bite, we said our goodbyes and headed back to my house.

On the way, Jamal and I concocted a story as to why I was traveling with him to Pakistan. In this culture, it was one thing to have a lover and another to flaunt it in front of your family. Jamal said Heinz had left for India on a business trip and he would tell his family that I was Heinz's fiancée and Jamal was driving me to Lahore where Heinz and I would meet. Men and women are not allowed to travel together if not related, hence the "traveling fiancée" story.

Humming to myself, I packed my clothes.

I said goodbye to my servant knowing that he'd take care of everything and grabbed a taxi to Jamal's hotel. I was introduced to his relatives. His cousin, his wife, and their thirteen-year-old daughter were in Jamal's Mercedes along with Jamal's paternal aunt who flashed me a sly look as we were getting into the car. I instantly felt that this old lady saw through Jamal's concocted story of the "traveling fiancée." Jamal's brother, Bilal, and two of his teenage sons, who lived in Jalalabad, had come to see the party off. They were heading north on a business trip.

Jamal opened the passenger door of his Mercedes for me and got behind the wheel. His aunt, cousin, cousin's wife, and their daughter were already seated in the back. The cousin and daughter were asleep while his wife talked with Jamal's aunt. Soon his aunt was gently snoring. It was late afternoon as we drove toward the border. The ensuing dusk, the rocking motion of the Mercedes over the non-existent road, the quiet hum of the engine together with the silence in the car, succeeded in putting us all in a drowsy state. About an hour away from Jalalabad, the last town before the Khaiber, Jamal announced that he felt sleepy. His cousin's wife tried to start a conversation with Jamal regarding her purchases in the Kabul bazaars.

After five minutes, Jamal's yawns became more pronounced and he said in Urdu, *"Please, Bhaji (sister - a term of respect for women), I have very little desire to hear whether thou purchased blue or black shoes for thy mother."*

194

Appealing to his pride as a Pakhtun, and his explosive temper, I decided on the perfect plan to awaken Jamal.

"You know, Khan Sahib, several Parisian journalists went to Pakistan a month ago for the purpose of interviewing your President Bhutto and returned to tell me that he was a complete idiot."

Jamal sat bolt upright as if struck by lightning. "What?" he blustered, "How can you desecrate my company by repeating such things as these?"

Not waiting for my answer, he launched into a forty-five-minute diatribe in defense of Bhutto. By that time, we were in Jalalabad.

It was almost dark when we checked into a hotel. The border was closed for the night. It took us awhile to register and get to our respective rooms. Later, we all met at the restaurant for dinner. Jamal and I'd agreed that we'd wait until he was free of his relatives before we'd be together but our longing was just too great.

As I was saying goodnight to everyone, Jamal rose from the table and addressed me in English, "Ms. Parenti, since you will be living in our country for some time upon your marriage, it is only fitting that you become familiar with our customs. Therefore, we have taken the liberty of presenting you with a small book on the history of Pakistan for your perusal as a follow-up to our earlier conversation."

I was touched by his gesture and smiled at all of his relatives while thanking him. I went down the cold stone corridor to my room and unlocked its Chinese padlock. The room, a small square was equally cold without any means of heating it. I bumped my shin on one of the legs of the two *charpoys* that were too big for the room. Both beds were part way across the doorway with a tiny, wooden nightstand separating them. The walls were washed a pastel-blue in contrast to the brightly-lacquered brown door and window frame. A solid heavy, navy-blue drape covered the window. The battered armoire stood off to one side, its door slightly ajar to reveal three bent wire hangers scattered on its rack.

I explored the bathroom to discover an ancient toilet and a tiny sink. A single cold water tap about five and a half feet off the ground passed for a shower. The floor was slanted towards one corner where there was a loose strainer over a drain hole. This room was even colder than the bedroom. I undressed quickly and squatted under this tap to wash, chills running up and down my spine. Shivering, I wrapped myself in the hand-towel and put my shoes back on to avoid standing barefoot on the freezing floor. I stood at the sink to brush my teeth. As I turned on the one working faucet, the water shot out from the detached pipes underneath the sink, soaking my shoes. Drying them as best as I could, I dressed quickly and sat down on the *charpoy* (rope bed). When I opened the book, there was a key and a note. It said I was to go to his room and he would be up as soon as he was able. I locked my door and ran surreptitiously to the end of the hall. His room was identical to mine. I climbed into one of the beds and promptly fell asleep.

I was awakened by a scratching at the door. Jamal wrapped me in his arms and I lay against his shoulder, cool from the outside. His whiskers felt like feathers as he kissed my forehead. The smell of his skin, the barely perceptible odor of jasmine hair oil, his French cologne and the remnants of a cigarette, permeated my nostrils. He carried me to a *charpoy* and went into the bathroom. When he reappeared looking like some Asian demi-god, he completely captured my heart.

Jamal's passion poured through him. He held onto me with a vise-like grip while he ravished my mouth. I felt his maleness harden against me. I responded lavishly to his lovemaking, feeling weightless, drifting in another time and space. We clung together, and when we withdrew we stared at each other in wonder. I dived into the chocolate pools of his eyes, wishing to be inside of this man so I could possess him and be completely possessed by him.

The dream or vision of my adolescence blazed through my mind again and I became rooted to the spot.

Before I could utter a word, Jamal, his face at once fierce and tender, whispered in Urdu, *"Command me, Oh Life of Mine, for I am thy slave."*

We made love again, and I told him of the dream that haunted me until now. With eyes alight with amazement, he admitted to me that the moment he saw me in the club, he had fallen in love with me. We satisfied ourselves with Tantric love many times that night.

I awoke near dawn, to see Jamal standing over me saying in Dari, *"Who art thou woman, that thou disturb my soul!"* His voice vibrated with passion. His face was as fierce as a panther's. Thunder poured from his brows and lightning flickered in his eyes.

"I am thy beloved that thou hath been seeking these many years just as it was thy face I saw in my dreams since age thirteen."

196

He stared at me, and exclaimed in a heated rush in Urdu, *"And what dost thou require of me?"*

"I require thy person to be mine alone. I require a house and a child by thee."

His entire demeanor softened and he replied in a very gentle voice, *"Very well, thou wilt have it. Inshallah, I shalt seal my business and we shalt take a house in England and I shalt give thee my child, Janni mine. Oh Janni, dost maree heh,"* he whispered in Urdu tenderly caressing my face.

I looked up at him with his gentleness permeating my entire being and asked, "And what does that mean, my love?"

"It means that for you, I would do anything!" he replied with heartfelt emotion. "*'Janni'* means 'Life of Mine' and truly you are my life. I can't imagine how I lived before I met you. The *'dost'* is more precious than family. For family is a duty and an obligation that must be carried out, but the *'dost'* is a love that is freely given. Therefore, one must give everything even life itself for the *dost*."

And if I had any doubts about how he felt, this sentence alone told me how much he loved me.

I smiled and said tenderly in Urdu, *"And wouldst thou give thy life for me, Janni?"*

"Yay, my love, that and more. Command me as to what thou wouldst have me do," he said in a voice resonating with passion as we turned towards each other again.

We melted into each other like oils on a canvas and made ecstatic heart-opening love with exclamations of, "Oh *Janni! Janni!*"

When we were done he kissed my eyelids and whispered in Dari, *"I love thee with one thousand lives."*

The depth of our emotion awed us. The nakedness of our souls' shone in our eyes obliterating the nakedness of our bodies lost in our own world beyond time. Words could not express the degree of our feelings. Dumbstruck, we merely gazed at each other in total wonder.

He propped himself up on one elbow and recited the first of many Urdu poems to me:

"Every leaf on every tree in the garden knows that I love my beloved

My beloved knows it not,
But every leaf on every tree knows."

I was incredibly touched and kissed him tenderly. We fell asleep in each other's arms.

When we awoke at dawn, he told me to get ready for the border. We kissed each other deeply and he left to check on the vehicles. I washed, dressed and fell back to sleep.

Jamal returned at eight thirty. He said that his car had broken down and we would be staying here until it was repaired. Sattar had gone for a mechanic. His aunt had suggested I go with them in another car, but Jamal quickly interjected that he'd received a telegram from Heinz saying he was on his way to Jalalabad so he must remain to look after me until Heinz' arrival. The rest of Jamal's retinue continued to Pakistan.

We got undressed and went back to bed and Jamal told me that it was the first time that he had ever slept in the same bed with a woman, and pronounced it a "delightful experience."

I asked him why and he said, "Sex before marriage is forbidden and even after marriage, couples do not sleep in the same room."

"But why, *Janni?*"

"My *Jon,* marriage is a contractual agreement between two families. Marriages between cousins, often first paternal cousins as in our family, are arranged, sometimes in infancy, by our parents. This is our duty to our family and our bloodlines. When we marry, the bride comes to live in the groom's house but both husband and wife have their own sleeping quarters and drawing rooms. Although there is respect and affection for one another, there is not the same romantic attachment as in the West. Men and women do not share confidences with each other. Sex is usually for procreation purposes. The wife comes to the husband's room and then returns to her own quarters. In our family, once the wife knows she is pregnant, she returns to her parents' home and, until the child is two years old, no sexual contact takes place."

This actually gives the woman time to heal and bond with her child as well as preventing continuous pregnancies that take a toll on women aging them quickly, I thought.

"Even in my experience with European women, each maintained their own bedrooms or at the very least their own beds. The idea of sleeping in the same bed is novel to me."

"Then why are you sleeping in the same bed with me?"

"Because I <u>love</u> you!" he exclaimed hugging me to him.

"Have you never loved anyone before?"

He stiffened and pulled away to smoke a cigarette. I watched him as he looked at me sideways, deciding whether or not to open up a painful episode in his life. He sighed and asked me to hold him. I did staring at him in anticipation, and then he began.

Jamal continued in English, "Know that when I was sixteen, I was in love with my first cousin Semina. She was fourteen. We lived in an extended family compound with our parents, siblings and many relatives. Spacious gardens with mango, lime and orange trees surrounded us. There was a profusion of beautiful flowers. My father and my paternal uncle, Semina's father, built this house when we migrated from India to become part of the newly-formed state of East Pakistan. My uncle died soon afterward. Semina was very beautiful and we wanted to marry. We spent many hours walking in these gardens and holding hands.

"One afternoon, Semina's mother, who was with us in the car yesterday, found us seated on a *charpoy* (rope bed) facing each other, planning our lives. My aunt flew into a rage. She demanded to know what I was doing alone with Semina. She threatened to tell my father that I had dishonored Semina, and she would have me ostracized from the family. She slapped Semina hard and called her a prostitute. We were both very young and very frightened. We protested vehemently that nothing had occurred. We loved each other and wanted to be married.

"However, my aunt had other plans for her daughter. She told me to come to see her later in her rooms. I felt confident that when I told her that we were serious about marriage, she would come around. My aunt was once very beautiful. After my uncle died, she became obese. When I entered her room, she was smiling and she held out her hand to me. I took and kissed it, and she asked me to sit down on the bed with her. I felt that Semina and I had a chance. While talking in a very pleasant manner, she suddenly threw open her sari and put my hand on her nakedness. I froze and tried to get away but she said that if I didn't do what she wanted, she would tell my father that I tried to rape Semina. I would be flogged in public, and thrown out of the house."

I understood what Jamal had just said. To be an outcast from the family is the cruelest act that can happen. Family is everything from cradle to grave. They live under one roof watching the passing of the generations as new ones replace them. There is no, 'I am getting my own place.' They are a collective culture rather than an individual one. The threat to have him thrown out of the family was tantamount to a death sentence.

"As for Semina, my aunt had already talked with a very wealthy Muslim prince in India, who, although thirty years older, would set her up for life when she became his wife. My aunt demanded and got the promise of a huge marriage settlement in the event of divorce or his death based on Semina's lineage, education, and great beauty. You see, *Janni*, my aunt never got over our loss of wealth and power when we had to leave the kingdom of Oudh in India. She saw a chance to regain some of her prestige.

"I had never seen a naked woman. I was horrified but knew that if she just raised her voice, servants would appear, and it would be difficult to justify my presence in the women's quarters. I could hardly think of intercourse but my aunt remedied that by performing oral sex. I could feel pleasure, but it was mingled with hatred and disgust. I closed the light so I would not have to see my aunt and pretended it was Semina. After this, my aunt told me to come to her once a week. This continued for two years until I was rescued by my parents' declaration that it was time to attend my grandfather's university in India.

"By this time, I had sworn never to love anyone again and never to marry. Sex was an act of disgust, performed only to satisfy my needs. I carried out my plan having intercourse with a different woman every night. I also swore that no woman would face me when we had sex. I have kept my oath .... until now," he faltered.

My heart broke at the thought of an innocent child being raped by an adult and I began to cry. And now I knew why his aunt had given me an unbelieving look when I entered the Mercedes as the "traveling fiancée." Having intimate knowledge of Jamal, she could intuit what was really going on between us.

"*Oh, Janni! Why dost thou weep,*" he asked in Urdu.

"*For thy suffering all of these years and for having no love. I cannot live without love,*" I cried.

"*Weep not, Janni, for I have found thee at last and never more shalt we be apart,*" he said cradling me in his arms.

"*Janni,* what happened to Semina?"

"She was wed as her mother planned. She lives on a huge estate in India. They had one child before her husband died several years ago."

"Did you ever see her again?"

"Yes, I waited for a decent interval after the mourning period and then I thought maybe there was still a chance for us." He blew a smoke ring into the air.

"What happened when you saw her?"

"She had aged considerably because her husband took many drugs for pleasure and insisted that she participate with him."

"You stopped loving her because she aged?" I asked in surprise.

"No Cath-ay, it was more than that," he paused, "I embraced and tried to kiss her. She refused and told me that she wanted to perform oral sex on me. She said that after their child, her husband became impotent hence all the drug taking. The only way he was partially aroused was through oral sex, and she too received some gratification. Unfortunately, this revived all of the memories of her mother, and how she stole my youth and my sexuality. I told Semina nothing about this of course. But I was so repulsed that I left and have never contacted her again."

"How sad for her, what a wasted life," I said.

I realized that Jamal never experienced true intimacy and pleasure although he had plenty of sex. The wonder on his face when I made love to him betrayed his innocence.

Jamal mused, "I never thought I could love again."

"Before I saw you, Jamal, I was drawn to you. I felt your energy reach out to me when you were sitting at the bar in the club. I was so happy when Heinz brought me to meet you. But you surprised me with your rudeness."

"Because darling mine, the minute I saw you at that club, I thought to myself, 'that's it, I am done.' To fall under a woman's spell after all these years was unthinkable! The first thought that popped into my head when I saw you was, 'If she is not married, I shall marry her and if she is married, I shall have a child by her.' Flustered and betrayed by my own thoughts when you spoke to me in Dari, the only response I could muster was to tell you that I wasn't a Kabuli, meaning a Persianized Afghan, but a Pakhtun who has kept his bloodlines pure for five centuries. 'We speak the pure Afghan language, Pakhto, not Dari which is the language of the court of Kabul.' After this non-sequitur, I had to force myself to remain composed for the remainder of the evening fearing that I'd appear an idiot in your eyes. I was smitten and dumbstruck by you, but couldn't let on. You know British stiff upper lip and all that."

I burst out laughing at all these mental contortions and before long Jamal joined me. I told him that, when I saw him in the club, I had the same exact thought about marrying him or having his child. And then we made long and blinding love.

CHAPTER TWENTY-ONE

Pakistan

"I love thee with one thousand lives." An Afghan saying

When the car was ready, we drove to Pakistan. Weeks of intimacy and tenderness followed. We walked through the conservative Muslim world with its rigid conventions and restrictions as if in a dream. We always managed a surreptitious look or secret touch when we were in company. Even when separated, we were conscious of the other through that electromagnetism that pulsed between us no matter how far apart we were. Jamal was the center of attention, not only because he was royalty, but because of his incredible looks, regal bearing, and natural charisma. Whenever our eyes met for the briefest of instants, an electric message flew between every cell of our bodies.

My mind was focused only on Jamal and our time together. I watched him out of the corner of my eye as he drove the Mercedes. No matter how many times I saw him, his overpowering presence, masculinity, and his physical beauty stunned me. Even his immaculately tailored clothing, and his cologne, intrigued and enthralled me. At the same time, Jamal was trying to understand his own feelings. He knew that my response to him was far more than just animal magnetism and that he too, felt the same, continued to amaze him.

Each moment we spent together was filled to the brim. We had so much to discover, to discuss, to know and to give to each other. Time was suspended. Afghanistan receded into my memory, along with my business, and the same thing happened to Jamal. We were in love. Several of his friends began to complain of his recent inaccessibility ... no mean feat in a society in which all of one's waking hours are spent in the company of family or friends. Days passed with a sameness that most people would find boring.

Jamal retained only his servant, Sattar, who was a deferential man and always spoke in a kind voice to me. He slept on the veranda of our bungalow, ever ready to see to our needs. Each day, Sattar presented Jamal with a pair of newly shined shoes, saw that our clothing was washed and pressed and cleaned Jamal's rifle and small revolver. He spent the rest of the time tinkering with the Mercedes that always seemed to be in various stages of repair. Sattar was instructed to reply to phone calls with "The Sahib is out," and no one could discover where! Most of the time was spent in each other's arms and with occasional brief appearances in the company of Jamal's business acquaintances.

Jamal and I got up at eight o'clock in the morning, and read the Pak Times while having *chai*. As we bathed, Sattar laid out our clothes and brought breakfast. I loved the green chili pepper omelets with grilled chicken livers. Sometimes it was rice with curried chickpeas and vegetables, plus a fried puffy bread called *poori*. We spent the remainder of the morning driving outside of the city into the hills. We meandered through small villages perched in niches of the pine-covered mountains where the air was cool and sweet, and Jamal was unknown. Occasionally, he went to his office. This was a room on the second floor of a two-storey building located in the center of town that housed a company he owned. He imported pharmaceuticals from the West. From the moment Jamal left for work, I missed him and couldn't wait for him to return. I relived our time together until he came back.

One day, bored with reading, I decided to take a walk. I put on a beautiful robin's egg blue *shelwar kamiz* (tunic and pantaloons) that Jamal had made just for me. The tunic had yellow embroidery with tiny mirrors on the front and the cuffs. I strolled down the boulevard for about ten minutes hoping to find a bazaar to amuse myself.

I saw a group of young men, their stares hostile, standing in their khaki-colored *shelwar kamiz* (traditional clothing) on the other side of the road. I smiled and nodded. Their faces turned curious and they began to relax and talk among themselves as they walked towards me. An eerie feeling squirmed through me. Then they jostled each other and some openly grabbed their crotches!

I had used Afghan behavior as a yardstick and that was a horrible mistake! I picked up my pace and started back in the direction of the motel trying to quell my rising panic. They quickly surrounded me, smirking tittering and groaning as they massaged their erect penises through their pantaloons.

Terrified, I looked around for help but there was no one on the street! I pushed them out of my way and ran blindly as a teenage boy on a bicycle veered towards me slipping his fingers across my mouth making his intentions clear that he wanted oral sex. To touch a strange woman's face was the utmost insult. But in their minds, I must be a prostitute since I was alone walking the streets. The laughter from the group of young men mounted as they shoved and hung all over each other congratulating themselves on having "gotten off" on a foreign woman.

Not knowing where the motel was, I kept running headlong as a *tonga* (horse-drawn cart) pulled alongside me. A woman's voice said, "Come, I can help you." She extended her hand and pulled me aboard. I couldn't thank her enough. Assma and I were the same height and build. She had blunt cut short black hair, pinkish coloring, heavy black eyebrows and large round eyes. Her nose was straight with flaring nostrils and her lips were full. She was dressed in a pastel pink *shelwar kamiz* embroidered with silver threads. She flung her white scarf over her shoulders with her heavy mannish hands.

Assma said in her slightly British accent, "Come, come, my dear, don't mind those boys, they are very ignorant. Where are you staying?"

I told her. She spoke to the driver, and around we turned. Assma said that she was the wife of a minister and added that when in Pakistan, I should travel in the company of women or with a man. She smoothed my hair and said that I was very pretty.

"Would you like to come to my house for tea," she asked.

But before I could answer, Assma slipped her hand in the opening of my shirt and caressed my breast.

Sickened, I lunged from the *tonga* and ran into the motel. I heard Assma calling for me to wait. Jamal grabbed me as I plunged through the doorway bursting into sobs. I blubbered out my story.

"*Janni, Janni,*" he said tenderly in Urdu, "*Tell me thy desire to go out and I shalt arrange a car and a driver for thee.*"

"That woman was a lesbian!"

"Most likely my *jon,*" he said in a matter of fact way.

The shocked expression on my face caused him to laugh. "Cath-ay-jon, homosexuals exist the world over. Have you never seen such people before?"

"Yes, in Afghanistan and New York. But I never had a lesbian grab my breast!

After I calmed down, I asked, "What does the Quran say about homosexuality?"

"It is expressly forbidden by the Holy Book as I am sure it is by the Bible. But homosexuality still exists."

"But she was married, *Janni*," I exclaimed in alarm as if that prevented homosexuality.

"Yes, darling mine, many male and female homosexuals are married and have children. As long as people observe custom, we don't make a distinction in our society."

That ended my solitary walks. Allowed in Afghanistan, they were prohibited here.

Jamal usually returned to our room around two o'clock in the afternoon. He would order grilled chicken or lamb kebabs, creamy yoghurt, salad, *roti*, and *chai*. We spent the rest of the day in the room talking, reading and making love to escape from the over one-hundred-degree heat and its ninety-five-degree humidity. The weather made walking even a few steps from the door to the car, like taking a steam bath. Our clothes clung to us as if we had walked through a waterfall. The day seemed to be punctuated by taking numerous showers.

Our bungalow looked out on many flowers in a huge garden surrounded by fifteen foot high hedges. At six o'clock in the evening, Jamal and I would go out on the veranda to watch the sunset. It tried to hide behind the white dome of the mosque that peeped from the hedge across the way. An old, scratchy, record blaring the call to prayer, punctured the hum of the city as it wound down for the night.

Jamal called room service and got Pak beer for us while we talked and enjoyed the night air until around ten o'clock. Some of Jamal's friends appeared, and we went out to the Intercontinental Hotel for a late supper. Frequented by tourists and wealthy Pak businessmen anxious to make Western contacts, it was busy until one o'clock in the morning.

The Hotel was very modern with all the comforts of twentieth-century living. It also had nice touches from the country where it was located. There were beautiful Pakistani and Indian carpets on the floors and hand-embroidered wall coverings. The food was very expensive by Pak standards. One meal cost from two to five dollars whereas traditional Pak meals only cost fifty cents to a dollar.

The Intercon was one of our favorite late-night haunts, away from inquisitive eyes and wagging tongues. I feasted on French onion soup and grilled cheese sandwiches ... a welcome change from Pak food. After supper, we walked in the hotel garden by moonlight or took a short drive around the now silent bazaars, and then to bed around two o'clock in the morning. Jamal and I had become friends as well as lovers and dreamed of a future together.

Pakistan was still very much an internal, family-oriented society. There were no places to eat outside of the home for men and women. Couples were confined to the Intercontinental Hotel and the Shezan Restaurant. In the Shezan, there was a separate area reserved for families where the women were protected by screens so they could lift their veils to eat. If they wished to eat in the bazaars, women remained in the cars while the men bought the food and brought it to them.

Several weeks later and still bored with sitting in the hotel all day waiting for Jamal, I decided to solve the problem of my walking alone outside by wearing a *burkha,* the Pak women's veil. Jamal sent a servant to the bazaar to get one for me. I was delighted and the very next day, I slipped out of the hotel in this disguise after Jamal had gone to work. Walking alone on the street was no longer a problem. It was as if I didn't exist, no one even glanced my way.

As I came to a crossing, a horse-drawn cart collided with a rickshaw. A crowd of about thirty men and boys gathered to argue and gesticulate with the two drivers. In the throes of the accident, the woman who had been riding in the cart was thrown out. She was very beautiful with exquisite local garb, pounds of jewelry and extraordinary make-up. I knew she was a prostitute. She picked herself up from the ground and suddenly a small group of eight young men noticed her. One made a grab for her but she slipped out of his hands and started running, with the men after her. I kept close to the walls of the buildings and followed them slowly at a distance. The woman ran down an alley with the men in hot pursuit. It was a blind alley filled with open carts bearing quilts, pots and pans, firewood and other household goods. No one else was around. I peered around the corner of one of the carts near the mouth of the alley. I saw the prostitute climb up on the cart filled with quilts, pull off her pantaloons and lay on her back. Without a sound, the men fell over themselves to be the first to penetrate her. Fired up, they took turns, each one spending no more than 3 seconds.

I thought to myself, perhaps this was the best way for her to protect herself from a beating, a mauling, rape by thirty men or God alone knew what else. But then she did what I thought was an extraordinary thing. As the young men were adjusting their clothing, she got on her hands and knees lifted her tunic presenting her bare bottom to them. The men lost no time in using her mouth and her anus coming on a gasp or a sigh. The entire procedure took about two minutes. Whether she did this to be sure they were satisfied and wouldn't come after her again or just as part of her normal service. I guess this is the role of the prostitute in a society where sex outside of marriage is prohibited. She served as a relief for men's pent-up sexual tensions.

When they were done, they quietly walked out of the alley without a passing nod or a sound. What amazed me most was that all this was done in complete silence on the part of both the men and the prostitute.

I didn't fear for her life because I felt that she was making the best of a bad situation. I also felt that because she was a prostitute it was less traumatic for her than if she had been an ordinary woman. I also realized the protection afforded by the *burkha*. I began to wonder if she needed help and what kind of help I could possibly provide. After a few minutes, she got up, put on her pantaloons, straightened her clothing and calmly walked out of the alley. Stunned, I stayed hidden for awhile absorbing that incredible scene and wondering if the same thing would have happened to me if I had submitted when I was trapped in a circle by the group of teenage boys several weeks ago. I never mentioned any of this to Jamal, knowing he would prohibit my outings as too dangerous and he'd be right. However, this scene abruptly dampened my curiosity about what went on in the streets.

Because Jamal and I were not married, we were prohibited visiting the homes of his friends, denying me access to Pak women. For unmarried wealthy Pak males, this limited them to the "Gymkhana

Club," based on the British club. We fared no better there. The appearance of a woman, particularly a foreign one, was greeted with lascivious stares and started tongues wagging as to whom I was, and what I was doing in the club. This was the very thing we wanted to avoid. I felt very restricted here. Living in the men's world, I was considered a prostitute or at least fair game by Pak men.

In Afghanistan, I rented my own house, kept servants, moved freely in the city in the company of Afghans or foreigners. Here, no women except prostitutes were found alone in hotels. So when Jamal was out, I was guaranteed several daily propositions from the hotel clerks, waiters and any Pak men who spied me in the restaurant. If I told Jamal, he would confront them and be told that I was absolutely mistaken. I gave up telling him since he got very angry and was powerless to do anything in the face of their denials.

Whenever I entered a restaurant, every eye was upon me. All I had to do at any given moment was raise my eyes from the menu or the table to meet the gaze of everyone present. In the West, men at this point look away so as not to be caught staring and wait for an opportunity to approach. However, since there is neither a way nor a place to meet a woman, a Pak man makes his intention clear by never lowering his eyes. It was impossible for me to finish a meal without some diner sending a note propositioning me with many polite phrases. At first, I was amused, but then began to dread the restaurants, and took to eating in my room just to avoid the constant unnerving scrutiny of my every movement and the inevitable propositions.

After a month in Pakistan, I had to return to Kabul to finish my shipments. The time of my departure for America was drawing near. Jamal booked a flight on the tiny twelve seat plane that crossed the Khaibar from Peshawar to Kabul. He promised to come to Kabul in a week's time and then we would return to Pakistan to be together until I had to leave for good. Our sorrow at parting was mingled with the joy of knowing, that in a short while we would be together again. We remained on the airfield several yards away from the plane, watching the snake of Pak men in their Western suits of brown, gray and black. First, they showed their boarding cards to the steward and then identified their luggage for the baggage handlers.

Curious I asked Jamal, "Why *Janni* are the men pointing to their luggage before they board?"

"Because my *jon*, if you do not do this, the baggage handlers, bugger them, sell your luggage in the bazaars, and declare it 'lost or unclaimed.'"

I had to laugh at the ingenuity of these people! The steward approached Jamal and said, "Please your Highness, allow this Lady to board so we may take off."

As I mounted the steps to the plane, after pointing to the last luggage left on the cart, I heard Jamal call in Urdu, *"Khoda ha'fess* (Go with God), *darling mine, inshallah, I shalt see thee soon."*

I turned to see him waving, standing in the hot sun on the red earth that gave off its acrid odor mixed with diesel. My heart contracted and I wanted to rush into his arms once more, but I just smiled and waved as the steward, a slim young Pak began to plead with me to enter the cabin.

I settled into my seat and an Urdu song filtered into the cabin from the loudspeaker, *"Alas, it was only when we hath passed over that we learned everything we hath seen was a dream and everything we hath heard was but a short tale."*

I thought of the impermanence of life, and I made up my mind to enjoy my time with Jamal as long as I could.

CHAPTER TWENTY-TWO

The Eṽnṽchṣ

"Oh, Moon! Moon!
The face of my lover is like the moon
On its fourteenth night,
Nestled in the heavens of his jet black hair,
His eyebrows, the bow that sends his lashes
As arrows into my heart."
The Author

I returned to Kabul the day after Christmas and rushed to check on my tailors. I wanted to finish my work so Jamal and I could spend some time together before I had to return to New York.

Deciding to use Afghan fabrics to create western-style clothing for export, I hired a tailor named the Merciful Master. My Afghan friends assured me that Merciful Master was indeed a master tailor. What I didn't realize was that his expertise was only in the department of Afghan clothing.

Most Afghans had little concept of tight-fitting Western clothing with buttons and zippers. Theirs was a tradition of drawstrings, folds and boat-neck style necklines. Putting a tiny stone in a piece of cloth and sewing it closed, made the rare button. The buttonhole was a loop of braided string or leather at the other end of the neckline. The Merciful Master's lack of tailoring techniques, let alone that of Western designs, was soon made apparent when I requested short bodice summer blouses with balloon sleeves. I purchased soft white Afghan cotton for the blouses themselves and had it dyed in the bazaars in the current American fashion colors of maroon, royal blue, and black. I also purchased the white Kandahari wedding embroidered shirtfronts from my friend and brother, Servant-of -the-Creator, and dyed them as well.

I gave the "master tailor" a sample of the finished product that I wanted and he replied, *"Very well, Khanum."*

The results of his handiwork were incredible. Some of the embroidered pieces were too long for a bodice blouse. Undaunted, the Merciful Master and his two apprentices, an adult dwarf and a boy of twelve, brilliantly cut off the bottom inch of embroidery that ended in points. As if this weren't bad enough, they put this amputated leftover upside down on the back of the blouse! Actually, if you never saw the original embroidery, you would marvel at the Afghan cleverness of having small mountains starting up your back from the waistband of the blouse. Fortunately, there were only a few of these "masterpieces" and I absorbed them into my personal collection. Oddities abounded in every job I gave them, but none was more serious than "the Chinese brocade cowboy shirt escapade." This occurred when the Merciful Master was ill, and sent his brother, Lamp-of-the-Most-High, to replace him. When I went to Pakistan, I had left the tailors to work on cowboy shirts from expensive Chinese brocade.

One fine morning, I stepped onto the mud embankment of Merciful's shop, wiped my boots as best as I could, and crouched to enter the five-foot doorway of the one-room shop. Immediately all work ceased, and the three tailors smiled at me while we exchanged the greeting.

Lamp-of-the-Most-High was a carbon copy of Merciful minus the rakish grin. They were obviously twins. He stood up and put his right hand over his heart, and we began to greet one another more formally in Dari.

"Oh Khanum, may thou never tire."

"May Allah grant thee long life, Oh Master Tailor."

"If it please thee, be seated, Oh Khanum."

"May I be acquainted with thy name," I asked as I sat down.

"I, praise be to God, am Lamp-of-the-Most-High, the brother of the Merciful Master who sends his greetings to thee. He hath taken an illness and cannot honor thy presence this day."

Merciful sometimes took a day off here and there, especially in the month of fasting (Ramazan) when neither food nor water was allowed from sunrise to sunset for the entire month. This is to remind Muslims that there are people in the world who suffer hunger and thirst daily.

Food and drink were no problem for Merciful, but it was the relinquishing of his daily snuff that put him in a bad mood. He needed a day or two off in the bosom of his family where he could do as he pleased while feigning illness to the outside world.

"*Ill?*" I cried in Dari in mock surprise. "*Oh this is very bad, may Allah preserve him. Inshallah, he will be whole again when the sun makes itself known tomorrow.*"

"*Inshallah,*" he conceded solemnly.

When I asked Lamp-of-the-Most-High about the Chinese brocade cowboy shirts, I noticed a subtle shift in the room and the apprentices suddenly became very busy. The master tailor asked the boy to bring a shirt. He deferentially, almost humbly with downcast eyes, held it out in his two hands for my inspection. The collar, pocket, and front of the shirt looked fine. I unfolded it to see the rest of it and my eyes bulged out of my head in shock!

I addressed Lamp-of-the-Most-High in Dari, "*Oh My Dear Sir! What may I ask is this? This shirt is no good! One sleeve is too long and the other is too short!*"

Rushing to defend his tarnished honor, Lamp-of-the-Most-High replied, "*Oh no Khanum! This is indeed very good. The long sleeve is good if thy hand becomes cold and the short sleeve, why, this is excellent if one wishes to study thy timepiece!*"

At this explanation, I couldn't contain myself any longer, buried my face in my hands and began to laugh hysterically.

Seeing this, Lamp-of-the-Most-High, King-of-the-Adepts, and Servant-of-the-Rose lost no time in joining me in my hilarity.

Half choking, I told Lamp-of-the-Most-High in Dari, "*If thy mother were present, she wouldst declare that this specimen must have been created solely for thee who hath the mind to conceive of such a monstrosity!*"

At this, they fell about the shop in helpless hysterics, and shrugged their shoulders exclaiming, "*But Oh Khanum, whiten our faces with thy forgiveness!*"

I counted the days until Jamal was due to arrive. New Year's Eve found me at the club in the company of my friends. I was in a champagne haze, mentally with Jamal. They tried to cheer me up with "Maybe the flights were delayed," or "Maybe his car broke down." I was not to be consoled. New Year's Day came and went as well as January second and third. The fourth was the last day he could arrive since the next flight from Pakistan was not due for three more weeks. By that time, I would be back in New York.

I busied myself in the old bazaar, collecting antique jewelry and visiting the shops of merchant friends, to avoid going back to my house, since I felt he hadn't arrived on the one o'clock flight.

To cheer myself, I called on my Hindu friends, the two brothers and their families who ran a travel agency here. They made me feel welcome my first time in Kabul. I was a woman alone among what they described as a "barbarous people," compared to India, who at least had been the recipient of "Britain's civilizing influence." They appointed themselves my protectors and telephoned my hotel room every few days asking how they could be of service to me. Out of respect and affection, I addressed them as Uncleji, Daddyji, and Auntieji. Daddyji's son Shashi and I, sometimes on a Friday, took Uncleji's dilapidated Volkswagen Beetle outside of Kabul for a picnic lunch of Indian delicacies prepared by Auntieji.

So familiar with them and their daily routine that without telephoning, I walked the one mile to their travel agency and residence, assured that they would be at lunch. Their street was one of the few paved ones in Kabul. The travel agency was the first floor of a smooth white stucco building with a painted brown wood trim. It had a large window with their name on it in dark blue letters outlined in gold. To reach their residence, they had only to leave their office, follow the side of the building into the alley, and climb a set of large stone steps to the next storey. I knocked on the wooden door of the house only to hear Uncleji ask in Dari, *"Who art thou?"*

I replied in English, "Oh Good Sir, I have come to ask your assistance."

Without opening the door Uncleji again repeated, *"Who art thou and what is thy wish?"*

I laughed and said, "It is Cathy, Uncleji."

He slipped the bolt right away, opened the door, and said with a laugh, "Well, well, well!"

Auntieji came out of the kitchen; the familiar vermilion streak following the part in the center of her hair matched the red flowers on her pale yellow sari. Her large brown eyes sparkling, Auntieji came towards me palms together, and we both said, "Namaste," the traditional Indian greeting to each other. This day, everyone else was in India except Uncleji, Auntieji, and Shashi, who was tall and well-built with thick black hair, and a ready smile. He adopted an American accent and tried all the latest slang on me. He, too, wore only western clothing like his father and uncle. Auntieji was a tiny woman with kind eyes who was always adorned in the traditional sari.

As I entered the *saloon*, a soft fragrance of curry and sweet hair oils transported me to Pakistan and Jamal in a flash! When I was seated, Shashi rushed into the room and extended his hand. He boomed with an American accent, "Hi Cathy, what's happening," while he shook my hand. I laughed and replied, "*Namaskar, bhai-jon* (Hello, dear brother)." Shashi laughed in delight and rushed off to bring us orange sodas. Auntieji returned to the kitchen putting the finishing touches to lunch. I was happy that I had guessed correctly, and they had not eaten yet. Of course, it was assumed that I would stay for lunch. It would have been an offense if I left before eating with them. Auntieji returned from the kitchen, sat on a chair beside me and showed me her palm with the words, "Please, you tell me."

I started laughing. It seems that it had been bandied about Kabul that I was a palm reader just because I read several of the women's hands at a party recently. Palm reading here was very simple, the women only had two questions, the first one was when would they marry, and the second was how many children they would have. Auntieji asked several questions, and then I was treated to a wonderful lunch of spicy ground lamb kebabs and a vegetable and chickpea stew. After lunch, I got up to leave, and they all pressed me to stay so I had another cup of tea. Shashi wanted to know when we could go on another picnic. I promised him it would be soon, thanked them all, and left. I spent the rest of the afternoon in the club, harmonizing with Tony, a Chinese from Singapore, while he accompanied me on his guitar. He was the leader of the club's band that consisted of an Italian piano player and two Afghans on sax and drums. Around five o'clock, I was so depressed, and could not face my empty house alone. I dragged Tony home with me.

When Mowlowdowt answered the gate, I knew that Jamal had not arrived and felt heartsick. My throat locked, and I had a dull ache in my stomach. Tony and I went into the bedroom. He perched cross-legged on one end of the bed and began strumming his guitar as I sat in front of from him on the carpet near the blazing stove.

After a while, I heard a banging at the gate and my heart skipped a few beats. The bedroom door was thrown open. There stood Jamal with that familiar fierce look on his face! I was so stunned that I remained frozen to the floor. In an instant, I grasped the situation of Tony, a "strange man," sitting on my bed, and that propelled me forward. As I hugged and kissed Jamal, all his familiar scents filled my nostrils. I could feel him trembling from the uncertainty of finding me still in Kabul. Silent as a cat, Tony eased himself out of the room.

Jamal threw himself down on the carpet, and exclaimed in Pakhto, *"Praise be to God, I am with thee at last!"*

He told me that he decided to drive over early on December thirtieth to surprise me, but his uncle died, and he was forced to turn back to pay his respects. After a few moments of silence, we jumped on each other, hugging and kissing until, unable to be apart any longer, made mad, passionate love.

Settled on the bed with the wine in our glasses perfumed by amber essential oil and sandalwood incense enveloping us in its gauzy embrace, I said to Jamal in Dari, *"Oh my Lord, tell me more tales of thy lineage."*

"Yes My Lady," he replied in English, "I shall tell you of the treachery of Gulzar's great-grandmother, Rani (Queen) the chief courtesan of Sultan Noureddin Yusuf Khan, ruler of Oudh and my great grandsire. My great grandsire, may peace be upon him, had four wives, and more than one hundred concubines. He sired seventeen sons and many daughters by three of his wives. The number of children by his concubines was not recorded. Noureddin's first wife, Latifa Begum, was my great-grandmother. She was childless and ruled with an iron hand, keeping peace among the women and children, and thwarting most of the intrigues among the eunuchs."

"*Janni*, what exactly is a 'eunuch?'"

"Eunuchs, *Janni* mine, are men who volunteer to be castrated. Some were castrated against their will by rulers when they were appointed as guardian of the Sultan's *hareem* (women's quarters). Many were born as hermaphrodites, and rejected by society for being neither male nor female and chose to be women."

"Why does a Sultan want eunuchs to guard the women in his *hareem*?"

"To ensure that he alone impregnates his wives and concubines. The eunuchs also act as a police force to deter different forms of mayhem committed by those inside the *hareem* who bear jealousy towards one another."

"What jealousy occurs since according to the Quran, all wives must be treated as equals?"

"That is true, but no one can control the Sultan. If he deems one of his wives or concubines as his favorite and spends months or even years with her ignoring the others, jealousy raises its ugly head and strangulations, 'accidental' falls, poisonings and suffocations occur. The eunuchs gladly participate in such doings. They are filled with hatred and revenge for what has been done to them and are capable of aiding such crimes. The eunuchs also form strong ties of loyalty and devotion to their mistresses and are willing to suffer much for their sakes. They actually run the inner court and are masters of intrigue.

"Oh My Lord, and what says the Holy Quran on the subject of eunuchs?"

"It is forbidden by the Holy Book to create castratos. But rulers resorted to purchasing already castrated slaves or prisoners from other countries where it was not forbidden."

"What role has the eunuch in society," I asked.

"Some eunuchs are confidants or advisors to the Sultan, some act as chauffeurs to the children, others are escorts for the women of the household, going to parties, weddings, births, and the like.

"Still others are cooks, and most are very talented in this area. Eunuchs also had a large role in the education of the princes, who after the age of seven, were cared for by the eunuchs in the men's quarters who although castrated chose to remain men. They were the best teachers in the land in the military and liberal arts."

"What is their role today, My Lord?"

"Most are employed as cooks, dancers, or musicians at births and weddings."

"Know, My Beloved that Rani, the courtesan, was beyond Latifa's control. The apple of Noureddin's aging eyes; she plotted and schemed to advance her son's position at court. Noureddin fathered Kamal, Rani's son, she also had a daughter by her first patron who lived somewhere outside the palace grounds. She found her chance when Noureddin's army, headed by his sons, went to conquer a nearby kingdom. She conspired with the eunuchs who would do any heinous crime for a price. One, Rashid *Bibi*, masterminded the plan.

One of ten children, he was born in a small village. He had both male and female genitalia. Teased and abused by both his family and the villagers, at the age of twelve, he ran away from home to the nearest city. It was no time at all before he was taken in by the eunuchs. At the age of fifteen, Rashid submitted to voluntary castration and began to dress as a woman, adding the title of "*Bibi*" or "Lady" to his name. Given a choice of a vocation as a singer, dancer, musician, nanny, or cook, he chose to learn how to play the *sitar*, an instrument with over twenty strings. His fame spread and the various eunuch communities vied with each other to have him reside with them to increase their renown and their earning capacity.

When Rasheed *Bibi* was invited to the four year and four-month ceremony of one of the sultan's daughters, his craftsmanship so delighted Noureddin Khan that he was made the chief musician of the *hareem*."

Tell me more, Janni mine," I prompted.

"Eunuchs in the royal household were in a unique position. They acted as a bridge between the *mardana*, men's quarters, and the *zenana*, women's quarters. Eunuchs were relied upon to carry information between the two worlds as well as supply goods and services and were paid handsomely in bribes, in addition to the large salary and upkeep they already received. The majority of the women in any ruler's *hareem* were young women. After the sultan bedded them, and they became pregnant, they were relegated to the *zenana* as new favorites took their place. Conjugal duty is mandatory with wives but not with concubines. Lonely and bored, they bribed the eunuchs with money, jewelry, and land to smuggle lovers and hallucinogens into the *zenana*.

"Rashid *Bibi* set himself up as a conduit for whatever the concubines needed and amassed a small fortune. Rani, the courtesan, bribed him with a very large piece of well placed, arable land with a palace on it. Motivated by greed at the thought of what he could do when he retired; Rashid *Bibi* agreed to eliminate the princes for her. He and several other eunuchs fed the army wrong information on the enemy's positions and the majority of Noureddin's sons were killed.

"Even though Latifa Begum was childless herself, she adopted Noureddin's son by his second wife who died giving birth to him. Jalaluddin (Divine Fire of the Faith) was her favorite, and she spoiled him unmercifully. Prior to the battle, Latifa had a premonition from a dream and begged thirty-year-old Jalal to refrain from the fight. Jalal, hot blooded for battle, scoffed at his mother's alarms and took off on a hunt with his servants. The Begum gathered her trusted emissaries who bribed some men to act as bandits, killing Jalal's favorite horse, and taking him prisoner. Bound, gagged, and blindfolded, he was returned to the palace and thrust into an underground room.

"In preparation for the family gathering at the fortieth day of mourning, Rani again bribed the eunuchs to poison the remaining male children. Then she went to Noureddin who was bedridden with grief and pretended hysteria over these tragedies. She put forward her son as the legitimate heir. Noureddin's bereavement took precedence over sense, and he agreed that Kamal would be the sultan of Oudh upon his death.

"But Rani did not reckon with the power of Latifa Begum who also bribed the eunuchs until one of them reported Rasheed *Bibi*'s activities. Discovering Rani's treachery, the Begum arranged for Rani to fall from a great height. She sustained many broken bones as well as a concussion. The Begum had her locked in an unused damp latrine where, five days later, she died a slow death from her untreated injuries. Without his mother, Kamal, age seventeen, was no match for the *Begum*. She had him imprisoned where he died five years later on the day of his mother's death.

"The Begum then had Rashid *Bibi*, and his cohorts brought before her. The other eunuchs, terrified of their punishment, groveled and crawled on their stomachs in her presence while Rasheed *Bibi* entered humbly but remained standing. He knew that Noureddin was near death over the loss of his sons, and would probably decree a public beheading."

"Latifa Begum said in Pakhto, '*Thou hath spilled the blood of our future for thy own gain.*'

'*Oh Begum, what punishment hath My Lord set for me and these ones?*'"

"The crying and begging of the other eunuchs rose to a crescendo. But Latifa commanded silence with a quick movement of her hand. She turned to the guards and cried, *'Behead them in the courtyard!'*

Rashid Bibi smiled to himself, and bowed low, starting to back out of the room."

'Oh Rashid Bibi!' commanded Latifa, *'Thy Lord is facing the angels of judgment and is in no mind to punish thee. Therefore, it is decreed that thy punishment be decided by the sultanas* (queens) *whose sons thou hath destroyed.'*

"Rashid *Bibi's* blood froze, and he turned to stone. To be beheaded by the king was to die a swift and honorable death. But to be given to the women meant a fiendish end. He fell on his knees and begged the Begum to take his life now. She turned her back to him and left the room as the guards grabbed him, and carried him screaming and fighting into the *zenana.*

"The mothers fell upon him with their knives, and several hours later when they had removed the top layer of skin from his entire body, they had him dragged into the courtyard where a huge pit was dug under their direction. He was buried up to his chin, and one of the guards pinched his nose. When his mouth opened they jammed a stick between his upper and lower teeth, and the women took turns urinating into his mouth until he drowned.

"Then Latifa brought out the one son she had saved, Jalaluddin Yusuf Khan, and placed him on the throne when Noureddin died. Her last words to her husband as he lay dying were: *'Behold, thy son lives!'* and *'Never trust the words of a harlot.'*

"After this incident, it was decreed that courtesans could never establish living quarters on the premises, but must arrive after dark and leave before dawn. Also, any courtesan who became pregnant must abort the fetus or be killed to prevent such machinations again.

"When the British arrived, the eunuchs were seen as sub-human and lost all status and pensions. Then, we the rulers were deposed, and our princely estates were broken up. Mimicking the manners of the English, we rulers only married once, burying the ancient practices of polygamy and concubinage," Jamal concluded.

I was enthralled and loved hearing Jamal's history. Many Americans can only trace their ancestry back through their grandparents or great-grandparents.

CHAPTER TWENTY-THREE

The Face of My Lover

"Alas, it was only when we hath passed over
that we learned everything we hath seen was a dream
and everything we hath heard was but a short tale."
Urdu song

One day, I suggested that we take a bath together. At first, he protested, but soon he submitted, exclaiming, "Oh you and your odd ways!" Then without another word he tenderly began washing me with a mystified expression on his face.

I threw him a perplexed look, and he burst out, "By God, I swear! I must love you, woman! When His Highness Jamal Mahmood Yusuf Khan takes a bath with a female ... !"

We both laughed until our sides ached.

One night after we made love, he looked at me and said in Pakhto, *"I wouldst have a son by thee, Oh Life of Mine."*

We kissed tenderly and I glowingly asked, "And what would you call this son of ours?"

"If he were thy child, I wouldst call him Sahibzada Jamal Mahmood Yusuf Khan," he whispered in Urdu in a voice filled with passion as we turned to each other again.

The Afghans, including my servant, were delighted and awed by Jamal's regal bearing, his beauty, and the fact that he was a nobleman. Mowlowdowt, when he spoke of Jamal, put his right hand over his heart and said, "He is a <u>very</u> good man, Lady Mistress."

After two weeks in wintry Kabul, we decided to head for the warmth of Pakistan. Jamal hired a car and driver, and we leisurely drove back to Pakistan through the corkscrew road of the now snowy Khaibar. We descended in an ever downward spiral to the plains of Pakistan. All the while, the driver sporting a golden mirrored skull cap and an ancient dusty western suit jacket kept his hand on the horn. It was impossible to see around the curves. The road was just wide enough for two vehicles one in each direction.

Once we were brought up short by an overcrowded bus with goats and sheep bleating on its roof. A leftover from World War I, it eased passed us, inch by inch. Its back tire was not even on the road as rocks and dirt cascaded with a clatter, into the abyss below.

We were only in Pakistan a short while when Jamal was invited to have dinner at a friend's newly purchased hotel. The owner, Faizal Khan, a Pakhtun, an American acquaintance, Jamal and I were sitting at the bar that was decorated like all the Hilton Hotel chains around the globe. The room was very dark. The only light came from the stage lights in the ceiling around the square bar that stood in the center of the room. There were small round tables each with a tiny candle in the center. Four leather armchairs huddled around each table. Sharif was very proud of his hotel and hoped to do a brisk tourist business, as well as attracting Pakistani businessmen. Sharif asked if we wanted drinks, and called over a blonde English waitress to take our order. After she had gone to fill the order, Sharif said that he decided to hire western help as a further inducement for foreign business.

After a few drinks, the American, George, remarked that he found our waitress very attractive, and everyone agreed. When she delivered a new round, George raised his glass and proposed a toast to her. We all raised our glasses. The waitress smiled, raised her empty hand in a toast and said, "Cheers."

Jamal held his glass up to her and said, "You may take a sip from mine."

She replied that she was not allowed to drink on duty, smiled and left. Angry because in this culture only beloveds or husbands and wives share the same utensils, I took a deep breath and turned to Jamal. I pulled his shirt collar open with my left hand, took his full drink with my right, and poured it down the inside of his shirt. Everyone froze. Jamal jumped up and started brushing off his soaking wet shirt and pants. The others were speechless.

Then I said, "And now being a true Pakhtun, and a Yusuf Khan, the Sahib will apologize to you gentlemen for having forced me to act in such an indecorous manner in a public place."

"The lady is quite right. I do apologize," said Jamal.

"Thank you, gentlemen, for accepting his apology. I will now retire for the evening."

I walked out and took a taxi to our hotel. A short time later Jamal entered the room, took off his wet clothes and sat on the edge of the bed.

"Hath thou forgiven me, Janni?" he asked in Pakhto.

"Nay. 'Twill take some time."

"Thou must have a lot of patience to love a Yusuf Khan, for we art very difficult to get along with. But no one can love thee as we do."

Then he puckered his magnificent mouth, and brought his head down, and pressed his closed lips on mine from side to side until my lips parted to admit his tongue. He used it to caress my gums and teeth very slowly while my soul met his.

He whispered, "Don't go away from me, *Janni*, I need you forever.

"Forever is too short a time for us, Jamal," I whispered back.

And then he began to sing that song in Urdu that Muni *Begum*, the courtesan sang in her youth when she gave court performances for his father. *"Nakaray"* meaning "Don't leave me."

One day, when Jamal was called to the office, I went to the Intercon to enjoy the pool, and have some lunch. I struck up a conversation with a tall, slim, dark Pakistani from Karachi who had just returned from a business trip to Saudi Arabia. Since I knew that Jamal would not be back until the late afternoon, I was glad of some pleasant company that would eliminate the ever-present stares, and propositions at the restaurant. Afterward, when Iqbal and I discovered that we were in the same hotel, we decided to share a taxi. He invited me to dinner later, but I excused myself telling him that I was not alone.

Jamal and I had our customary Pak beers as we watched the sunset. He was casual when he mentioned that he had invited a "certain Sahib" to join us. I was pleased, always eager to meet new company. Half an hour later, Sattar ushered Iqbal into the *saloon*. I was very surprised as I glanced at the man's uneasy expression, and then at Jamal's face. Jamal seemed calm but underneath I detected a restless current, like that of a panther about to spring. Before I could say anything, Jamal and Iqbal began the traditional greeting, and introductions were made. Iqbal accepted a drink, and we all made polite conversation. After an uncomfortable amount of time, Iqbal rose to leave. He offered many thanks and polite expressions as he backed out of the room. No sooner had he turned to put his hand on the doorknob, than Jamal rose, and with two strides overtook him. As Iqbal turned in surprise, Jamal gave him a blow to the jaw that almost embedded him in the door! I sat there horrified, unable to move, as his unconscious body sank to the floor. Sattar took the man over his shoulder like a sack of wheat and carried him to his room.

Then Jamal turned and came over to me, his fierce face within an inch of mine, and said in a low voice accentuating each syllable, "Know that I am possessive! I have the preemptive right to act as I wish because I love you, woman!"

Switching to Pakhto, he said, *"How dare thou break bread with another man? If thou felt the necessity of this, then thou shouldst have paid. He should never hath been allowed to pay!"*

"But why, *Janni?*" I asked totally perplexed.

"You are my guest, *Janni*. No one has the right to feed you but me. I am your host in my country. This man has offended my honor by transgressing the law of *melmastia* (hospitality to the guest)."

Then eyes smoldering, Jamal rubbed my fingertips against his lips and mustache over and over, gently nibbled them, and sat down to his drink as if nothing had happened. Even though Jamal grew up in India with its British influence, away from Pakhtun culture, I saw that he still observed the rigid code of the Pakhtuns *"Pakhtunwali."* Beneath this very westernized exterior, beat the heart of a true son of the Yusufziais. I had no idea who had informed Jamal. It could have been anyone from the hotel personnel to any of the Pak men who were having lunch at that time. Jamal was very well known, and I stood out as a foreigner.

After that episode, Jamal and I spent our every waking moment together. One day I asked him, "What is good about being a Muslim, *Janni?*"

He smiled and replied, "Oh my love, the best of Islam is that you feed the poor and offer salutations to those you know and those that you don't know."

"But, *Janni*, why would you offer salutations to those you don't know?"

"Because my darling, this shows my respect for God and humankind for being born a nobleman. Besides, to be born a nobleman is a gift but to die a nobleman is an achievement."

"So *Janni*, why do some men in the Muslim world beat their wives?"

"Because my love, they are ignorant, and don't know the true meaning of Islam. Don't people in the West abuse their wives?"

"Yes *Janni*, unfortunately, they do."

"Our Prophet Mohammad may peace and blessings be upon him, said, 'No person should be hurt by the tongue or by the hand.'"

"What other things did Mohammed say of women?"

Jamal leaned towards me and said in a gentle voice, "If you say the name of your father with reverence once, you must say that of your mother twenty-five times."

"And why is that, *Janni*?"

"Because, darling mine, she gave her body to nourish you while you were inside her, and then she gave the milk of her breasts to give you strength to live. Do you know that a man must supply his wife not only with the necessities of food, clothing and a home but luxuries within his means? The more beautiful the wife, the more luxuries must be given. And I am afraid that with you, *Janni* I will be very broke," he said with a chuckle.

I lovingly kissed him and said, "Tell me more, *Janni*."

"After my grandfather founded the university, in the great state of Oudh, he made the decision to first have us educated by a private tutor in the ways and customs of the English. Grandfather sent one of his sons to England to find a proper tutor for all of us boys and girls. My uncle returned with a Miss White. She was an excellent instructor. We all grew up in the *pukka* (correct) English way with language, customs, and manners. Miss White never married. She was paid handsomely. She lived with us for thirty years.

One day, she went to my grandmother, and through an Urdu interpreter said, *'Oh Noble Lady, 'tis time for me to retire, and return to my home in England.'*

"My grandmother replied, *'Thy home? This is thy home. Who is left in England to care for thee? Thou must stay with us, and we shalt care for thee as thou hath cared for us these many years. Our hearts are thine, do not abandon us now.'*

"You see *Janni* mine, once we have given our hearts, tis forever. We shall never abandon you, whether a servant or a beloved."

Several weeks later, our idyllic life was brought to a halt. I received a cable from my Afghan shipper that my goods were ready to be taken to customs and sent to New York. This was a sad reminder that my visa would soon be up, and I must return home. I told Jamal. At first, he made light of it and told me that he had to go to Japan on a shipping deal anyway, and would be gone for six months. Jamal was a cargo ships' broker in addition to having the pharmaceutical business. Then he patted me on the back in the "stiff-upper-lip" manner of the British. But I could see that he was as shaken as I was over our impending separation.

After an unusually silent breakfast, Jamal rang up Amanullah, a close friend, who lived with his wife and family in a newly-built house in the suburbs of Peshawar. Amanullah was educated in the United States. He was chief of the Afridi tribe. This was the second largest Pakhtun tribe, after the Yusufziais, in northwest Pakistan. A short, stocky man with a boisterous air and an American accent, he was quick to get things done, a rarity in this part of the world. Also, he had many American colleagues and friends. So he understood and accepted the relationship between Jamal and me. He put himself at our disposal. Jamal asked him to check on flights to Kabul. He turned up one hour later, in his white Mercedes, and drove us to the ticket office in the center of the city. Upon our arrival, we were told that, due to the snow in Afghanistan, all flights to and from Kabul had been canceled until further notice. Amanullah drove us back to our hotel.

Jamal decided that I could return to Kabul through the Khaibar, and went about ordering a car and driver for the following morning. After this, he slept most of the day, and when he was awake was silent and withdrawn. He sat in the living room on the pale gray sofa, his back to me, facing the windows with the drapes closed. He face wore a fierce frown, eyes like chocolate beads as he chain-smoked slowly and deeply. He held the smoke in for fifteen seconds before expelling ragged, Chinese clouds from his nostrils. Emotions churning, I kept to my bed. At dusk, I heard him telephone several friends to come and have a drink with us. Then he went out to watch the sunset. I was heartsick since this was the first time I was not by his side. I heard Sattar moving about the room and the familiar clink of glasses filled with scotch.

After a while, Jamal came and stood by the side of the bed with a drink in his hand. He stared down at me for a long moment, the fierce expression still upon his face.

Then he put the drink on the nightstand and cried in Pakhto in a voice filled with anguish, *"Oh Life of Mine!"* as he threw himself upon me with a deep sigh. *"The thought of thy departure hath rent my heart in two! I canst scarcely bear to look upon thy countenance! I must steel myself from the pain of separation. But this thing is impossible to me!"*

"Oh My Life, I love thee with my very breath, and dost not wish this unbearable sorrow," I replied. *"I shalt be without anyone if I canst not be with thee! But I must return home!"*

"Then take my son with thee in thy belly that thou return to me swiftly, inshallah," he whispered in a choked voice.

I was deeply moved by Jamal's asking me to bear his child and groped for the correct response. Jamal took my hesitation for a "no" because we were not married.

So he said in a rush in Pakhto, *"I am as a slave to thee. 'I shalt be as the dust under thy feet'. There I have uttered the words of the groom to the bride. I swore that I wouldst never love nor marry, but by God, I am helpless with thee."*

"Yay My Lord, my life, my love, put thy child in my belly so I shalt have a part of thee wherever I am!" I exclaimed with intense love and joy as I surrendered to him.

We swore undying love and made impossible vows. He promised that he would give up his title, and leave his country if the furor of his marrying "one not of the blood" couldn't be quelled.

Having heard his companions' violent opposition to marriage that "diluted the bloodlines," I knew that this was no careless statement on Jamal's part. So this is why he was so quiet all day! He was struggling with whether to follow his traditions or to risk opening his heart a second time. He vowed to me that nothing could or would prevent his happiness. Unspoken was the thought of his first love, Semina, who was taken from him.

"Thou art my life and I canst not be without thee any more than without my breath," he said in Pakhto.

He promised to talk to his parents and arrange everything, so I would return to Pakistan as his bride.

Our friends arrived, and we spent the remainder of the evening drinking and telling stories. I noticed that Jamal was drinking much more than usual, and by eleven o'clock had consumed the better part of a bottle of Scotch by himself. He was oblivious to his friends' requests that we go for supper. Instead, he kept suggesting another round. Then he rose to go into the bedroom. I saw his walk was unsteady. I went after him, begging him to stop drinking and go to supper. He looked at me. His face, a mask of exquisite torture, pierced my heart as he whispered with urgency, "But I must darling, for tomorrow we part!"

We embraced painfully, and only then did he agree to go to supper.

The next morning after breakfast, Amanullah appeared. He drove us to the center of the city where a white, 1955, Plymouth and driver were waiting. The full impact of my leaving Jamal descended upon me. My body became like wood, my ears were buzzing and my legs felt as if they were encased in cement. While my eyes filled with tears, I shook Amanullah's hand with a mechanical motion, deaf to his goodbye. I forced myself to remain standing straight.

Then, with the utmost difficulty, I faced Jamal. I looked at his shoulder as I shook his hand.

I feared that if I saw his face I would break down completely and be incapable of leaving him. He was wearing sunglasses, so I could not see his eyes, but as I started to move away, my glance fell on his mouth, and I saw that it was trembling. Tears blinded me as I groped for the car door and climbed in. Only after the driver pulled away and I heard Jamal say, "Go with God," did I allow the dam inside of me to burst.

I sobbed and wept for about an hour when suddenly something forced me to look up and I saw Jamal standing in the road! He motioned for me to stop. There he stood, his eyes narrowed to chocolate beads, his lips pressed together curved downwards. He blushed with effort as he ran towards the car. His mustaches bristled, and his Roman nose became the dominant feature of his face. I screamed "rookshah" in Pakhto for the driver to stop as Jamal flagged the car down. Against the background of the white clouds tinged with gray, his hair seemed blacker than ever.

The car braked violently. I got out and ran like a wild woman through the churning cloud of dust to Jamal who was striding towards me.

The next thing I knew I had his big, shaggy head in my hands and I was kissing his mouth, and smelling the cologne on his skin as we embraced and laughed.

We spoke in Dari, *"I had to see thee once again before I would release thee, Oh Life of Mine!"*

"Oh Jamal, I canst not bear the pain of separation! My fear is that I shalt be forever deprived of thy presence," I cried, my head buried in his chest.

"Oh Janni, Janni, I swear by God, I shalt die without thy love! Know that our parting is only a temporary thing, inshallah," he said as he kissed my head and my eyes.

Then he helped me back into the car, took my hands, squeezed them and said, "It is *kissmet* (fate), Janni mine that we shall be reunited again very soon."

As the car pulled away, I watched him standing on the dun-colored, barren plains. The massive, brown, bulk of the mountains with their mauve folds jostled the intense blue of the clearing sky. With his right arm upraised wishing me "Godspeed," he receded into the distance as I once again headed towards the corkscrew crags of the Khaibar.

In Kabul, I set about making preparations for my departure. I concluded last-minute business with my merchant friends. They took my right hand, held it over their hearts and pressed me to remain. They made me swear "by my eyes" that I would return. It was the same when I went to bid goodbye to my friends in their homes with the addition of tears from the women and children who clutched my clothing and implored me to stay. Crying also, I vowed that I would return to them again.

The morning of my flight, four of my merchant friends, including Servant-of-the-Creator, turned up at my home to wish me goodbye and send me off to the airport in a taxi. My servant, whom I had left in charge of the house for the next three months, saw me to the taxi with tears in his eyes saying in Dari, *"May God shower all blessings upon thee, Oh Khanum!"*

I stood surveying these open-hearted, beautiful people with whom I had made lasting friendships on the basis of trust and loyalty. I swallowed the lump in my throat as they wished me a safe journey and a speedy return and then we all cried like children. As the taxi drove up the road, I saw them follow on foot, a sign of respect while waving and sending me off with blessings amidst swirls of talcum powder dust.

* * *

During my time in New York, I longed with a physical ache for the barrenness of the plains and the vastness of the mountains. I spent my time selling my goods, and feverishly planning my return. During this time, I had a couple of experiences related to Servant-of-the-Creator. It was then I realized that Creator was a Sufi Master. I had read many books on Sufism (Islamic mysticism) since I went to Afghanistan. The books showed the miracles the Sufis wrought in everyday life while living as normal people.

I was in a seat on the New York subway. I suddenly felt as if I were leaving my body. I put my head back against the wall and closed my eyes. The next thing I knew I was in Kandahar, on the flat adobe roof of Creator's house, sitting cross-legged in the late morning sun. We were facing each other with tears of joy cascading down our faces. Our hands were raised, palms facing one another's about one inch apart, and an incredible white light was circulating back and forth between them. I heard Creator's voice so gentle and tender in Dari even though he was not speaking, *"I was desirous of thy presence, oh Amshir-jon, and the sight of thee hath gladdened my soul."*

I opened my eyes and I realized that I was still on the subway. The other passengers, normally oblivious to their surroundings were staring at me. When they saw that I was all right, they went back to their newspapers. This experience told me that it was time to return to Afghanistan.

While I was getting ready for my journey, I had another out-of-body experience. I dreamed that I arrived in Kabul, and went down the street to Creator's shop. He wasn't in his normal place in the main room ... seated on a small carpet surrounded by his embroideries. I went to the back, and there he lay on his bed of stacked carpets with a high fever. He opened his eyes and looked right through me. I put my cool hand on his burning forehead. A silver, white light shot out from the palm of my hand, and I felt that he would be all right. I woke up and hastened my preparations.

Jamal was always in my thoughts. I had only to look at his picture, to be transported to him where I could see, hear, smell, and taste Afghanistan and Pakistan. Usually, within minutes, he would call me. We exchanged brief, loving letters ... his always written on blue aerogram stationery.

I was sitting on my bed reading in the late afternoon when suddenly a powerful urge impelled me to look up at his picture on the mantel. I experienced a surge of love, and a warm feeling in my heart. Several minutes later the phone rang, and I heard his voice say, "Cath-ay-jon!" We both started talking and laughing at once. I told him of my upcoming return and he asked if it couldn't be sooner.

"Why, *Janni?*" I asked.

"Because, darling mine, when you finish your work here we will drive to England to buy a house."

"Oh, Jamal! That would be wonderful!" I exclaimed.

Excitement overtook us as we made plans to meet in our usual Pak hotel, and then the connection broke.

This was annoying but typical of Pak international phone service. I tried to call back, but it was impossible to get through. Anyway, we already knew how and where to meet.

CHAPTER TWENTY-FOUR

Bollywood

"The heart of the Pakistani motion picture industry is in Lahore. One star will work on forty or fifty films per day for twelve to fourteen hours. This is relatively easy since all of the movies have the same storyline: Boy meets girl, boy and girl fall in love and are separated by their families. Finally, all is reconciled and the couple is reunited."
Told to the Author by a Pak woman whose brother was a film star.

It was a hot, sunny afternoon when I arrived in Lahore only to be disappointed by Jamal's absence at the airport. I had the porter get me a taxi, and started on the short ride to our hotel. I anticipated my usual argument with the driver over the fare, and he lived up to my expectations.

The taxis have tiny, toy-like meters that they keep hidden behind a small multi-color curtain under the dashboard so they can charge whatever they want.

At the end of the ride, I said, "Let me see the meter."

The taxi driver's reply was invariable, "There is no meter, My Lady."

At that point, I leaned over the seat and reached for the curtain. He laughed, acknowledging that I had won that round, and showed me the meter stating five *rupees*. Sometimes, there really is no meter. Unfortunately for them, I know the fares. This particular ride began with the driver asking my country of origin. When I said America he began praising it, and I could see the dollar signs in his eyes. Then he told me that he had a wife and four children, and she was ill, and he was not earning much money, etc. By the time we arrived at the hotel, the fare jumped from the usual five rupees to fifteen! I offered him five. He refused it and said we should consult the hotel manager as to the proper fare.

After hearing the driver's complaint, the assistant manager who was behind the desk said to the driver, in Urdu, *"No, it is five rupees, friend."*

Then he turned to me and said in English, not realizing that I understand Urdu, "Give him ten *rupees*, Madam."

I looked at the driver, gave him seven and sent him on his way. Then I looked at the manager and asked if he gave ten *rupees* for a ride from the airport, knowing full well that he probably gave only six if that.

He laughed and said in reply, "But Madam, you are American; you are rich so it does not matter!"

"Well, if you want to use my country of origin as a criterion then I must apply Muslim law to my room charges in this hotel. According to your law of hospitality to the guest, I should be charged nothing for my room."

At this, he doubled up in merriment and quickly changed the subject. Just then the manager himself appeared. His hair was heavily oiled and he oozed charm and smiles as he handed me the key to one of the best suites in the hotel. I immediately thought, "Aha! Jamal's been at work here!" However, I found it strange when the manager said that there were neither messages nor phone calls for me and that he hadn't seen "Khan Sahib."

Despondent, I went to my suite and began taking a bath. There was a knock at the door, it was Jamal. I refused to open it because he wasn't at the airport to meet me. He replied in an indignant tone, "I have just returned from that accursed place! Your plane must have arrived early."

I told him through the door that my plane arrived exactly on time at two-thirty. Then I heard him explode, "Son of a swine! The manager told me three-thirty when I asked him to check up on the flight!"

I threw open the door and asked, "What manager?"

"The manager of this bloody hotel where thy arrival hath been pressing upon me for five days!" he hissed in Urdu in a fury.

I dressed quickly so we could confront the manager. Of course, the manager swore that the airlines had given him the wrong flight time, and abjectly apologized for the stupidity of his countrymen.

When I asked why he told me he hadn't seen Jamal, he denied it right to my face.

"Are you calling this lady a liar?" Jamal roared.

"No indeed, Khan Sahib, she must have misinterpreted my words. I beg forgiveness for this misunderstanding."

I was astounded at first. Then I realized what all that managerial charm meant. The manager was jealous of Jamal and made us aware of it with this petty annoyance. I looked at Jamal, who, knowing we had lost this battle, took my arm and, with heads held high we went back to the suite.

After we closed the door, I was scooped up, kissed and nibbled on the back of my neck, ears, fingers, and eyes, over and over, amidst growls of pleasure. I embraced him, and we fell onto the bed where we remained for hours in each other's arms. We gave each other the minutest details of our lives since the last time we were together and declared our love for the thousandth time.

One early summer day, when the humidity glued my clothes to my dripping body, Jamal took me to visit some of his friends.

The Wali Khans' home was outside of Lahore. They were a very famous family who worked in the film industry. Mrs. Victory Wali Khan was five-feet-eight, medium build with a regal bearing. She wore a navy blue and tan sari. Her graying hair was in a large bun at the nape of her neck. She had thick black eyebrows and penetrating black eyes in her mocha-colored face. Her generous nose and mouth and dazzling white teeth made her a handsome woman.

"Welcome to my home," she said in perfect English after Jamal introduced us. Her two daughters Honeysuckle and Nectar appeared. Honeysuckle was tall and thin in a ropey way with dark skin and huge, luminous, black eyes in a beautiful face. She had the proud carriage of a nomadic woman resembling her Afghan ancestors. Nectar was a little shorter than her sister with medium height, and heavy set. She had café au lait skin, small pointed eyes, prominent heavy cheekbones, a medium nose with flaring nostrils and a wide mouth with full lips. There could not be more of a contrast between two sisters!

After introductions were made, and we were settled with tea, I asked them to tell me about the Pakistani film industry.

Honeysuckle began, "The heart of the Pakistani motion picture industry is in Lahore. One star will work on forty or fifty films per day for twelve to fourteen hours. The star rushes from set to set. This is relatively easy since all of the movies have the same storyline: Boy meets girl, boy and girl fall in love, boy and girl are separated by their families who don't want them to marry. Finally, all is reconciled and the couple is united. The male stars, like my brother, Wisdom, all come from "film families," like ours who have been in the industry for years and whose children follow in their footsteps. The women come from the red light district since no self-respecting woman will bare her face to the public. Top stars get ten to fifteen thousand dollars per picture. Secondary actors get six to twelve thousand and the remaining get fifteen hundred to six thousand dollars."

We heard a blur of words that signaled that someone had entered the house. Several minutes later, a tiny, beautiful young woman glittering like a jewel in a gorgeous pink and gold sari bowed and stepped into the room. Precious was adorable, five-feet-tall and curvaceous with huge black eyes, a pert nose and full lips with cascades of black hair that she kept in a huge chignon. Her vivacious greeting was returned in equal measure. She excused herself for interrupting. Everyone was very pleased to see Precious and Nectar made room on the bed for her to recline with us. She was Wisdom Wali Khan's wife.

With a radiant smile, Precious said, "I heard that we had a foreign guest and I came to meet you."

After tea drinking, I asked, "How did you meet your film star husband?"

"I am from an upper-class Yusufziai family who lives in Karachi. I majored in English at the University and after graduating took a clerical job in Pakistan International Airlines."

"This in itself is very unusual as most Pak women return to their homes after graduation to await their parents' choice of a suitable marriage for them," I said.

"That is true, but my parents are quite modern. Around Eide, a Muslim holiday occurring after Ramazan (the month of fasting), I persuaded my parents to allow me to visit my cousins here. After much arguing and pleading, since single women do not travel great distances alone, they consented. Honeysuckle, Nectar and I spent our time paging through the latest film magazines. I saw a picture of her brother Wisdom. This family is also Pakhtun Yusufziai that originated in Balkh Afghanistan. Their last name indicated a long illustrious lineage originating from the union of Ali, the fourth Caliph of Islam, and his wife Fatmah, the daughter of the Prophet Mohammed. Any descendants of the Prophet Mohammed and his family hold a high place of respect in our society."

"I was smitten by Wisdom right away and told Honeysuckle, who replied that her brother was in Rawalpindi visiting some relatives for Eide. We started scheming how to arrange a meeting and decided to give an Eide party."

"Wisdom and I were introduced at the party and became inseparable until I had to return to Karachi. At that point, we announced our engagement."

"What did your parents say?"

"My parents raged, 'An actor!' they spat with contempt. Wisdom's parents objected too."

"My late father-in-law was a great playwright who spent fifteen years working with theatre greats in Europe. Wisdom followed in his father's footsteps. He went to Europe after graduation to find work and married a European against his parents' wishes. Eventually, they divorced. So now his family said with sarcasm, 'He has found another love match! Once was not enough!'"

"The bickering continued for several months until I went on a hunger strike. It is still difficult to meet anyone outside of the home since there are very few clubs, no dance halls, or theatres like in the West where young people can meet. I met my husband because I saw a picture of him in a magazine! With the introduction of photography, less orthodox parents allow their children to peruse photos of future mates."

"What happened next?"

She said, "Oh Kitee (the Pak version of 'Catee') when my parents saw that I would take my life for love of Wisdom, they cried and said that if he is my choice, so be it. So they came to Lahore and met with Wisdom's parents, and the engagement papers were signed. This allowed my future husband and me to spend time together in public. My parents wanted us to wait to marry, but Wisdom and I couldn't. Since I was already finished with my studies, they could give no excuse to hold us back. So they made the *ruksatee* (public marriage), with five hundred guests! It was so exciting to meet all of our relatives and receive so many presents!" she exulted with childish glee.

"If you hadn't graduated," I asked, "what would your parents have done?"

"My parents would've said that we couldn't marry until I graduated and I would've remained at home. Or they may have agreed to the marriage in name only. The Quran says that there is no true marriage unless it is consummated."

At that point, she showed me the gold and pearl earrings she was wearing and some matching bracelets and said that these were part of her wedding gifts. She also showed me her wedding picture; a very tall, well-built young man who had a ruddy complexion, hazel eyes, a Roman nose and full lips was standing beside her. He was as striking as she was beautiful.

Precious' mother-in-law, Victory, was a recognized painter, her brother-in-law a sculptor, one sister-in-law, Golden, a journalist and Nectar was an aspiring playwright like her late father. Honeysuckle was still at the university majoring in art.

Victory said, "My husband had a vision when he was young that he would go to study in Europe. He said that it was his mission in life to bring European theatre to Pakistan. Over a period of thirty years, he began his studies and successes in Europe and then in India and Pakistan. He also was able to predict his own demise. He claimed that our son Wisdom would not be present for the funeral. Of course, Wisdom swore that there was no way that could happen. My husband also promised to stay in contact with us after his death."

"True to his prediction, eight years later he died in his sleep. Wisdom was in Europe making the film that launched his career. We knew he was at a critical stage of filming so we didn't tell him about his father's death. But the director called a two-week break and Wisdom had an inexplicable urge to return to Pakistan wanting to surprise us. He arrived at Karachi airport. While waiting for his connecting flight, his glance fell on the newspaper headlines mourning the death of his famous father. My husband's prediction had come true."

"You must stay with us since Jamal has to travel to Karachi today," said Victory.

I was exuberant in my agreement. No boring hotel rooms and daily propositions! Instead, I discovered that Honeysuckle adored tribal silver jewelry as I do and we spent many happy hours searching the bazaars for such treasures.

Riding back from the bazaar in a *tonga*, we talked about her father and she confided in me that sometimes the aroma of his cologne pervades his study. At the house, she took me to his room that has been kept in the exact same way as when he was alive. I felt a great peace there.

Honeysuckle said, "At times when I pass my father's study, I see him standing by his desk and he smiles at me."

"I am sure that you were a very close family," I replied.

I stayed with the Wali Khans the obligatory three days and was feasted and regaled with many stories about their lives.

On the afternoon of the third day, when the electricity went off for its daily rest, I was moved to tell Nectar and her husband Warrior about the recurring dream I had since age thirteen.

"My father told me that those are prophetic dreams," said Nectar.

"Yes! And I have finally met him in the person of *Sahibzada* Jamal Mahmood Yusuf Khan!" I exclaimed.

"What was your dream?" Warrior asked.

"I am living in a country far from my own. I am married to a very tall man. His country is at war and I am helping him. How I am helping is not clear nor are his features. But the minute I saw Jamal, I knew that this was the man! However, there is no war."

"Ooooh! I have shivers!" exclaimed Nectar. "That is definitely prophetic. Did Jamal recognize you also?"

"Yes, he did and he asked me to marry him."

Nectar squealed with delight. "When is your wedding?"

"We have not planned that far ahead yet."

Just then the lights went on and I heard Jamal call. He had returned from Karachi. After having tea, we said goodbye to the Wali Khan family and walked outside to find a taxi. A crisp yellow crescent moon ascended the lapis lazuli sky. As we walked, a flashing galaxy of multi-colored stars and planets visible to the naked eye illuminated the dirt road.

CHAPTER TWENTY-FIVE

Lady Fawzia

"Take thy horse and ride from sunrise to sunset in one direction.
Then make a circle, and this land wilt be thine to rule."
Babur Shah, King of Afghanistan 12th Century

When we reached our motel, Jamal said in Pakhto, *"Come with me woman, I wish to lie with thee."*

Always ready to give him some of my Brooklyn language, I replied, "How would you like a bust in the schnoz?"

He stood there silent.

I said, "Well?"

"Can't comprehend you," he stated in his most British of accents.

I showed him my clenched fist and said, "Bust." Then I pointed to his nose and said, "Schnoz."

He drew himself up to his full height, brows furrowed like the edge of a crevice, eyes like chocolate beads and said in a fierce voice, "Madam! Do you mean to attempt to strike my proboscis exteriori?"

I blinked and the next moment I was doubled up on the bed in hysterical laughter. He looked even fiercer which increased my hilarity.

I gasped out, "Your what?" knowing exactly what he meant.

His expression changed to one of attempted condescension as he said, "Oh! Can't understand proper English?"

I rose, took his hand and love bit his lower lip.

He sucked in his breath with a hiss releasing all of his Britishness and exclaimed, "Whyuuuuuuuuu!"

He was an Asian once more. We fell onto the bed and didn't get up until dawn.

The following day, Jamal and I went to see one of his relatives. Her husband, who was thirty years older than she, had died several months ago.

On our drive over, Jamal informed me, "When a person dies in this country, the family members run around the property to put their own locks on anything they want to 'inherit.' In the mad scramble that followed Rafi's death, Ameeda managed to get a good deal of property. She is living in her husband's house with a young man who is her lover. I am sure that this was a welcome change after fifteen years of marriage to an impotent alcoholic."

"Well good for her," I said.

"Not really. Her husband's son Selim hates Ameeda."

We arrived at the house and a servant ushered us into the *saloon* (living room).

After the amenities, Jamal said, "My dear Ameeda, how are you? You look well."

"By the grace of God, I am well. Oh my dear cousin, you also look well. And who is this lady?"

"This is my fiancée Cath-ay, from America."

"Welcome to Pakistan, my dear. Do you like our country?"

Taking the shortest way out of the trap, I replied, "Yes, it is very lovely."

In Urdu, Jamal broke in with, *"Oh Ameeda, I am come to advise thee for thy own safety."*

"And what pray is this advice and on what matter, oh cousin of mine?"

"Thou know full well thy stepson's feelings against thee art very strong. He believes that thou hath given the drink of poison to thy husband robbing him of a father."

"I swear an oath on the Holy Quran, oh son of my uncle, that no such thing hath been done! Never wouldst I do harm to my husband!"

"I know this of thee, but thy husband's son hath this thing in his mind and wilt not leave it."

"What be thy advice, oh cousin of mine?"

"My advice is to invite thy stepson to go before the kazi (judge) and hold him to a very large cash settlement. Accept nothing less, no thing of property nor of land for then he wilt have a claim upon thee. When he grants thy wish before the kazi, leave this property and make a new life for thyself."

"But why must I do this? This property hath been my home for fifteen years!"

"In three years, Selim will have reached his majority inheriting his father's title and all with it. At that time, if thou art still in his way, he wilt arrange to have thee killed for what he believes to be thy part in his father's death. He wilt do this grievous thing to thee especially if he finds thou hath taken a lover disgracing the name of his father."

"Oh son of my uncle, inshallah, I shalt do this thing thou hath advised. It were better that my life is still with me than all the property in this world."

After we left, I asked Jamal in Pakhto, "Oh Janni, wouldst Selim really take the life of Ameeda?"

"Yay, that and more My Beloved, if he thinks that Ameeda hath made some gain from his father's death. Widows, especially second wives can have everything taken from them by the husband's children from his first wife. This is especially true since Ameeda hath no sons by her second husband. According to Islamic law, when the father dies, the sons inherit two-thirds, the daughters, one-third, and the wife nothing. It is incumbent upon the sons to care for their mother. Some widows hath been killed by their own sons when they try to marry again. It is considered a disgrace upon the husband's family for his widow to remarry."

One afternoon, Jamal and I went to visit an old aristocratic family in Lahore. The parents, the son, his bride, and the two daughters all spoke excellent English. Both daughters were college graduates, but the girls did not have jobs, according to custom.

"It is considered immodest for a young unmarried woman to 'consort' with men in a public place," they chorused.

After tea drinking, the father took Jamal into the garden and confided in him. Curious, I pleaded a headache so they would show me to a bedroom. All of the bedrooms faced the garden. I listened to the conversation even though I knew that Jamal would tell me later.

"My oldest daughter, Shaheen was 'formally married' (engaged) to a Pakistani living in New York City. He was supposed to come to consummate the marriage two months ago. He called to say that he could not leave his job and would arrive in six months."

"My son who just got married was studying in New York at that time. He did some checking and found that Shaheen's fiancé was already married to an American. That would place my daughter in the position of a second wife. You know that we have eschewed this custom for several generations."

"Good GOD, what a disgrace!" Jamal exclaimed. "What did you do?"

"The only thing I could. I dissolved the marriage."

"You have saved the family's honor," Jamal replied.

I came out of the room a few minutes later and joined the family and Jamal. They were still talking about this.

Shaheen said, "It is too difficult to meet someone of my station, so I must look to my parents to choose."

Her mother replied, "Now, it will be even more difficult to find someone since she was already married. She belonged to someone else even though the marriage was never consummated. A man must protect his honor by not assuming someone else's property."

I was shocked by the fact that this young girl probably will never be able to marry. After we left I said so to Jamal.

He replied, "But *Janni*, this is our culture."

"So if you and I break up, no other man will marry me because I belonged to you?"

"I will kill any man who looks at you," he replied evenly.

"Do I have a choice in this matter?"

"No my *Jon*, you are mine and mine alone," he said with his fierce panther's face.

I thought to myself, "Talk about machismo!"

One day, Jamal brought one of his employees to meet me. Brilliant Star was from an upper-class family. He was a little older than I and engaged to a girl who lived in Karachi. His parents' home was here in Lahore. He stayed with his parents four days a week to work in Jamal's pharmaceutical company. Brilliant Star invited me to lunch to meet his mother.

I looked at Jamal and he said, "His mother will be company for you when I am at work. I think that you will like her."

Lady Fawzia was a well-educated woman in her early forties. She was very striking with huge black eyes, a slim, tall figure, and shoulder length, blunt-cut thick black hair. She wore traditional clothing of the finest silks and pounds of gold jewelry. Lady Fawzia was interested in all things foreign and lived vicariously by spending time with women from other countries. Fawzia, her son and, I shared wonderful meals prepared by her cook. Afterward, Brilliant Star went off presumably to nap in his room, but actually to phone his fiancée. Fawzia and I went to her bedroom to talk and rest until the heat of the day was over.

She questioned me about my life. "Are you married?"

"No, I'm not."

"Do you wish to marry Jamal?"

"Yes, I believe that we will marry," I replied.

"I do not think his parents will agree."

"Why do you say that?" I asked.

"You are not of the blood and you have neither great wealth nor position."

"He will convince them. We are in love!" I retorted as anger brought a rosy blush to my face.

She laughed, "Do not forget that social and economic standing are very important in this culture."

Seeing that I was upset she changed the subject. "Tell me, what do you like about Pakistan?"

"I like the bazaars and the clothing," I mumbled.

"And what about the people?" Fawzia asked.

"Not very much," I shot back.

"Oh come darling; let us talk of other things. Is there anything that you want to ask me?"

I calmed down and said, "Yes, I haven't met Brilliant Star's father."

"Aah!" she exclaimed in disgust, "Him!" I settled back on the bed, propped up on my side with cushions. I knew a story was coming.

"I came from a well-educated family who gave me proper schooling. However, families still arrange our marriages," she said through gritted teeth.

"When I was eleven years old," she continued in her perfect British accent, "my parents had me engaged to my husband, my first cousin who is twenty-two years older than I am. I have always hated him. He is so black and ugly! I was forced to marry to him at age fifteen and at sixteen I had my first child, a daughter. I named her Silver Moon because the full moon was my favorite color. The birth experience was so traumatic that I studied contraception methods available from British doctors. I chose the diaphragm and I was happy for several years until one night, my husband came home drunk and forced himself on me. I became pregnant again and had Brilliant Star, my son. I hated my husband even more now and when the children were ten and thirteen years old, we stopped speaking to each other altogether and spent as much time apart as possible. He said I could stay in this house and he would go to his lands and live in the house there."

"Why do Eastern peoples engage and marry their children off so early?"

"Darling," she replied, "on average, people die at thirty-five. After twenty, a woman is middle-aged and cannot produce as many children. Now back to my story. Five years later, my husband married a European woman whom he met on one of his frequent business trips abroad. He brought her back to Pakistan. At that time, my father died and I went to the south of Pakistan to spend time with my family. I decided to initiate a divorce. I did this by remaining with my family for four consecutive months. You know that in our culture if we remain away from our husband for more than three months, it is a sign that we want a divorce.

"During this time, my husband left on another business trip and his European wife was sent to my house to stay with my children. She set her eyes on my son because he was so physically mature for his fifteen years. When I returned to my home, my son would not speak and my daughter was hysterical.

"I discovered that Madeleine forced herself on my son. Silver Moon could do nothing to prevent this and when she tried, Madeleine locked her in her room.

"First, I confronted Madeleine and then Chief, my husband, when he returned. He divorced Madeleine and sent her back to Europe.

"Then and there I decided never to leave the children again. I have remained married to Chief all these years. We never speak except out of necessity. Both my son, who is engaged and my daughter, who is married, have chosen their own spouses. Praise be to God! I vowed that they would never suffer as I have."

"You know there is a younger man interested in me," she said changing the subject with an oblique smile. "But I do not wish to marry again."

In my naiveté, I said, "You should divorce Chief so you may be free to pursue this relationship."

"Nah!" she exclaimed with vehemence. "I have come so far that I can wait a few more years for the old man to die and to claim my share of the inheritance! Besides, according to Muslim law, the son inherits the lion's share. Since both my children have made wealthy alliances, Brilliant Star who is very successful in business, promised his share to me."

One afternoon, Fawzia and I were having tea when she was visited by another lady, Bilqueess. The woman only spoke Urdu. She stayed for a half hour and drank the obligatory three cups of tea. When she left, Fawzia told me her story.

"Bilqeess and Ayesha were best friends and married to two cousins. Bilqeess's marriage worked whereas Ayesha's did not. Her husband spent a great part of the time away from home in the company of other women. Both Ayesha and Bilqeess had sons, Jaffar and Sayeed, who were like brothers and visited each other's houses all the time. After the birth of Jaffar, Ayesha's husband never touched her."

"The boys went away to separate private boarding schools in England. When they grew up, Sayeed got a job and an apartment close to home, so the boys were again reunited. Sayeed had a car accident and Jaffar insisted on moving him into the house where he could be looked after by his family until he was well. All the care of Sayeed fell to Ayesha. Sayeed and Ayesha began a love affair. They managed to conceal this from everyone. However, when Bilqeess arrived to visit her son, she took one look at him and knew everything. She confronted Ayesha who said that she loved Sayeed and couldn't bear to give him up. Bilqeess set a time limit for both of them to break it off. She told her son she would look for a wife for him."

"Several months passed and Sayeed called his mother to announce that he wanted to marry Ayesha's younger sister Aneela. He said that they were very much in love. However, Aneela had confided to Sayeed's sister that she didn't want to marry Sayeed. She was being forced to by Ayesha. This way Ayesha could share Sayeed with Aneela."

"Bilqeess was infuriated and made another trip to Ayesha's home. A huge argument ensued and Bilqeess demanded that Ayesha end the relationship. Ayesha claimed that she could not live without Sayeed. Bilqeess threatened to tell Ayesha's husband but she never got the chance to carry out her threat. Ayesha hanged herself before her husband found out."

"I saw Sayeed several months later when we were both on the train from Karachi. I spoke to him and he said he was going to marry Aneela."

"'Do you love her?' I asked him."

"'I will only love Ayesha for the rest of my life.'"

"'Then why are you doing this?' I asked."

"He hung his head and replied, 'Because Aneela will do anything I say since she has been compromised. Everyone knows that we were supposed to marry.'"

"Then, with a defiant look, he said, 'Besides, she has a very wealthy uncle who lives in the States and perhaps in a few years he would be willing to bring me to America.'"

How awful, I thought. All these lives ruined.

Just then Jamal appeared and Lady Fawzia and I said goodbye.

One evening, Jamal received a cable saying that his shipping deal went through and he must fly to Japan right away. He asked if I wanted to accompany him, but I declined since I had orders from New York stores that had to be fulfilled in Afghanistan. We were both unwilling to part but knew that it was only for a short time before we'd be reunited. He purchased a ticket for me and I flew to Kabul.

CHAPTER TWENTY-SIX

İnnŏcĕncĕ

"Circumcision is a very old custom
showing loyalty to one's, blood, tribe or clan.
All men art then brothers.
They hath sacrificed the skin and hath shed blood together.
When this occurs, we art bound by blood to aid each other."
God's Gift

My friend Brian was back in Kabul again. He invited me to a party with some French people. There I met God's Gift. He was a handsome young man, who was very European looking with auburn hair, green eyes, and a rosy, creamy color like the northern Italians. He spoke Dari, Italian, French, and English. His father, who had an Italian mother and an Afghan father, was an exporter of sheepskin coats and often took God's Gift to Italy on business trips with him. God's Gift, in true Afghan style, took me home to meet his family. The Light family lived in a very wealthy modern section of Kabul called Wazir Akhbar Khan.

His father, The Knower, was distinguished looking with tan skin, liquid black eyes and a mustache flecked with gray. He was not quite as tall as his son. The Knower wore very fashionable European suits. His wife Innocence had alabaster skin and knee-length straight black hair and wore the latest western clothes. They had two sons and three daughters. I remarked on the youth and beauty of his mother, and when we were alone, God's Gift told me some of his family background.

"My grandmother, Queen of Flowers, is a northern Italian woman who married a very wealthy Kandahari against the wishes of her family, who were in the diplomatic corps in Kabul. She bore one child, The Knower. At seventeen, he fell in love with my mother when he saw her hand through a lattice window on a balcony in his neighborhood. He begged his father to marry him to her. Innocence was fourteen and the last child of the Lord of Kandahar. Negotiations took place through the parents and The Knower got his wish. After The Knower was married, Queen of Flowers urged him to buy his own house in Kabul since she no longer wished to live with her husband who had taken several wives over the years. Queen of Flowers' husband agreed to this and she, together with the newlyweds, moved to Kabul. When my mother was fifteen, she bore me, the oldest of her children. She soon became pregnant again with the rest of my siblings, my brother, and three sisters."

Innocence and I became good friends, and we spent a lot of time together chatting, tea drinking and clothes shopping. One time she suggested that we remove the hair from our legs together. I knew that Muslims remove the hair from their armpits, legs, and genitals for hygienic reasons. She laughed at the look on my face when I told her of the barbers I saw on the street corners scraping dull razors over the stubble on the heads of customers. She told me to sit down and called for her servant.

Aminah was a fifteen-year-old pretty petite Hazara girl, brought to this house by her parents when she was still a child. The entire family worked for the Light family. They lived in the servants' quarters inside the family compound. She was the children's nanny and cooked and served food as well. She was very patient and kind. Innocence said that Aminah was a family member who would never be sold unless she committed some crime. There was a cousin of hers that was interested in marrying her and Innocence promised to help pay for her dowry.

Aminah boiled up honey and lemon juice. She cooled it until it became the consistency of soft taffy. Innocence applied this to my legs and let it set for a few minutes. When she peeled it off, the hair came with it. The sting was uncomfortable and Innocence commented in Dari with a grin, *"Thou wilt think nothing of this when thy first child comes."*

"I swear by God I shalt never bear children if it is more pain than this," I jokingly replied and we both laughed.

Switching to English, Innocense said, "I started having children when I was fifteen," she confided.

"You were very young."

"I did not want many children too quickly because I was so young, but I became pregnant easily. It is by the grace of Allah that they are all healthy. My last pregnancy was very difficult and I cannot have any more children."

After our hair removal session, Innocence said, "Come, Catee-jon, we will visit a friend of mine."

We walked a few doors down to another large three storey stucco and glass house. A servant answered the door, smiled and bowed when he recognized Innocence. We were led into the *saloon*: a beautiful room with a French sofa and chairs and two end tables with lamps encrusted with marble and gold. A fourteen-by-fourteen foot carpet depicting hunting scenes lay on the floor. Here we were greeted by Sweet Intoxication and her two daughters, Light-of-the-Heavens and Wedding Sweets.

Sweet Intoxication was gorgeous. She had natural dark chocolate-brown hair, dusted with auburn and huge turquoise eyes. She was five-feet-eight with a willowy figure and was dressed in the latest western fashions. Her daughters, fifteen and thirteen, were very beautiful. Light-of-the-Heavens asked direct questions and seemed to have the personality of one who took no nonsense from anyone. Wedding Sweets was polite and shy. Light-of-the-Heavens had her mother's turquoise eyes.

After tea with *gosh-ay-feel* (a deep-fried dessert dusted with sugar and ground cardamom seeds), Innocence told Sweet Intoxication in Dari that I was afraid of the pain of childbirth.

"*Oh Catee-jon, the wonder of the child wilt make thee forget thy pain,*" Sweet Intoxication said as she laughed.

"*How many children hath thee?*"

"*I hath been given two daughters that thou canst see and one son who hath seventeen years. He attends Kabul University.*"

"*What dost he study?*"

"*Electrical engineering.*"

Switching to English, Innocence chimed in with, "Sweet Intoxication would have had more children, but she took matters into her own hands."

"What do you mean?" I asked.

Sweet Intoxication said, "I didn't want to have too many children so soon. My husband travels abroad for months at a time, and I wanted his company when he was here. After the birth of Farhad, my son, I became pregnant again. My husband was on a business trip to France. I tried to abort myself with a kebab skewer. I was bleeding too much and my servant sent for the doctor. The doctor brought me to his private clinic; he is the doctor for all the noble women and even the queen. I got an infection and my life was uncertain for two weeks. But then I recovered. The doctor and I had a secret; he would not tell my husband if I told no one especially my husband. I also promised him that my first born daughter would be his wife. Firman would be in France for at least two more months and by that time I would be totally well the doctor assured me."

"Oh Catee-jon, it is not unusual to engage people before or soon after birth," said Innocence, noticing the surprised look on my face.

"Why did the doctor ask you not to tell your husband, Oh Sweet Intoxication?"

"It was for my protection as well as his. Abortions are illegal in Afghanistan. My husband could claim that the doctor killed our child. Also, my husband could divorce me if he found out I aborted our child."

At that point, Farhad entered the room. He was tall and handsome with his mother's looks. He greeted us, had one cup of tea and asked to be excused. By this time, late afternoon shadows were gathering. Innocence and I left after a few more cups of *chai*.

It was Thursday, the equivalent of our Saturday, when Innocence suggested that we go to the bazaar to get the latest western fashions. We grabbed a taxi and set out. I was sure that she was going to bring me to a very high-priced shop that sold European and American clothing. We whizzed by the new part of Kabul and headed straight for Jad-i-Maiwand, the old bazaar. My face was a question mark when Innocence laughed and said, "Come, Catee-jon. I shall show you our 'secrets.'"

We trudged through the twisted alleys until we came upon the Nixon Bazaar. This consisted of piles of used American and European clothing strewn on wooden carts where the highborn women of Kabul in their western clothing, scarves, and sunglasses rummaged around in these heaps, avoiding surrounding puddles too odious to describe.

Innocence said, "Every Thursday, the noble women are found here looking for the latest western fashions for themselves and their families. They will take these purchases home, wash and mend them if necessary.

They and their families will wear them on Fridays at their own or friends' parties and picnics."

She picked out several outfits for herself and her family and we returned to her house.

One afternoon, I came to the house but Innocence was not there. God's Gift was very upset. I asked him what was wrong and he told me about his eleven-year-old male cousin who was recently circumcised. God's Gift was present for the circumcision party. A *hakim* (healer) came to the house. After tea drinking, Mohammed's foreskin was first pulled over his penis and then tied very tightly with some thread for the circumcision. The *hakim*'s knife was blunt and this procedure took quite some time. God's Gift said that he could see by the agony on Mohammed's face that the pain must have been unbearable. Afterward, some ashes were rubbed into the wound to seal it. That was about one month ago. Mohammed still hasn't healed and he is reportedly delirious.

"*Oh God's Gift*", I asked in Dari, "*What means this cutting of the foreskin?*"

"*Oh Lady Catee, 'tis a very old custom showing loyalty to one's, blood, tribe or clan. All men art then brothers. They hath sacrificed the skin and hath shed blood together. When this occurs, we art bound by blood to aid each other.*"

"*And if a man dost not submit to this?*"

"*Then he hath not our belief and all manner of crimes canst be put against him with a lack of fear of the judgment of God or man.*"

I knew that in the United States, circumcision was performed when the baby was just born or soon after. I couldn't imagine a teenager or adult undergoing such a painful process.

Taken into the bosom of this family, I participated in their daily life. The first Friday that I was with them, we all piled into their car and went to the village of Paghman.

It was a small village several kilometers outside of Kabul with very beautiful gardens. Every Friday, the Kabulis came here to picnic with their families and friends. They spent their day in the gardens playing *tokhum jangee*. The goal of this game was to break the other's hardboiled eggshell first. They grilled kebabs and ate them with boiled potatoes and the hardboiled eggs that were dipped in a light sauce of yoghurt with garlic and cayenne pepper. Of course, there were plenty of melons and grapes for dessert. Musical instruments were brought. People sang, played and laughed until the food was eaten and the sun went down.

Innocence confided in me that she had a weak heart. When I asked her what made her say that, she told me the following story.

"I had another son whom I lost to electric shock. He was three years old. He was running around the house playing. Queen of Flowers was making lunch on the electric plate that sat on the floor in the kitchen. The metal pot with lid was cooking away with a metal spoon on the floor nearby. My son came into the kitchen when Queen of Flowers was not there and used the spoon to lift the lid of the pot. The pot boiled over and some soup spilled onto the floor. You know, Catee-jon, that we have direct current in Afghanistan. The water, the metal spoon, and the metal pot, shocked my son to death. Queen of Flowers found him dead on the floor by the pot and she has refused to cook since then."

"I am so sorry, Innocence," I said as I took her hand. Grief over her son's death had weakened her heart.

She wiped the tears from her face and said, "Enough. Let us talk of other things. Come, Catee-jon, let us get ready for our guests tonight."

One day, it was late morning when I heard Innocence call for Aminah. Then she called my name and I went into her room. Aminah appeared with *chai* and a smile, several minutes later. Innocence told her to prepare her bath and some bread and jam for our breakfast.

Innocence lay back to smoke a cigarette and to drink tea, chatting with me about what outfits I thought suitable for her to wear that day. We selected several that she had Aminah lay out while she had her bath. Aminah then straightened the room, dusted, aired the bedding, emptied the ashtray, and put on the radio. When Innocence returned, breakfast arrived.

Her two youngest daughters had just come back from school. They greeted me in a loving way while arranging Innocence's thick black straight hair. After this, they massaged her arms and legs and gave her a manicure. Then Innocence tried on the various outfits from the Nixon bazaar for all of us to approve. She consulted her mirror on her final choice.

She brought out a pile of Pak film magazines; the most recent was only a few months old. We gossiped about the stars while paging through the magazines lying on our stomachs like teenagers on Innocence's bed.

She asked me which actors I thought were attractive and she pointed out her favorites. Then Innocence went on to praise or criticize the actresses for their personal lives which were vividly described in the magazines ... especially their love lives. Meanwhile, Afghan music swirled around the room from the radio as we smoked cigarettes and drank tea. All this talk of favorite actors and their lovers reminded her of Sweet Intoxication's lover. She told me that he worked in the tourist visa office. This didn't surprise me. I remembered the old saying, "You can control who you hate, you can control who you fear, but no one can control who they love." In a culture of arranged marriages, I imagined this was more common than we would think.

I asked in Dari, "*Oh Innocence-jon, how canst Sweet Intoxication meet a lover?*"

"*Oh Catee-jon, 'tis not difficult. Thou know of the parties and picnics on Thursday nights and Fridays?*"

"*Yay, Oh Innocence-jon, I hath attended many with thee and others.*"

"*There is the place where they canst see each other and decide if they wish to meet alone.*"

"*But Innocence, Sweet Intoxication, and others art always in the company of their husbands?*"

"*Yay Catee-jon-ay-qand, (sugar cone) they are both free to look and choose. No one wouldst ever bring shame or hurt to their husbands. A husband wouldst never bring harm or shame to his family.*"

"*But how dost the lovers choose each and another?*"

"*A man wilt never choose, since all women art in the company of their husbands. The women must choose.*"

"*But art there no unmarried women at these parties?*"

"*Yay, Catee-jon, but thou know that a girl must be a virgin to marry. Only married women choose lovers. If a woman sees a man who hath interest in her, she sends a note to his place of business. No servants can read so there is no fear of discovery. As you know, servants grow up with us from generation to generation; they art not concerned with the contents of our errands. The note tells her lover where and when to phone her. After their relationship hath been established, the woman's daughters will be the contact.*"

"*Dost not the husbands suspect, Oh Innocence-jon?*"

"*There is certainty that he knows but as the lovers art very secret about their time together, nothing is said. Besides, husbands hath their own lovers.*"

"And the wives hath no objection to this behavior?"

"Catee-jon, when thou hath been married since the age of fourteen or fifteen to the same man for twenty-five years, for some it grows wearisome. Husbands and wives art very respectful of each and another. There is no desire for conflict or the involvement of their families. They art happy with life."

"Hath thou taken a lover?"

"Nay Catee-jon, my love for my husband hath been since we first met when we were very young. And I know that he loves me deeply. We both enjoy going to parties together."

It reminded me of Victorian England, where people took lovers, but it was kept secret from their husbands and wives.

The servants and children did all the housework. Innocence painted her nails, read old Hindu movie magazines and changed outfits several times each day. At five o'clock, she readied herself for the night when she and The Knower partied alone or with friends at home. The jokes at these gatherings were quite ribald. They were always in the form of double entendres. One of their favorites is the use of the words "key" and "lock" or "box" for the genitals. One woman casually mentioned that she could not find the key to an important box in her bedroom. A man asked if she had lost the key. Amid laughter, another chimed in that the key is still there but no longer fits that particular box. This was furthered by another comment that claimed that the key was seen in another box and it "surely must be bent by now" and this is why it does not fit the original. All this was accompanied by laughter, shouting and applause.

I attended many of these evening parties. The ever solicitous Knower always took the drink from Innocence's hand when he felt it might compromise her health, but only after she already imbibed several glasses. He clearly adored his wife.

CHAPTER TWENTY-SEVEN

Ṣḥaykḥ Liǧḥt öf Ṣälväṫiön

*"Roses are the favorite fragrance of the Sufis (Islamic Mystics),
and have the most powerful ability to heal."*
Afghan belief

During my stay with the Light family, I met John, an American who was interested in helping me expand my handicraft business. He said that he had an Afghan business partner who would back us and assist with shipping. John asked me to accompany him to Kandahar to meet him.

While John and I were waiting for John's business partner in one of his shops there, I became restless and took a walk outside the walls of the city. There I saw the black butterfly tents of a nomadic encampment. Curious, I drew closer until I was spotted by their young children. They laughed and chattered like excited birds while they pulled me to their camp by my hands and my long Afghan tunic. I was led to their chief and his wife and offered green tea with dried mulberries to sweeten it. Holding the mulberries in my mouth and sipping the steaming tea, I smiled and nodded as the chief spoke to me in a dialect I didn't understand. I could see by the light in his eyes that all was well.

After a while, the children again surrounded me and pulled me to my feet. We walked around the camp where the people smiled and greeted me. I rounded a tent corner and there, in the distance, were the purplish brown mountains, the ocher-colored plains, and a fourteen-year-old girl in a black and red dress, heavy with embroidery and silver coins. She wore red pantaloons and her hair was a mass of braids. She stirred a metal pot over a fire with a wooden spoon the size of a yardstick.

A star exploded in my forehead! There was a tremendous blast of white light, and my childhood vision from age three returned full force! I knew then that I had been here before in another life.

I turned my back on the encampment to hide my tears that I was allowed to behold another part of myself in this lifetime. I walked the wild, savage, lone landscape. It touched me with an unbearable ache. Standing by myself on the barren plains, I felt my soul throb with an indefinable longing. Tears of gratitude streamed from my eyes as I beheld in awestruck wonder the mightiness of the Creator's work. A poignant feeling of having come home at last bubbled up inside of me. I stood straight into the wind; its strong fingers caressed me as it buffeted my clothes. Suddenly I experienced a tremendous surge of power and freedom as if I were master of the universe. Then a blaze of light illuminated my thoughts, and I knew that I had stood this way before as a warrior, a priest, or a queen in some distant past. A sense of majesty and peace descended upon me. I remained standing there for some time until the winds died, and the sky began to turn royal purple and then indigo. A peace crept in to soothe the turmoil that raged within my soul for as long as I could remember. I had finally come home.

John's business partner, Amir owned the hotel where we lodged and had a bodyguard, Habib. Both of them reminded me of New York gangsters. I later discovered that Amir was one of the largest hashish exporters in Afghanistan, hence the bodyguard. No wonder he had money to invest. Perhaps he and John were scheming to send kilograms of hashish in my shipment of clothing! I resolved to keep my eyes open.

The hotel, a whitewashed two-storey high adobe was near a main crossing. It boasted about its electricity: the ever-present forty-watt bulb in each of its rooms plus a telephone and a radio in the office. The office was a cubbyhole with a large battered desk and an old wooden chair. The building was similar to the government buildings in Kabul. The guests were lodged on the upper storey that had ten rooms, the majority of them empty. Both Amir and Habib were married and had several children. However, because I was with John, in their minds, this excluded me from their homes since he was a strange male who was honor bound to protect and provide for me.

The "hotel" was actually a series of offices left over from the British who were here in the late 1800s. For the entire floor, there was only one room with indoor plumbing, used as both bathroom and a kitchen. This was a square room with a stone floor and an overflowing squatter along with a bucket of questionable liquid standing beside it to wash it down. The flush system was broken. A filthy sink with one trickling cold water tap occupied one corner. Dirty dishes from the restaurant were piled high in another corner of the room with spoons scattered about. A gray and white kitten was busy licking one of the plates. Nearby was an old five-gallon water tank with vegetable remnants looking like splayed feet at its base.

John and I each had a medium size room with two single beds covered with cotton-filled pallets. Two scratchy old army blankets with two rock-like pillows decorated these beds. There was a *bokharee* (wood-burning stove) in each room. The flues were blocked and they belched forth black smoke at any attempts to make a fire to relieve the nighttime chill. In one corner behind the doors were old armoires where John and I kept our suitcases, not daring to unpack our clothes. The floor was cement and the walls whitewashed a pale blue. The wood around the casement windows was painted a faded brown. From the window seats, we could look out onto the main street at what we called "television." Once we were settled, Habib brought a *chillum* (a vertical, hand-held clay pipe) and the three of us smoked. This hashish was very good and soon the bodyguard's and John's conversation grew dim as I took off for other spheres in the galaxy. My reveries were interrupted by a knock on the door. It seemed like a small eternity before we tacitly decided that, because I was a woman, there would less likely be trouble if I answered the door.

I came face to face with a young Afghan woman in a western skirt, blouse, and sweater with her husband arrayed in a second-hand western suit with an old button-down shirt and pullover. He was holding their little boy who was about a year old. She smiled and said, "*Selam Aleikum*" and proceeded to tell me that they were our neighbors next door. I invited them into the room. They arranged themselves on one of the beds as Habib, John, and I sat together on the other one facing them. The woman immediately launched into a conversation about hashish, and how it was abused by foreigners. I guess that unmistakable aroma gave it away. She finished her talk by telling us that just a few minutes ago her brother, a policeman, came to their room to find out if there were any foreigners in the hotel and she told him that only Afghans stayed here. At that point, Habib got up and left the room. Our "friends" began to grill us as to who we were, where we came from, where we were going, when, why, and how. Before we could respond to the barrage of rapid-fire questions there was another knock on the door. Habib poked his head in to announce that the "food is ready." We said goodbye to our neighbors. Of course, dinner had not even begun to see the kitchen. We thanked Habib for rescuing us.

He replied in his half English, "Talk, talk, talk! *Parwa nist*, bullshit *hast!*" which meant, "Never mind it is only bullshit."

John and I laughed at his "Americanism" and over the next several days we repeated his words and laughed again. Later that evening, we presented ourselves in the "dining room" for the evening meal consisting of a greasy *pullow* made by Habib's own hands showing honor to the guests. This "stunningly attractive" room was ten-feet-by-ten. It had rickety wooden chairs and tiny battered wooden tables that had pieces of colored Pakistani magazines glued to their tops. Each of the five tables boasted a candle in a dish covered by a perforated ceramic dome. During this barely edible repast, I asked where the bathroom was.

Habib jumped up and led me to another room where he threw open the door with a proud grin and the words, "*Now hast!* (It is new or westernized)."

I was greeted by a filthy backed up toilet minus its seat, a naked six-foot-high pipe with a faucet on the wall for a shower, plus a grimy sink with two trickling cold water spigots. In Habib's mind, I guess this was a veritable palace compared to squatting outside or in an adobe out house.

Sometime after I retired for the night, Habib knocked on my door with an unmistakable look in his one turquoise eye. The left one had been gouged out in a fight, years ago. I kept my foot against the door and told him I would see him tomorrow. Undaunted, he pressed himself against the door to reveal that it was okay for me to let him in since he had already slept with John on several occasions. Knowing John's preference for men I didn't bat an eye but congratulated Habib on his accomplishment while assuring him that John's choices were John's and had nothing whatsoever to do with me. I closed the door on an astonished turquoise eye and went to bed. I laughed at Habib and at myself for getting mixed up with a "foreigner," John, and not sticking to my usual routine of only associating with Afghan families.

The following days were uneventful and I got some shopping done in the bazaars while John wound up his business with Amir. The evenings were spent talking and joking with Amir and Habib. No mention was made of my handicrafts business. I noticed that I was getting more and more tired and sleeping later every day. I attributed it to Afghanistan's high altitude versus New York's sea level climate. One morning we took the bus back to Kabul and I slept most of the time. When awake, I had absolutely no appetite. I was so exhausted that John put his arm around me and I put my head on his shoulder to soften the jolts of the old bus over the rocky dirt roads.

Suddenly, someone tapped me on the shoulder through the space of the seats. I woke up, turned around to see this granite-like fanatical sunken face with blazing eyes talking rapidly in Pashto while shaking his index finger at me. I glared at him and John and I tried to go back to sleep when a few moments later the same thing was repeated only with a more insistent shove on his part. Thoroughly dizzy and annoyed, I began telling him in Dari that I did not understand his Pashto and to leave us alone. I sat down and John asked me what was happening. I told him I had no idea but hoped it was over. Five minutes later as I was about to drop off into a dream, this finger roughly tapped me again. I got up in a rage whipped out my knife and started to step into the aisle. What I thought I was going to do, I don't know. A young student from Kabul University came to our rescue from the back of the bus and told us that this man was a *mullah* who thought that John and I were "making out" in public! If I were not so sick and angry, I would have laughed uproariously at that statement! I explained to the student that I was ill with a headache and dizzy and that I was only trying to cushion my head from the jarring ride.

Since Afghan men and women do not come into physical contact in public, I could see what disturbed this *mullah*. He was still talking and gesticulating at the top of his lungs. I further told the student, who was translating my Dari, that it was our custom for a woman to rest her head on her male companion's shoulder. Furthermore, since we were not Afghans we should not be disturbed.

Upon hearing my words, the *mullah* said the equivalent of "when in Rome." The discussion came to an end because the bus stopped in Ghazni for lunch. The young student, Shahbaz Khan, insisted on taking us to lunch showing honor to guests in his country and to make up for any bad impressions we might form of the Kandahari people. But the mere mention of food produced such nausea that I begged to be excused and sent John and Shahbaz Khan off to lunch together. I walked around the town on uncertain legs trying to clear my head that seemed to be in a perpetual fog. I bought a kilogram of tangerines that I had developed a craving for all of a sudden.

After a while, we got underway again. As the fanatical *mullah* had gotten off the bus in Ghazni, I slept undisturbed on John's shoulder all the way to Kabul. When we arrived, I told John that I would be staying with the Light family until I felt better.

I called God's Gift from John's hotel and told him that I was on my way. I started walking down Chicken Street. My legs felt like two lead blocks. I thought I would black out any minute. My entire body ached like it had been beaten with a club. I put the blame on the old fashion bed springs in the Kandahar hotel. Unable to walk further, I took a taxi to God's Gift's house.

The gate was opened by his brother, God's Purity, who brought me into the house and led me to his brother's room. God's Gift jumped off the bed when I entered, and hugged me with delight. I sat down while he took the teapot off the *bokharee* and served us. I recounted my Kandahari adventure, and we both had a good laugh. He said that he always felt that John was a "*kunee*," a passive male homosexual. He added that there were many Kandahari men who would be glad to accommodate John as Kandahar was noted for homosexuality. He said families keep a close watch on their sons especially if they are particularly good looking for kidnapping was not unknown.

I told him about my constant sleeping, dizziness, and leg pains. He left the room to return with his grandmother Queen of Flowers who squeezed my hands in her own two, as we greeted each other. She pulled me to the window, pushed back the curtain, and turned my face up to the sunlight. Then she pulled my lower eyelid down and drew back with a sharp intake of breath.

"*Zardee giriftee!*" (Thou hath taken the yellowness!) She exclaimed in Dari. This is the way Afghans describe jaundice since everything eventually turns yellow: eyeballs, skin, urine, and stool.

Seeing my frightened look, Queen of Flowers put her hand on my cheek, and said, "*Be at peace, My Soul. The disease wilt not harm thee. 'Tis but Allah's way of removing past sins.*"

I remembered when John was ill; we discussed the possibility of his having hepatitis and I had looked to see if his eyeballs were yellow.

I sat down on the bed and cried out, "Oh no, hepatitis!" as a thrill of fear shot through me.

Queen of Flowers instructed her grandson regarding my diet. It was very simple, lots of fresh pressed juices including lemonade and sugarcane juice with vegetable soup and bread. God's Gift cared for me by preparing all of my meals himself. His sisters swept my room, aired the bedding, and brought fresh spring water. Thus I languished in their home, bedridden and dropping weight for two months. I looked like a yellow skeleton.

Innocence became alarmed at my appearance and called a family meeting with Queen of Flowers in the lead. They decided to perform a healing ceremony called *Panja Maryam* or The Handprint of Mary (Mother of Jesus). Afghans believe that Jesus and Moses are prophets as great as their own Prophet Muhammad. They also accept the virgin birth. Muslims believe that Jesus (Issa) was conceived by the angel Gabriel blowing on the womb of Mary (Maryam). Many miracles are attributed to both Jesus and Mary.

This ceremony called for the entire household to fast and pray for three days. On the third day, Innocence, Queen of Flowers, and her three daughters, Nobility, Goodness, and Mercy prepared a rice pudding to be baked in the oven. God's Gift carried me into the kitchen while his brother brought me an overstuffed chair from the *saloon* (living room). I watched as the women prayed, and prepared the rice pudding that was similar to ours but without raisins and cinnamon. They used ground cardamom seeds instead.

Queen of Flowers took out a large, earthenware pot with a lid and Innocence poured the pudding into it. Then Nobility took some flour and water and created an elastic dough that they used to seal the pot that was then put in the oven. They sat down, and began to pray again, and read from the Quran believing their prayers for my recovery would be answered.

Five hours later, they took the pot out of the oven. The dough had hardened into a crust similar to the puffy outside on a pizza. The women waited until the pot was cool enough to touch and then, all took turns breaking the dough seal. They asked me to come to see "the opening of the pot." When I approached, and they removed the lid, there in the center of the solid baked pudding was a handprint!

The women laughing and hugging each other and me gave shouts of "*Alhamdulillah*" or "Praise be to God," and "*Allah hu Akbar,*" "God is Great." *Panja Maryam* was proof that Mary had interceded with God, and their prayers were answered. I would be well.

The Knower, hearing the commotion entered the kitchen, and upon seeing the results of the pudding said in English, "Thousands of such and even greater miracles occur in our daily lives without us noticing them. We are surrounded by Allah's miracles, and we ourselves are God's greatest."

They all assured me that now my "yellowness" would leave. I was grateful and willing to have this happen. Several days later I was a lighter shade of yellow. In order to speed up my recovery, Queen of Flowers insisted that I should see a well-known *Shaykh*, a healer who specialized in liver problems. Bathed and dressed by the women, God's Gift found a taxi that took us to Jad-i-Maiwand. Unable to go farther, the taxi stopped at the mouth of the old bazaar. The narrow, twisted, rock-strewn, muddy lanes were negotiated only on foot or with a donkey. Anything with wheels remained mired in the taffy-like mud. After being bedridden for months, I began an excruciating ten-minute walk through the bazaar with God's Gift, Queen of Flowers, and Innocence.

We found *Shaykh* Light-of-Salvation sitting in a tiny wooden shop that was perched on an adobe embankment, two feet above the ankle-deep mud. He was in his seventies, five-feet-two with a foot-long, white beard, and close-cropped grayish hair topped by a *karakul* cap. He wore the white cotton white silk embroidered, long wedding *peeran* of the Kandahari Pashtuns, a white *tambon*, and was barefoot. He looked just like any other elderly Afghan man.

I was so exhausted by my first day out of bed that I just sat there against a huge pillow panting with my pale yellow face and eyeballs.

God's Gift spoke to the *Shaykh* about my obvious condition. The Shaykh came and sat down before me. He opened a worn copy of the Quran and picked up a wooden scythe that was inlaid with brass and mother-of-pearl. This he lay on my forehead, lips, and chest while reciting words from the Quran. He ended by blowing into my face three times. The whole process took less than five minutes. Then he rose, and taking a minute scrap of paper, he wrote some numbers on it with yellow color ink and gave it to God's Gift together with a tiny vial. God's Gift gave him twenty afghanis. We all thanked him, and he smiled and bid us farewell.

I made the debilitating trip back to the main road where we got another taxi and went back to the house. I fell asleep right away and did not wake up until it was dark. God's Gift came into the room and showed me the scrap of paper the Shaykh had given him.

I spoke to God's Gift in Dari, *"What meaning hath this, Oh God's Gift?"*

"Certain Shaykhs hath discovered passages in the Quran that remedy various ills."

I remember Jamal telling me of Sufi Masters and the many miracles they perform such as bi-location, distance healing, the ability to alter time and space, appearing in person, in dreams and meditations to help and guide people, as well as their knowledge of essential oils and herbs. These Islamic mystics view God/Allah as the Beloved. Afghanistan is the home of four major Sufi orders: Qadiri, Naqshbandi, Chishti, and Suhrawardi. They perform a sacred trance dance called the *zikr* believing that it unites them to Allah. Some study the Quran for the remedies for specific illnesses.

"And what says this paper?"

"These art the numbers of passages in the Quran. These passages canst be looked up by their numbers and read. They dost not scribe the words because they art too long."

"What may be the reason that these particular numbers hath been given to me?"

"The Shaykh hath related that these Quranic passages are specifically for the liver. Thou must take this paper, and put it in the bottom of a glass, and drink water from this glass three times each day for three days. Thou must also put one drop from this vial in each glass, and on the morning of the fourth day the illness wilt leave thee, inshallah."

"*So I shalt drink water and ink,*" I asked recoiling from the thought of it.

"*Nay, Catee-jon, thou wilt drink water and zafaron (saffron). The shaykhs only use ink made from things that art safe to consume.*"

"*What use hath the vial that Shaykh Light-of-Salvation gave thee?*"

God's Gift opened the vial, and the "smell of a thousand roses" (as the Afghan saying goes) uncoiled to fill the room. He smiled and said, "*Roses art the favorite fragrance of the Sufis, and hath the most powerful ability to heal.*"

I looked at him doubtfully. "*Imbibe rose oil?*" I asked perplexed.

"*Tis for thy health. Tis but one drop three times a day for three days. No harm wilt befall thee. All these roses art grown with much prayer and fasting and, when the oil is prepared, 'tis left in the presence of many old Holy Qurans that bring a blessing to the oil by their vibrations.*"

I was so weakened by hepatitis for what seemed like an eternity that I was willing to submit to anything that required almost no effort on my part.

On the morning of the fourth day, God's Gift came to me with my usual breakfast of lemonade, followed by a large glass of fresh orange juice and some bread warm from the baker. He entered my room, saw me sitting up in bed, and ran to me joyfully crying "*Praise be to God! The yellowness hath left thee!*"

I called for the mirror that Queen of Flowers had removed from my room. She didn't want me to see how sick I really was and to become afraid. God's Gift ran in with the mirror, and his mother, grandmother, and sisters excitedly accompanied him. They all began to weep and exclaim and kiss my forehead, praising God for my recovery. Sure enough, when I looked into the wavy piece of glass that passed for a mirror, except for my eyeballs, the jaundice had receded.

CHAPTER TWENTY-EIGHT

Marcellina

"The rising moon is half with a lacy ruffled edge
Amid tendrils of clouds in a slate gray sky."
The Author

I was ready to return to work. My shipments were two months behind, so I began working ten hours a day to catch up. Jamal cabled that he was stuck in Japan. I told him of my illness. He asked if I wanted to fly to Japan so he "could look after me," but I told him I desired to return home to my family. He wished me well as we renewed our vows of undying love, and I went back to New York.

About a month later, I had a relapse. This time I was hospitalized. My liver was so hard that the doctors couldn't take a biopsy. My good Catholic parents had the last rites administered. Word got out and all of my friends and relatives dropped by. A couple I barely knew came to see me. They said, "We have just returned from India where we saw a living saint called Sai Baba. Would you like some *vibhuti* (holy ashes)? Sai Baba manifests this with his fingers."

"Sure," I said receiving a tiny packet of sweet-smelling incense-like powder. "How do I use this?"

Amanda replied, "Take a pinch and add it to a glass of water, three times a day for three days."

"You will receive a healing," her husband Joe finished.

I smiled and told them about Shaykh Light-of-Salvation and thought, *"It worked once, why not a second time?"*

On the fourth morning, I sat up in bed and felt fine. The doctors and everyone else were amazed. My liver levels were completely normal and the jaundice had disappeared! I silently thanked God and Sai Baba for my recovery once again and went home with my family.

At that time, there was a series on television about Marco Polo. I saw similarities between Marco Polo and me. When he returned to Venice

269

and told the people his adventures, no one believed him. My relatives and friends spoke to me as if I had just returned from the beach, an hour away. I had changed drastically inside, but no one could see. Homesick for Afghanistan, I only talked about returning there to the few people who would listen to me.

Everything New Yorkers said and did seemed so trivial and ridiculous, including their homes and their cars. I hated living in a Manhattan high-rise apartment, with its tiny terrace that was exposed to the sun for only a few hours a day. The skyline was buried in smog and I had the grand view of seeing into other people's apartments across the street. This, plus paying outrageous rent, was laughable to me.

I longed for my two bedroom house and yard in Kabul. My greatest desire was to walk in Afghanistan where men on the streets had kind and welcoming eyes and smiles as opposed to the hoots and whistles that greeted me here. I gloried in the bazaars, returning the merchants' gentle greetings while viewing the distant, magnificent mountains, their tops puncturing the huge blue sky.

Months later, while Jamal was still in Japan, I returned to Kabul with new orders for handicrafts. My first visit was to the Light family. I was greeted with hugs and kisses and made to recount all that happened since I last saw them. They marveled at my story of the relapse and my second healing from Sai Baba.

The family was happy and in good health. However, Innocence was very sad about her sister's daughter. Wafa, her eldest niece, had fallen in love with a boy called Ibrahim, the son of a very influential family. However, the two families had little liking for each other and refused to allow them to marry. Ibrahim's family felt that Wafa's was beneath them. Undaunted, the couple continued to meet in secret, swearing undying love. Together, they came up with a solution to their problem. Wafa told her parents that she wanted to marry Ibrahim's closest friend, Wajid. They were certain this would meet with both families' approval.

Wafa and Wajid's family were very happy at such a good match, and the marriage took place. Ibrahim used up all of his inheritance bribing Wajid so he would not consummate the marriage. After a few months, Wajid and Wafa planned to go abroad, where he would divorce her and hand her back to Ibrahim. At that point, her parents would be overjoyed that someone wanted to marry a divorced woman.

However, Wajid went back on his word, demanding that the marriage be consummated in order to extort more money. Wafa, of course, refused his advances, and he refused to divorce her. So Wafa exercised her right to "visit" her parents and remained with them beyond the proscribed three months, indicating that she wanted a divorce. Wajid started blackmailing Ibrahim. He threatened to go public so Wafa would be forced to consummate the marriage since they were married in the eyes of the law. Of course, Ibrahim paid Wajid even more money to avoid this.

After his inheritance was used up, he went to Wafa's father and told him the truth since his own parents would have none of it. Through the Kabul grapevine, the knowledge of Ibrahim and Wafa's scheme brought permanent disgrace on both families. The gossip was vicious.

"Wasn't there anything that Wafa's parents could do?" I asked The Knower.

"What could they do? They were bound to protect my niece's honor. Because of this, they had to move from a large nearby house in Wazir Akbar Khan where they had three cars and five servants. They moved to a very small house and could only manage one car and one servant. Finally, they were forced to move to a tiny house away from the center of Kabul with no cars and no servants. Only when Ibrahim and Wafa's family were bled dry financially and emotionally, did Wajid relent, and agreed to divorce Wafa.

Soon afterward, Wafa went to Europe with her father supposedly to accompany him on a business trip. Ibrahim followed one month later. The couple was married in Germany, and remained there, not wishing to subject themselves to the scandal in Kabul."

"After this, did Wafa's family regain its wealth?"

"No Catee-*jon*, my brother-in-law lost everything when his partner cheated him. Marwan was in Europe selling sheepskin coats like I do and sending the money back to his partner. By the time Marwan returned to Kabul, Faruq had taken all of the money and left Afghanistan permanently."

Then The Knower, said, "Come Catee-jon, let us celebrate your return and talk of happier things."

My heart sang as I once again walked the streets of Kabul. The mountains were resplendent in their imposing vastness, while time caught by her delicate throat was once again hushed in mid-breath. Sitting along a main road was a line of blind dervishes who put out their eyes so they may only have the internal vision of God the Beloved. The Afghans called the dervishes "*Majnoon-ay-Khoda*" (Those Intoxicated with God) and treated them with respect.

Further along the road squatting in the dust was a knot of strong-faced, nomadic women in all their finery. Their proud, unveiled profiles defied the searing sun. Multi-metered red or blue balloon pants buttoned at the ankle, brushed the tops of their bare, bejeweled feet. Black short tunics, with manifold pleats, decorated with heavy, dark red embroidery, brass, silver, and bright glass beads glinted blindingly in the sunlight with their every movement. They wore all of their families' wealth in the form of silver jewelry on their arms, necks, ears, fingers, and toes. Their children swarmed around them and clung to the various folds of clothing.

The nomads lived in the warm climate of southeastern Jalalabad in the winter and trekked to the cool pastures of northwestern Pakistan in the summer. Their lives were guided by their flocks of sheep, goats, and camels that gave them wool for clothing and tents, as well as cheese, yoghurt, and meat for food. They only came to town when they needed salt, sugar or tea. The women sold a piece of their jewelry to purchase these necessities. Their chores done, waiting for their men, they chatted among themselves, oblivious to the children's clamor.

A boy of fourteen, with black wool western pants and a worn black turtleneck sweater, was selling American textbooks from the 1950's. He stood in front of a fissured adobe wall, his few books laid on a cloth in the dust. Greedy for something to read without having to make the rounds of the tourist hotels, I looked through all six books only to discover to my dismay that they were on engineering and mathematics ... not quite my idea of bedtime reading.

As I walked along, I passed a car crammed so tightly with eight men that their multi-meter turbans collided. Six more men were in the act of paying a small fee to sit in the open trunk. All smiled and waved.

In the throbbing sun, **a** sightless boy of eleven was sitting cross-legged on the stone bridge over the swollen Kabul River that separated the new section from the old section of the city. The boy wore a pale gray traditional *peeran tambon* over which sat a ragged, brown, tweed Western suit jacket two sizes too big for him.

In the 1920s, when King Amanullah was in power, he became enamored of Western architecture and clothing and decreed that Kabulis should adopt this mode of dress. Afghans true to their independent nature of resisting all interference in their lives, simply put western suit jackets over their traditional clothing. The women wore miniskirts, stockings, and high heels underneath their *chadorees*. In the cities, gray and dark brown traditional clothes were the norm for the men, just like the dark-colored suits of their Western counterparts. Their "country cousins" still retained their pale, colorful clothing of turquoise, mauve, pink, green and blue. The men represent the moon with its pale colors, and women represent the setting sun with vibrant reds, purples, and oranges. The upper-class men wear second-hand American and European suits bought by judicious wives in Kona Frushee (Used Items for Sale), the second-hand clothing bazaar.

The blind boy was small for his age, and the jacket made him look shrunken. He had a shaved head and his closed eyelids drooped over empty sockets. His palms were face up on his knees and he cried "Al-lah! Al-lah!" with a rhythmic one-two beat as he waited for alms.

There were several beggars to whom I gave money on a regular basis. One was an old man with a white beard and a wooden staff. He was palsied and lay in front of a small park. The other was an old woman with clever hands and a loving heart. Neither the man nor the woman ever asked for anything with gestures or words, unlike the small boys who always pestered foreigners for *baksheesh* (a gift or in some cases, a bribe).

I made my way to the bazaar. At eight-thirty in the morning, the day was already half gone for those who woke to the call to prayer before dawn. Dozens of scored, flat, oblong, brown *naans* had already been baked, sold, and eaten with countless cups of sweetened black tea, some tea perfumed with cardamom seeds. The butcher had sold the day's kill, and what remained were several enormous elliptical sheep tails hanging in front of his shop that people rendered for cooking oil. Poor people used this fat as a substitute for meat.

Only the fruit and vegetable stands still had an abundance of leftovers. As I perused the fruit, one of the merchants jumped off his perch and handed me half of the tangerine that he was eating. I thanked him, refused, and pointed to the apples. He picked out an apple, handed it to me and said, "*Baksheesh.*" I thanked him again and stood on the side of the road enjoying my sweet juicy apple.

A girl of twelve was in the company of a woman in her early thirties. The woman wore a dark, green *chadoree* with the front piece thrown back revealing her face. They both smiled at me and chattered in a language that I didn't understand.

The girl reached up to touch one of two charms that I wore around my neck on a gold chain. One was a scrimshawed whale's tooth and the other a Brazilian good luck symbol called a "figa." The girl's face turned into a question mark. I puffed out my cheeks, stretched my arms out as far as I could, and illustrated swimming and diving. Then I pointed to my tooth. Both the woman and girl grinned and nodded. Whether they understood my imitation of a whale or not (living in a landlocked country), I didn't know.

Then the woman reached up and touched the "figa." She asked me with her eyes what it was. This I did not know how to explain, so I showed them my own fist with a tip of my thumb sticking out. At this, both of them laughed outright and patted me on the back and arms. I later discovered that this was a very rude local gesture that I leave to the readers' imagination!

When they touched my arms, back, and hands, centuries of womanhood coursed through my veins. Primitive cries came to my throat with a powerful current generated by those simple but curious touches. I felt a deep kinship with all women. I smiled at them both, and tears filled my eyes for the lack of a common tongue. I so desired to speak to them, to ask and answer all the questions of life.

Modor-jon or Mother-dear, as I came to call her out of respect, sat cross-legged on the patch of cement between the bakery and the basket weavers' garage-like place. She had a small, straw color, woven basket at her side. She looked up at people as they passed by, and murmured a prayer of thanks to those who dropped one or two coins into her basket.

The first time I saw her, I was going to the vegetable bazaar and happened to look across the street. We both smiled at each other. Other times, I used to greet her aloud or put my right hand over my heart and incline my head if I was too far away.

Little by little I started speaking to her and gave her my change from my vegetable purchases after giving the merchant his customary tip. When the merchant saw what I was doing, he refused the tip and gifted me with extra vegetables or fruits.

Modor-jon thanked me with a smile, and some kind words like "*May God be good to thee,*" while calling me *dokhtar-jon* (daughter-dear). She beamed into my face, and her eyes shone and twinkled.

* * *

I had made friends with an Italian couple who also exported handicrafts. Marcellina and Pietro were from Milan. They had been traveling back and forth from Europe to the Near East for several years, buying small handicrafts in Afghanistan, Pakistan, India, and Nepal. They sold them in Europe. I met them in the shops when I made my rounds looking for antique jewelry and tribal costumes. We became friends and had several meals together.

One day, when I dropped by their hotel to visit them, petite Marcellina was curled up in a tiny ball in bed; her huge black eyes, enlarged by fear, dwarfed her face. The thick curly fringe of black hair around her face was wet with tears that had created rivulets in her olive skin. The rest of her waist-length hair was in a rope of a braid. Marcellina told me that she was about two and a half months pregnant, and was sure she was having a miscarriage. She said this happened before. She and Pietro had been trying to have a child for several years. I asked her where Pietro was, and she said that he left yesterday morning for Maimana in the north to look for carpets and *ghelams* (flat weave rugs). Given the travel time, I saw that he would not be back for a week. There were no phones or other ways to contact him, and Marcellina was very frightened. Someone had told her about an Afghan doctor who had studied in the States, and Marcellina asked me to accompany her. I suggested we leave right away. It was almost four o'clock in the afternoon.

We took a taxi from Shar-ee-Now to Jad-ee-Maiwand. On the way, I told her not to worry. I would remain with her no matter what had to be done. I kept my thoughts to myself. I was afraid for her and felt that she was in a terrible position. She was in a foreign country, and at the mercy of the people here. Their English and hers was shaky at best. Marcellina and I spoke Italian to each other.

The doctor's office was located in a remodeled *serai* or inn. We paid the driver his customary fifteen cents and walked into the dusty courtyard where only a few small shops were occupied. A dilapidated stairway took us upstairs where spacious offices had been created. The doctor's door was a bright turquoise, inset in a pale blue-washed adobe wall. We entered a large waiting room that was jammed with fifty women in *chadorees* in little groups of four or five, all chirping away in Dari. The color of their veils, pomegranate-red, sea-green, jet-black, royal-blue and sienna-brown, reminded me of the plumage of gaily feathered birds. A middle-aged woman wearing a white lab coat thrown over her western blouse and skirt was standing on one side of the room in front of a door that led to the doctor's office. She was the doctor's assistant. As she handed out small scraps of paper with numbers in Dari written on them, she told the women to be seated.

Marcellina and I looked at each other with the same thought, we would be there forever. When I told her that our numbers were fifty-four and fifty-five, we were positive. We shrugged our shoulders in typical Italian fashion and sat down on two straight-back wooden chairs to wait. We watched fascinated as the women talked and gesticulated. We studied their voices, feet, and hands trying to guess how old they were and what they looked like.

Then an incredible thing happened. The woman in the lab coat reappeared and called, "Number thirty-two!" in Dari. Eight women got up and disappeared into the inner office. It became apparent to us that there was only one patient, and the rest were relatives there for moral support! Fifteen minutes later, our numbers were announced, and we realized that the numbers weren't sequential either. Marcellina and I walked across the room and stood in the open doorway to wait our turn.

Dr. K was a middle-aged man with a kind expression. He was seated behind an old wooden desk with nine veiled women standing three-feet-deep in front of him. The patient was sitting on the edge of a battered, wooden chair as befits a "supplicant to the doctor's knowledge." The doctor asked what the problem was, how long was she sick, did she have a fever and other such questions. A short woman in a royal-blue *chadoree* seemed to be the spokesperson for the group. She did all the talking with occasional additions from the other women. The doctor's way of addressing her informed me that she was the patient's mother-in-law. She said that the girl was in pain and could not eat. This had been going on for over a month. She was joined by the others who told the doctor how they prepared her favorite foods, made different herbal teas, and purchased talismans for good health, all to no avail. So they brought her here as a last resort.

Dr. K. asked for the patient's hand. She produced a small, thin, hennaed palm that looked like it belonged to a girl of fourteen. The henna indicated that she was a bride. Dr. K spent quite some time on her pulse. Afghan healers, like the Chinese, can tell a lot about the person's constitution by the regularity and strength of the various pulses. Then Dr. K. proceeded to apply pressure with a pencil eraser to various points on her palm until he got an involuntary jerk from the girl when he hit a sore spot. He leisurely but firmly pressed and rubbed the sore spot for some time, and continued his examination with the eraser. Dr. K. was doing hand reflexology. When he was satisfied that there were no more sore spots, he prescribed some medication and vitamins that he wrote on his prescription pad and handed to the mother-in-law. He gave her oral instructions on the dose of the pills and when to administer them since none of the women was literate. They all thanked the doctor as the mother-in-law pressed a few coins into his hand. They blessed him and left. All this time, the patient never uttered a sound.

Dr. K. looked up as Marcellina and I entered the room. He smiled, stood up and asked us in English to be seated. I greeted him in Dari, and he congratulated me on my knowledge of his language while I returned the compliment regarding his English. Dr. K said that he had studied gynecology and obstetrics at Johns Hopkins University in New York. Marcellina told him her history in her Italian/English. He asked if she would permit him to examine her. She threw me a surprised look at his question and said of course. The doctor then opened the door of a tiny examining room where everything was covered in a thick layer of the ever-present powder-fine Kabul dust. The examination table had a filthy stained sheet over it. Dr. K's assistant, the woman in the lab coat, began to beat the dust off everything with a graying rag. Marcellina and I recoiled, and Dr. K saw the look on our faces. He apologized to us saying that Marcellina was the first patient he examined since his return from the States some fifteen years ago! What we saw in the other room was a typical examination of Afghan women.

I stopped his assistant from raising any more dust, and when it settled I put Marcellina's shawl on the table for her. Dr. K left the room while she positioned herself, and I covered her with my shawl. Dr. K returned wearing examining gloves. I gripped Marcellina's hand to reassure her. When he was finished, the doctor told her she must go to the women's hospital as she was indeed starting to miscarry. Dr. K emphasized that he would see what if anything could be done to save the child.

Marcellina was right to be frightened. Her huge, terrified eyes glued themselves to mine. She made me swear on everything I held sacred that I would come to the hospital with her. I swore her hand would not leave mine for an instant. Dr. K gave her a prescription and said he would see her at Zaeshkoh Women's Hospital tomorrow morning. I took Marcellina to her hotel, filled the prescription, made sure she had something to eat and was ready to fall asleep, and then left with the promise to return to go to the hospital together.

The next day, I picked her up in a taxi. The hospital consisted of a series of white-washed adobe huts, clustered together on the inside of a nine-foot-high wall. The halls were dingy. The rooms were small and lit with one naked light bulb. The beds were a conglomeration of bumpy springs, a cotton stuffed mattress, a hard pillow and one old rough blanket. The squatter toilets, as well as the area around them, were choked with piles of bloody pus stained bandages, rags, and excrement.

Hazara women walked up and down the halls haphazardly sweeping great clouds of dust with their homemade brooms. Others, dressed in simple cotton navy blue traditional outfits with gray aprons and headscarves, moved up and down the halls with full pails that resembled pig slop. This turned out to be lunch. The groans of the patients could be heard everywhere, and there was never a doctor to be found, except when they made their rounds at nine o'clock in the morning. My heart sickened at these sights. I clutched Marcellina's hand and strengthened my resolve never to leave her.

Dr. K met us in the hall and directed us to a small room with three empty cots. He gave Marcellina a hospital gown, told her to put it on and said that he would be right back. I sat down on the rough brown army blanket resting on the thin cotton mattress and a small puff of dust arose. Marcellina noticed this, and we both looked at each other. The absurdity of the entire situation overtook us, and we started laughing. Just as fast, Marcellina burst into tears. I rose, embraced her and cried too. I swore again that my hand would not leave hers.

Dr. K returned to take us to a room that was bare except for an examination table and a brown curtain that divided the room. Marcellina lay down on the table and put her feet in the stirrups. Dr. K brought a relatively clean sheet to place over her and walked out of the room. For the next hour, various Afghan doctors came into the room, lifted the sheet, glanced at Marcellina and walked out consulting each other.

I tightened the grip on her hand when Dr. K returned and made his examination. He said he could not save the child, and she would have to undergo a uterine scraping to remove the fetus. A look of sheer terror came over Marcellina's face.

I looked at her, squeezed her hand tighter, and said in a fierce whisper, "Don't worry. I will stay with you. You will survive!"

She relaxed in the face of my determination, and said in a strangled voice, "Si, si!" as she returned the grip on my hand.

We went together into surgery in a small room down the hall. The naked light bulb cast an eerie shadow around this pale green room. She refused Dr. K's offer to anesthetize her, and during the entire operation, her eyes were locked onto mine. If she began to whimper or cry, I bored into her eyes, tightened my grip on her hand, and willed her to feel secure and to bear the pain. It took all of my concentration and energy for an entire hour. When it was over both of us were exhausted but smiling.

Marcellina was wheeled into an empty room with two beds. She was assisted into bed by a nurse. I lay down on the other one. Drained, we both fell asleep before our heads hit the pillow.

I stayed with Marcellina until Pietro returned, and then I flew to New York to sell my handicrafts.

CHAPTER TWENTY-NINE

Heartbreak

"Command me My Lady, for I am thy slave."
Said to Author by Jamal

Six months later, after many loving letters from Jamal, written on his usual blue aerogram stationery, he told me that he had sent a formal letter to his parents requesting their permission to marry me. He was anticipating their answer. He was sure that he could overcome their objections to the fact that I was "not of the blood" and a foreigner. He sent me a ticket to come to Pakistan.

Jamal and I were not just happy to be together again, we were ecstatic. We drove to his ancestral lands in India for a month to plan our life. Jamal's parents, Muslims forced from India during the Partition, now lived in Hyderabad in Pakistan. As a ships' broker, Jamal lived all over the world: Japan, the United Arab Emirates, England, Pakistan, and Scandinavia. He returned to his ancestral home in India once a year if possible.

The huge, old palace, occupied only by caretakers, resembled a pink and white birthday cake. It became our home, and we spent every moment in each other's company ... away from Pakistan, and the prying eyes of his business acquaintances and friends, who were only too eager to carry tales back to his family. The hot afternoons were spent lounging on the bed. The wine in our glasses was perfumed with musk while incense of amber swathed the room. We bathed each other in essential oils, and Jamal regaled me with more tales of his lineage.

It was sunset when Jamal called for food. The servants brought a fabulous feast with many succulent dishes. There was curried chicken soup, rice with whole spices of cinnamon sticks, cardamom seeds and cloves, spicy ground meat in a tomato sauce with fried eggs on top, a salad of cucumbers, onions, and tomatoes with fresh mint leaves in yoghurt, and sugar cane juice scented with fresh lime.

We laughed, joked, teased one another, and made all-consuming love. No honeymoon could have surpassed this.

Looking into the depths of my soul after we made love, he said in Pakhto, *"Tell me oh Life of Mine, what dost thou wish of me?"*

"Oh, Janni!" I responded with an exquisite ache. *"I wish a child by thee."*

"There is no command but thy command. I shalt give thee my child with joy and gladness!" he whispered, the ferocity of the Pakhtun in his voice. I gave myself up to him again, and he poured all of himself into me.

The next morning, I went to the cloth bazaar wanting to buy some of their exquisite material to have some saris made. I was driven by his servant, Sattar, in Jamal's forest-green Porsche.

After making my purchases, we returned to the palace and I noticed that Jamal was depressed.

"What's wrong, *Janni?*" I asked concerned.

"Oh nothing, alcoholic depression, I guess," he said.

I rang the bell for a servant and asked him to bring us two beers. I sat down across from Jamal and noticed that he was avoiding my eyes. I came over, took his head in my hands, and gently kissed his mouth, smoothing his mustache. Then I asked him how I could help. Evasive, Jamal got up, walked across the room, and lit a cigarette. He inhaled deeply, and the smoke swirled from his nostrils like lazy hieroglyphics. He sat down on the edge of the armchair, took a letter from his pocket, and gazed at me.

"I can't marry you," he stated in a flat voice "my parents have denied their permission."

I drew back and looked at him, positive he was joking.

Stunned, I jumped up when I saw the gravity on his face. "B-b-but why?" I stuttered, the knot in my stomach tightening with every breath.

"Because you are not of the blood. You know that we only marry our first cousins."

Shocked to the core, I sat there staring at him while he continued smoking. After a little while, I found my voice, "Jamal! You're thirty-eight years old! You cannot allow your parents to dictate your life, can you?" I asked in shocked disbelief.

"Cath-ay, you don't understand. As long as my father is alive, I must obey or lose everything, my title, my lands, monies, everything! I would be an outcast!"

To be cast out of the family with their financial, emotional and physical support was unthinkable in this collective-minded society.

"Then come to America with me Jamal, and we will find a way!" I cried my panic rising like a surfer's wave.

"Oh *Janni, Janni!* I am a has-been, leave me, and make your life. I have lost everything before and cannot bear to go through it all again."

He was referring to the partition of India when the Muslims moved to the created state of East Pakistan and his family's subsequent loss of everything again when East Pakistan, reverted to India and became Bangladesh.

Fury rose up my spine as I cried out in Dari, *"Oh My Lord, thou wouldst abandon our love for wealth?"*

"Nay, Oh My Lady, for the dignity of my family. Terrible the shame 'twould bring. I cannot ruin an innocent life. Thou know my custom is such that a 'promised woman' who is rejected can never marry!"

Switching to English I screamed, "What are you talking about?"

"I am speaking about my first cousin to whom my parents have engaged me. We will be married in five days."

I was so outraged by his words that the only thing I could think of to spit out was, "So! It's all right to ruin my life even though you claim to love me, but not some first cousin whom you probably have never seen and for whom you have no feeling?"

"Cath-ay, Cath-ay, you're young and strong and not constrained by custom..."

Scathingly, I cut him off and shouted with tears stinging my eyes, "Why the hell did you make me come thirteen thousand miles around the earth to tell me this?"

"Because I love you so very much, and I wanted to be with you one more time on the chance that my parents consented. And if they did not, I wanted to impregnate you so you would stay with me in my situation, and I could take care of you and our child."

"And what exactly did you intend to do when I had our child? Move me in with your wife?" I shrieked.

"There is no question that I will provide everything for you and our child!" he snapped, not really answering my question.

"And how will you do that? With deposits into my bank account? I will be in America and you will be here!" I yelled.

He hung his head and there was no reply. Rage shot through the top of my skull. I flew across the room and slapped Jamal's face so hard that pain shot through my arm into my neck.

The words: "You selfish bastard!" burst out of me, "You coward! You will never see me again! If I ever return here I will never let you know that I am here! Paah! That is the last thing you will ever hear from me, that of my spitting on the Yusuf Khan name since it has produced only liars and cowards!"

Thunderclouds gathered in his face, and his eyes spewed lightning. Jamal grabbed me by the shoulders and threw me backward onto the bed, falling on top of me nose to nose. His growl was menacing, "If you ever set foot in my country without informing me, I shall have you jailed!"

The idiocy of his trying to control our relationship struck me funny but I said nothing. He got up, and we both dressed in silence. He opened the door and walked out. I slammed it shut with all the force I could muster. The building itself shook. Then I threw myself on the bed and pounded it in a rage. I cursed Jamal, my life, my luck, and everything else I could think of at that moment. I collapsed in tears and sobbed myself to sleep.

When I awoke, I showered and packed. I rang for a servant to call a taxi to the airport. I waited in the front room with my emotions, and intestines in turmoil. Only one thought kept running through my mind, to get as far away from Jamal Mahmood Yusuf Khan as I could. I never wanted to see him again. I prayed to God that I was not pregnant even though I always knew that when I became pregnant, it would be a conscious conception between both of us.

Glancing up, I noticed that I was getting the most peculiar looks from the servants. My fury must have shown on my face. When the taxi did arrive, the six-foot-three, heavy-set, usually jolly majordomo, his eyes bulging out of their sockets, stood well away from me and said, just above a whisper, "Madam, your taxi has arrived."

If I were not feeling so angry and betrayed, I would have laughed at how frightened of me this large man looked.

I booked a one-way ticket to Rawalpindi. I had stored some of my goods at my friend Brilliant Star's mother's house. I arrived at Lady Fawzia's and threw myself into her arms sobbing. She held me tight and brought me to her room ordering the servant to bring *chai.* I blurted out everything that had happened over the last weeks.

"I know, darling, I know," she said as she consoled me kissing the top of my head.

I pulled away astonished, stared into her eyes and repeated, "You know?"

"Yes, my dear. I was invited to the birthday party of one Jamal's parents' grandsons. While I was there, Zareen *Begum* (lady) and Shamsuddin, Jamal's parents, received his letter and I overheard their conversation."

"What did they say?" I asked.

"His mother, Zareen *Begum* said that she had found a first cousin, twelve years younger, for Jamal. I knew why she chose White Diamond. She is a very headstrong and ambitious young woman who will become the matriarch of Jamal's clan as soon as Zareen Begum dies."

"Why is this important to Jamal's mother?"

"She is a clever woman and knows that she will be the ruler after Shamsuddin's death even though the title passes to Jamal. She needs an ally so together they can bend Jamal to their will."

"But Jamal is not the oldest son, how can he rule?" I asked as some of the tales of family treachery that Jamal had told me rippled through my mind.

"Zareen's oldest son died in infancy. The second one is a reclusive Quran scholar. He has very little interest in anything 'worldly.' To suit her purpose, Zareen chose more demure wives for her other six sons. Despite what our culture appears to be on the surface, without women to promote them, the men don't stand a chance of doing anything worthwhile with their lives."

The Afghan saying in Dari, "*Poor, indeed, is he who hath no friend in the hareem* (women's quarters)" popped into my head.

Fawzia continued, "Zareen put up with Jamal's drinking, drugging and whoring until she found a suitable match. She was not about to let a foreigner ruin the plans she had so carefully crafted."

Then Fawzia proceeded to relate the conversation that she had overheard between Jamal's father Shamsuddin Mahmood Yusuf Khan and his mother Zareen *Begum*.

"Zareen said in Pakhto to her husband, *'Oh My Lord, Jamal's future wife hath the pride and the carriage of a true Yusufziai. She is strong and wilt bear many sons and daughters.'*"

"Shamsuddin replied, *'Oh My Lady, she is too headstrong, and wilt flaunt her beauty before my son 'til he becomes her slave.'*"

"*'As you wish, My Lord, but lest thou forget, her ambition to rule wilt override anything else. She wilt challenge and occupy Jamal's wits 'til no other thoughts of women and wine remain.'*"

"*'Ah Zareen, thou dost tire me with thy prattle. Choose as thou see fit. But marry him soon. Rumor hath it that his soul hath become ensnared by some foreign woman, an American no less!'* and he spat with contempt."

"*'Yay, My Lord' Begum* Zareen replied smiling to herself knowing she had won that round."

"I was privy to this information because my room was next to theirs. I left to return here the following day," said Fawzia.

"Oh Fawzia, how could Jamal just abandon me like this?" I asked through my tears.

"Darling mine, blood and honor are above all else in this culture no matter how much unhappiness it causes."

Grieving my loss, I understood her words even though I disagreed with these cultural commandments. I stayed with Fawzia for a few days, and then returned to America to heal my wounds.

THE END

Cat's story continues in Volume 2

The author experiences more love and even greater loss when she returns to her beloved Afghanistan and finds a changing landscape as war begins to grip the region.

After a horrific accident, she is forced to go on the run. She is rescued in a most unexpected way and given a place to hide and heal by someone who once considered her an enemy.

With love as her only protection, she dons the *chadoree* and enters the war zone in search of her beloved.

Then, she rallies Americans to help the women and children of war-torn Afghanistan, the beautiful country she had grown to love so much.

To find out more about Afghanistan and
when the next volume is available,
visit www.CatParenti.com
and join the email list.

If you enjoyed this book,
please visit Amazon and
give it a positive review!

Glossary

Afghanis –currency of Afghanistan

Amrika - America.

Angrezee - the English.

Awshak - small chive stuffed dumplings in a ground lamb and tomato sauce.

Badal - vengeance is the third great law of the Pashtuns (Afghans). Revenge is taken for stealing money, land or for rape.

Baksheesh - a gift of money (alms), can also be a bribe.

Bhaaji - elder sister, a term of respect given to women regardless of their relationship to you.

Bibi - Pakistani word for a lady.

Bokharee - a metal wood burning stove.

Burkha - the women's veil in Pakistan. It consists of a long black coat to the ankles with sleeves to the wrist and a 'nun's veil' covering the hair with a sheer black cloth from the hairline to the neck that covers the face.

Caravanserai - an inn that houses passing caravans.

Chador - a huge, sheet-like garment worn by women in Iran.

Chadoree - the full veil of the Afghan women. A minute pleated 'tent' dropped over the head that falls to the ankles in the back and to the thighs in the front. The front piece is not pleated, but embroidered and has a small 'grill' for the eyes. Prior to the Taliban, the chadoree was worn in the public streets by middle and poor class city women and by country women on arriving to the cities.

Chai - usually refers to plain black tea sometimes served with sugar and sometimes with crushed cardamom seeds. In Pakistan and India, chai is served boiled up with buffalo milk and sugar.

Chaikhana - tea house

Chapan - a quilted cotton or silk coat worn by men and women to keep warm in the winter.

Chapatti - a round flat bread usually made on a cast iron skillet without sides over an open fire.

Charpoy - a bed that consists of a wooden frame with ropes for the 'mattress.'

Charsee - a hashish addict.

Chillum - a clay cylindrical pipe held vertically between the fists to smoke tobacco or hashish.

Chubazee - a graceful circular dance with wooden swords performed by men and boys at weddings and other festivities.

Chacha - father's brother, uncle.

Chaka - drained yoghurt often mixed with garlic and dried spearmint and used as a sauce for vegetable and rice dishes.

Chowk - concentric rings in cities and towns (like roundabouts in the United Kingdom) where shops are found.

Chuddar - a voluminous shawl from head to knees worn by Pakistani women, sometimes, covering the mouth and nose.

Dastarkhan - literally means the 'hand of the lord or khan' meaning generosity and magnanimity. There is a popular saying "There is no khan without dastarkhan," meaning that if someone who claims he is a khan cannot feast you, then he is no khan.

Dhol - a huge drum like a conga drum played at weddings by the women while describing the groom to the bride who has not supposed to have seen him until the third night of the marriage. It is also played when the groom leads the bride to the bridal chamber and takes her maidenhead.

Dogh - an Afghan yoghurt drink with salt, pepper, and dried spearmint.

Dost - intimate friend or beloved.

Dussmol - the embroidered handkerchief given by the bride's relatives to the groom's relatives showing that he has been accepted as a future husband.

Feringee - a foreigner.

Flaneh, flaneh - the equivalent of 'yadda, yadda.'

Gel-ay-sashoy - an opaque sienna color liquid used as a shampoo.

Ghelam - the flat weave geometric design rugs handmade by the Turkmen nomads.

Gosh-ay-feel - the deep-fried dessert in the shape of elephant ears coated with sugar and ground cardamom seeds.

Gur - a hard candy made from molasses studded with fennel seeds, ginger, almonds, and pistachios.

Hakim - a natural or herbal healer.

Hareem - the women's quarters of the house.

Hookah - water pipe.

Islam - "submission" not subjugation. In many drawings, fabrics, and rugs, there is what we call the paisley design. This is actually the cypress tree blowing in the wind showing submission to its Creator. If a tree doesn't bend with the wind it breaks.

Ikat - refers to the creation of geometric and nature designs by hand tie-dyeing and hand looming silk. Often seen in the men and women's coats, chapans, and curtains.

Issawee - a believer in Jesus.

Janni - my life, a term of endearment.

Jezail - an antique wooden rifle inlaid with brass and mother-of-pearl.

Jihad - is each individual's internal struggle to strive for perfection to be closer to God/Allah. Yes, it can also mean a "holy war" for those who attack Islam.

Jirga - is a tribal council meeting where each man has one vote.

Jon - means 'dear' usually tacked onto a first name like 'Mary-dear.'

Jooey - the water trenches from the underground springs that crisscross Kabul.

Kamiz - a long tunic worn by both men and women. In imitation of the West, Pakistani men's tunics had collars and cuffs that sported gold cufflinks.

Karachees - huge, wooden plank open carts with tractor-size tires

Karakul - referred to the lambs' wool caps the men wore as well as lambs' wool vests with the fur inside worn by all.

Kar-ay-dast - eating by hand instead of using utensils.

Kazi - a judge.

Khaibar - the Afghan word for the Khyber Pass.

Khan - a lord.

Khanum - Afghan word for a lady.

Khoree – sister.

Khuh – good.

Khwar-dil - Sister-of-my-heart or best friend.

Kissmet – fate.

Kulcha - hard tasteless biscuits made to be dunked into sweetened tea.

Kunee - a passive male homosexual.

Labs giriftan - literally 'the taking of the lips' or the promise between male and female relatives is an agreement to move forward with the marriage.

Lawasha - a huge thin flatbread used as a plate.

Luhsee - a Pakistani yoghurt drink made with sugar and rose water or salt and pepper.

Luree – daughter.

Mantoo - dumplings filled with ground lamb and spices dotted with carrots and lentils with a sour yoghurt sauce, qrut on top.

Mardana - the men's living quarters.

Madrassa - a religious school that teaches reading, writing and arithmetic based on the Quran.

Maleeda - A whole wheat crumble made with oil and butter and depending on the wealth of the host, crushed cardamom seeds and rosewater.

Masjid - the mosque.

Mayrabanee - thank you in Urdu, the main language of Pakistan.

Melmastia - the first great law of the Pashtun Afghans 'honor to the guest.' Anyone can knock on any door and must be received, fed and housed for three days even if the host is starving. At the end of that time, the guest either leaves or states his business with the host.

Mufarah - a hallucinogenic comprised of spiced tea with milk, honey, and hashish oil.

Mullah - a Quran interpreter.

Muezzin - the man who calls the faithful to prayer five times per day.

Naan (pronounced 'nawn' - like dawn) - Afghan word for bread that also means food in certain contexts such as 'Nawn tieyar hast' meaning 'The food is ready.' It's a flat oblong whole wheat bread resembling pizza crust baked in a beehive adobe oven. Naan is primarily purchased from bakers in the cities but can be made at home.

Namak haram - a serious crime, one who is unfaithful to his/her salt meaning failure to protect a guest breaking the second great law of the Pashtun Afghans, asylum or protection.

Nanawatai - the second great law of the Pashtun Afghans is protection or asylum. Any person can ask another for protection and it must be given even if the protector forfeits his life in the process.

Nay nay – No, no.

Nesswar - the equivalent of our chewing tobacco. It is composed of green tobacco, lime, chalk and sometimes opium.

Pakoras - deep fried vegetable fritters.

Panja Maryam - the ceremony called 'Mary's handprint.' The Afghans believe in Mother Mary or the Blessed Mother of Christ and pray for her miraculous intercession. They fast and pray for three days and create a rice pudding whose crockery they seal with dough and bake in the oven for several hours. If their prayers are answered, when they break the dough seal, there is a handprint in the middle of the pudding.

Parwa nist - 'It doesn't matter' or 'Forget about it.'

Peeran - the long tunic of Afghan men and women. The neck is round, sleeves are to the wrist and it hangs to the calves with slits halfway up the thigh.

Pukka - correct.

Pullow - rice with meat or chicken buried in the center baked in an oven or steamed on the top of the stove.

Purdah - the practice of veiling.

Pyara - my darling or my love.

Qabili Pullow - the national dish of Afghanistan, prepared for weddings, births, feasts and even bets. If you lose a bet you must make qabili pullow, a dish of lamb, rice, carrots, raisins and whole spices for the winner.

Qand - an eighteen-inch-high sugar cone used in marital negotiations showing the bride's willingness to accept the groom.

Qawa – green tea.

Qaymak Chai - a green tea served on special occasions. The tea is thrown back and forth between silver teapots until its green color becomes pink. Then it is served with the equivalent of crème Fraiche on top. It represents the mountains in the setting sun with their snowy caps.

Qrut - is the third and last process in yoghurt making. First yoghurt is made, then drained of its whey, the remnants are formed into rounded balls that are left to dry in the sun. They are kept in a container until needed and reconstituted with boiling water producing a sour sauce to be poured over vegetable and rice dishes.

Rebab - a violin-like instrument in the minor scale.

Rickshaw – A three-wheeled vehicle.

Roos - the Russians.

Rooksha - a Pashto command to 'go back.'

Roti - the Pakistani word for bread.

Rukhsatee - the wedding party or public marriage, read: guests and feasting.

Ruyibar - the matchmaker, literally, 'the one who sees the face of the prospective bride.'

Saloon - the equivalent of our living room where entertaining is done. Europeans use the word 'salon.'

Samowat - the Afghan equivalent of the Russian samovar, is a huge copper urn placed over an open fire that keeps the water boiling for tea.

Samosas - are fried turnovers with meat and/or vegetables.

Selam Aleikum - may peace be upon thee.

Shamol – The north wind.

Shelwar - the Pakistani version of men and women's long voluminous drawstring pantaloons cuffed at the ankles.

Shir baha - 'milk money' is demanded by the bride's mother for her nurturing and raising her daughter. The more talented and beautiful the girl, the higher the bride price.

Shir Chai - Unlike Hindus and Pakistanis, Afghans are not a milk-drinking culture. Shir chai is a tea served with milk on special occasions.

Sitar - a stringed instrument played in the minor scale.

Swara - a woman given in marriage to stop a blood feud. You cannot kill your own relatives.

Tabla - a small drum played with the hands.

Tambon - the voluminous drawstring pantaloons worn by Afghan men and women that are tapered at the ankles. The Kabuli women wore white cotton or silk drawstring 'elephant leg' pantaloons that had white lace for cuffs.

Tashakor - thank you.

Tassbees – A 99 prayer bead rosary, each one denoting an attribute of Allah.

Tobah - the equivalent of 'God protect me.'

Tokhum jangee - a game played with hard-boiled eggs. The goal is to break the shell of your opponent's egg first.

Tonga - a two-wheeled horse-drawn cart to carry passengers.

Tulwar - a sharp sword.

Turkic - the language of Turkey Azerbaijani. It is also spoken by the Turkmen, Qashqai, Gagauz, Balkan Gagauz, Crimean Tatars, Macedonians, Siberians and people in Western China.

Uzbek - a Central Asian people living in Uzbekistan one of the former Soviet Socialist Republics. They also live in Tajikistan, Kyrgyzstan, and smaller numbers in Kazakhstan, Turkmenistan, and Sinkiang in China.

Voh – Bravo.

Wali - a governor.

Zakat - alms. The Muslims believe that this is the third and last step into Paradise. The first two are prayer and fasting.

Zenana - the women's quarters in the house.

Index

About the Author

Cat Parenti was born in Brooklyn New York and majored in Russian Studies at Fordham University. After graduation, she worked as a part-time translator for a Russian lawyer in the United Nations, taught English to foreigners in Berlitz School of Languages and worked as a private secretary to a Japanese vice president of Panasonic.

Subsequently, she went to Afghanistan where she started collecting antique costumes and tribal jewelry that she sold to museum and museum shops on the East coast. Parenti has been radio and newspaper interviewed, given many presentations on Afghan culture to the royal Afghan women in the U.N., the Pakistan Literary Society, written articles for the Arizona Republic and the Christian Science Monitor and taught Afghan culture and cooking classes in the U.S. and abroad including ones to the royal Afghan women in the U.N. and the Pakistan Literary Society.

After the Soviet invasion, Parenti joined the Afghanistan Foundation and became the Director of the Afghan Women's Work Project. With the help of the Girl Scouts of America, she collected sewing kits for the Afghan women in the camps of Pakistan helping them to restart their handicrafts. She then did fundraisers in the U.S.A., sold their crafts returning 90% of the money to them. Parenti also had grade school children collect packets of vegetable seeds that were flown to Pakistan and taken over the Hindu Kush Mountains into the liberated areas of Afghanistan where she personally distributed them.

She also collaborated with the International Committee of Migration in Washington, D.C. to bring wounded Afghan fighters to the U.S. for free medical treatment. She housed, fed and took them to their doctors' appointments seeing them through their surgeries and recuperation before sending them back to Afghanistan.